America Unfinished

America Unfinished

250 Years of Law and Governance

An Essay Collection from Harvard Law Faculty

Edited by Alexandra Natapoff and
Guy-Uriel E. Charles

The MIT Press
Cambridge, Massachusetts
London, England

The MIT Press
Massachusetts Institute of Technology
77 Massachusetts Avenue
Cambridge, MA 02139
mitpress.mit.edu

This book was set in ITC Stone Serif Std and Trajan Pro by New Best-set Typesetters Ltd. Printed and bound in the United States of America.

Library of Congress Cataloging-in-Publication Data is available.

ISBN: 9780262060431

10 9 8 7 6 5 4 3 2 1

EU Authorised Representative: Easy Access System Europe, Mustamäe tee 50, 10621 Tallinn, Estonia | Email: gpsr.requests@easproject.com

We dedicate this book to the principles and promise of academic freedom, and to all the people who have risked and sacrificed so much over the centuries so that we may still exercise it.

CONTENTS

Acknowledgments

We owe an enormous debt of gratitude to all our colleagues who helped bring this collection to fruition. They did so not only by contributing essays but by discussing, questioning, challenging, brainstorming, and otherwise sharing their time and wisdom with us. The final product reflects their collective insights.

Many students helped individual faculty members with research. Since the essays have no footnotes, they lack the traditional mechanism for thanking individual research assistants by name, so we thank these students collectively on behalf of all contributors. Our thanks also go to Dean John Goldberg for his leadership and encouragement, to the staff in his office, and to all the extraordinary faculty assistants and staff of Harvard Law School who provided superlative support and who make our work possible every day.

We are deeply grateful to the MIT Press, in particular to Amy Brand, Janice Audet, and Lorelei Horrell, for their enthusiastic support, vision, and imagination. This was an unusual project requiring speed and flexibility, and they worked creatively and tirelessly to make it happen. Throughout this process, the MIT Press has exemplified the very best of the nonprofit academic press ideal, with its unique rigor, commitment to academic freedom, and the advancement of human knowledge. We have been beyond fortunate to work with them.

Also thanks to the MIT Press, this book will become open access so that anyone in the world can read it for free. We are thrilled—this commitment to the sharing of knowledge reflects the essential spirit of the volume. To the extent that the physical, published version of the book generates editorial royalties, we are donating them to our local Cambridge Public Library.

Declaration of Independence

In Congress, July 4, 1776

The unanimous Declaration of the thirteen united States of America, When in the Course of human events, it becomes necessary for one people to dissolve the political bands which have connected them with another, and to assume among the powers of the earth, the separate and equal station to which the Laws of Nature and of Nature's God entitle them, a decent respect to the opinions of mankind requires that they should declare the causes which impel them to the separation.

We hold these truths to be self-evident, that all men are created equal, that they are endowed by their Creator with certain unalienable Rights, that among these are Life, Liberty and the pursuit of Happiness.—That to secure these rights, Governments are instituted among Men, deriving their just powers from the consent of the governed,—That whenever any Form of Government becomes destructive of these ends, it is the Right of the People to alter or to abolish it, and to institute new Government, laying its foundation on such principles and organizing its powers in such form, as to them shall seem most likely to effect their Safety and Happiness.

Prudence, indeed, will dictate that Governments long established should not be changed for light and transient causes; and accordingly all experience hath shewn, that mankind are more disposed to suffer, while evils are sufferable, than to right themselves by abolishing the forms to which they are accustomed.

But when a long train of abuses and usurpations, pursuing invariably the same Object evinces a design to reduce them under absolute Despotism, it is their right, it is their duty, to throw off such Government, and to provide new

Guards for their future security.—Such has been the patient sufferance of these Colonies; and such is now the necessity which constrains them to alter their former Systems of Government. The history of the present King of Great Britain is a history of repeated injuries and usurpations, all having in direct object the establishment of an absolute Tyranny over these States. To prove this, let Facts be submitted to a candid world.

. . . .

Gettysburg Address

Four score and seven years ago our fathers brought forth, on this continent, a new nation, conceived in Liberty, and dedicated to the proposition that all men are created equal.

Now we are engaged in a great civil war, testing whether that nation, or any nation so conceived, and so dedicated, can long endure. We are met on a great battlefield of that war. We have come to dedicate a portion of that field, as a final resting-place for those who here gave their lives, that that nation might live. . . . It is altogether fitting and proper that we should do this.

*But, in a larger sense, we can not dedicate, we can not consecrate, we can not hallow this ground. The brave men, living and dead, who struggled here, have consecrated it far above our poor power to add or detract. The world will little note, nor long remember what we say here, but it can never forget what they did here. It is for us the living, rather, to be dedicated here to the **unfinished** work which they who fought here have thus far so nobly advanced. . . . [W]e here highly resolve that these dead shall not have died in vain that this nation, under God, shall have a new birth of freedom, and that government of the people, by the people, for the people, shall not perish from the earth.*

Abraham Lincoln

Gettysburg, Pennsylvania

November 19, 1863

INTRODUCTION

ALEXANDRA NATAPOFF AND GUY-URIEL E. CHARLES

Sometimes a moment in history invites you to pause and take stock. That's how this book got started. Many of us in the legal academy have been grappling recently with our roles as legal scholars and teachers, and our relationship to the American legal experiment. At some basic level, the job of being a "law professor" intrinsically embraces the view that law and legal institutions are central to our society, to our economy, and to our republic. But you don't need a law degree these days to realize that this view raises some big, messy, challenging questions. Does law really work the way it purports to? For whom does it actually work? Do our foundational legal and governance institutions still do a good job? Did they ever? Is our particular brand of constitutional governance a good way to run this ship?

These are the bread-and-butter questions of the legal academy, and members of the Harvard Law School faculty have been working on answers now for over 200 years. Legal scholars do this work not only for the intellectual satisfaction, although it is often deeply satisfying, but because at some level we *believe* in the legal experiment. We believe that law is an indispensable tool for a polity that values individual liberty, equality, and human dignity. We believe in law as an engine for elevating collective democratic decision-making over exercises of raw, unchecked power. And we believe that law is a uniquely inviting vehicle through which to address basic, pressing questions about our communities and our society: Is this fair? Is this just? Should we do this differently?

And so, on the 250th anniversary of the Declaration of Independence and this entire democratic experiment, in the face of enormous shifts in many of our legal rules, norms, and institutions, we paused. We took stock of our opportunities as scholars and teachers at Harvard Law School, and our commitments as members of the legal profession, and we decided to try to make better sense of this moment collectively.

Hence this book.

This endeavor was inspired in large part by a year—2026—which means it was inspired by history and politics, culture and conflict, legal rules and democratic ideals. As the United States turns 250 years old, it is grappling with foundational challenges to its laws, institutions of governance, and ethical commitments. It faces structural questions about the power of the executive branch, the capabilities of Congress, and the proper scope of judicial review. As a result, the presidency, Congress, and the federal judiciary are locked in new conflicts. The balance of power between the states and the federal government is likewise shifting. At the same time, longstanding divides between public law and private ordering, between workers, consumers, and markets, create thorny obstacles both to economic flourishing and to democratic accountability. And then there is the quintessential challenge of state violence. America's willingness to use force within our borders tests the entire domestic fabric; its willingness to use force beyond our borders tests the entire international order. How we respond today to these legal and institutional challenges will profoundly shape the trajectory of the republic.

Against this backdrop, American identity is also hotly contested. Values of equality, tolerance, and pluralism are being challenged in numerous ways, including by the rise of antisemitism and anti-Muslim bias, by aggressive anti-immigrant policies, and by deep political polarization, all of which exacerbate perennial divides created by racism, sexism, and economic inequality. The Declaration of Independence had its own famously conflicted relationship to our multicultural democracy: Two hundred and fifty years later, the meaning of the phrase "all men are created equal" has yet to be fully resolved. These civic tensions are unfolding, moreover, amid deepening distrust of institutions of knowledge and expertise, and accelerated by the disruptions caused by technological and informational revolution. Even as we grapple with changes and challenges within our polity, the very nature of the world around us is changing.

Taken together, all these weighty developments underscore how much of our legal framework and governing ethos remain unfinished, contested, and thus in need of serious evaluation after 250 years of constitutional governance.

The sixty-two essays in this collection are each responses to this dramatic historic juncture in some form. Each essay provides a short, clear, expert analysis, proposal, prediction, theory, or other insight into the challenges facing American law and governance. As you will see, our faculty have a wide range of often conflicting views and approaches. The essays are very different from one another in content, tone, and substance. Collectively, they do not represent the position of Harvard Law School, or of the Harvard Law School faculty. Rather, each one is an expression of the individual scholarly expertise and academic freedom of each author.

We would be remiss if we did not acknowledge that our parent institution, Harvard University, is currently in conflict with the federal government over the scope and operation of academic freedom itself. As professors, we are each privileged to be beneficiaries of that freedom. We are also scholars of the legal infrastructure that makes it, indeed all legal entitlements possible. In ordinary times, faculty mostly exercise that freedom individually—in our own work and within our own fields. But these are not ordinary times, and so it seemed to us especially appropriate to come together now to share our knowledge, views, and concerns, to examine the American legal infrastructure from many different angles, and to exercise collectively and in full the expressive entitlements that our university is defending. Put differently, we think the best way to appreciate our academic freedom is to exercise it. Law and academic freedom walk hand in hand; neither can survive without the other. We hope that this collection contributes to both foundational endeavors.

This volume includes reflections from some of the nation's leading legal scholars. Many are global experts. Their backgrounds span an enormous range of disciplines, professions, and experiences. Everyone is a lawyer, but some are also economists, philosophers, and historians. Many have served in the federal government, in agencies including the Department of Justice, Securities and Exchange Commission, Environmental Protection Agency, Office of Information and Regulatory Affairs, National Labor Relations Board, Treasury Department, Department of Labor, Homeland Security, Department of State, and the Pentagon, as well as in Congress and in the White House, under both Democratic and

Republican administrations. Other contributors have worked as public defenders, prosecutors, judges, civil rights and human rights attorneys, labor lawyers, law firm partners, Supreme Court litigators, counsel to global corporations, and advisors to international institutions. There are best-selling authors, prominent opinion columnists, and recipients of Guggenheim, MacArthur, and Pulitzer prizes. And, of course, everyone is a teacher. Among us, we have taught hundreds of thousands of law students over the decades, not only at Harvard but also at many other law schools.

Given this breadth of expertise and experience, it is not surprising that the sixty-two essays cover an enormous amount of ground and span dozens of legal subjects. These include: the presidency, Congress, the Supreme Court, constitutional law, criminal law, corporate regulation, free speech, election law, civil rights, immigration, labor law, international law, national security, the legacy of slavery, democracy and authoritarianism, economic inequality, climate change, new reproductive technologies, and AI. The collection also explores, both directly and indirectly, what it means to teach law students and to be a lawyer at this moment in history.

Taken together, the collection offers a dynamic, colorful, contested engagement with the entire U.S. legal and governance apparatus. Our faculty is diverse and, as you can see from the essays, we disagree about many things. But we nonetheless share the view that these ongoing challenges to American law and governance demand sustained attention, reflection, and care, not only from legal experts but from everyone affected by and invested in our constitutional democracy. As teachers, scholars, and members of the legal profession, we hope these analyses will advance the kinds of core public conversations needed for a thriving polity, both at this historic moment and for decades to come. We also hope that this volume will convey to students—our own law students as well as those at other institutions—that it could not be a more important, exciting, challenging, and meaningful time to enter the legal profession.

Sixty-four professors—over half of the Harvard Law School faculty—contributed essays. To our knowledge, this is the first collective work of this nature from this faculty in our own 200-year history. Every full, active member of the Harvard Law faculty was invited to contribute, including all tenured professors, full clinical faculty, and professors of practice. As editors, we exercised no selectivity among our colleagues: If a particular professor did not contribute an essay, it was by their choice. Likewise, perhaps obviously, we exercised no editorial control over our colleagues' decisions about what to say. Each individual contributor is entirely responsible for the substantive content of their essay. Given the production demands of the collection, we could not accommodate footnotes, so our colleagues were prevented from including sources and attributions as they typically would.

As editors, it was a privilege to collect and edit these essays. We learned an enormous amount from our colleagues in the process, both substantively about their areas of legal expertise, and also more personally about their intellectual commitments and struggles. We are proud to be part of a faculty that, notwithstanding our many differences and disagreements, is willing to come together in this way.

Alexandra Natapoff and Guy-Uriel E. Charles

Cambridge, Massachusetts

May 2026

PART I
DEMOCRACY

Although the Declaration of Independence nowhere uses the words "democracy" or "republic," the document gave us many of the principles and values that constitute the essential DNA of American democracy. This first section, although also in some sense this entire book, is a meditation on the nature of that DNA, the ingredients that a democracy needs to flourish, how far we've come, and how far we have to go. Noah Feldman opens with a reflection on the dialectical nature of our republic—both a revolutionary transformation and a commitment to stable constitutionalism—and the tumultuous role of the Supreme Court in mediating that ongoing tension. Annette Gordon-Reed lays out the historical competition between "warring viewpoints on American identity": Are we a democratic nation bound together by creed and ideals as envisioned by the Declaration, or a heritage nation rooted in blood, identity, and religion? Martha Minow reminds us that "democracy is a process, not a static condition," and charts the institutional preconditions for meaningful self-governance, including education, information, and safety. Sheila Heen points out that democracy is also a negotiation, sometimes a delicate one, reliant on our collective ability to govern through persuasion rather than the raw exercise of unilateral power. And Rachel Viscomi argues that we have moved as a nation from an original ethos of independence to a reality of interdependence: an increasingly interconnected global economy, community, and physical environment, all of which shape our polity and its future. Taken together, these five authors take us on a grand tour of the origins, nature, potential, and challenges facing our and perhaps any democracy.

1

The Unending Work of Democracy

Noah Feldman

Two hundred and fifty years ago, the Republic was brought forth in resistance and rebellion. That revolutionary birth stands as a reminder of the American penchant for unruly and disordered transformation—our collective inclination to move fast and break things.

The Constitution, drafted eleven years later and ratified a couple of years after that, reflects a different side of American nation-building. It emerged through planning, research, heated rivalry, negotiation, compromise, and extended, engaged, literate national dialogue.

Looking at the state of the constitutional republic today, you can discern both the warp and weft of this fabric. National polarization is at levels reminiscent of the 1790s, when the first national political parties were formed by James Madison and Alexander Hamilton. If we are not quite at the levels of alienation that led to the Civil War, that says more about the practical impossibility of dissolution than about mutual respect. The sense that we could come apart violently has persisted from Charlottesville (2017) to Minneapolis after the killing of George Floyd (2020) to the Capitol on January 6, 2021, to Minneapolis (again) in 2026. Donald Trump's second presidency has featured attempts to change the structure of government that feel revolutionary both to his supporters and his opponents.

At the same time, the constitutional model featuring the rule of law and stable institutions is also in evidence. Trump was twice impeached by the House of Representatives and twice acquitted by the Senate during his first term in office. Those events followed the playbook laid out by the Framers, even if both outcomes would have astonished them. The judiciary has worked hard to keep the constitutional order functioning. The Supreme Court's decision striking down the unlawful tariffs that were Trump's signature policy initiative (both domestically and internationally) is a highly salient example.

To be sure, the Supreme Court finds itself in the more than slightly awkward position of defending the existing constitutional order even as its conservative majority is in the middle of changing that order. In a series of high-profile decisions in recent years, the Court overturned important precedents that had lasted roughly half a century. It ended the constitutional right to abortion and outlawed the use of racial diversity as an objective for higher education admissions decisions. The Court is poised to kill independent agencies, defined as those whose leadership cannot be removed except for cause. Independent agencies had been an important feature of governmental design for roughly a century.

This is not the first time the Supreme Court has self-consciously evolved the constitutional order. Something roughly analogous happened during the presidency of Franklin Delano Roosevelt, when the Court first blocked and then dramatically reversed itself to unblock New Deal legislation, then repudiated its libertarian jurisprudence that had prohibited state regulation of wages and working hours and conditions. The Warren Court of the 1950s and 60s similarly transformed the constitutional order, outlawing segregation, establishing the principle of one-person-one-vote, and substantially expanding civil liberties.

Nor is this likely to be the last episode of judicial transformation of constitutional norms. The Court has, over the last 150 years, assumed an increasingly central position as arbiter of constitutional limits within our governmental system. Exercising this function has, over time, earned the Court an implicit public mandate to evolve the constitutional system. Because some degree of systemic evolution is required for a constitutional system to flourish as the world changes, the Court can be expected to continue guiding that evolution, even when it purports to follow an originalism that denies evolution altogether.

Although the Court's guiding role is not a historically necessary feature of liberal constitutionalism, its stability demonstrates the value of rule-of-law structures in creating legitimacy and (modest) predictability.

By now, the Supreme Court has no choice but to protect basic rights, ensure the rule of law, and supervise the electoral process—simply because no other governmental institution is capable of delivering on these requirements.

Sometimes, the Court's role in managing the constitutional order seems to come into tension with the revolutionary pull of polarization and executive action. The *Trump v. United States* decision, handed down during the interregnum between Trump's two presidencies, has facilitated radical executive action by insulating the President from criminal charges for official conduct. Yet seen in context, the decision is best understood as an attempt to stop the United States from falling into the situation of a banana republic in which each subsequent president prosecutes the one who came before.

The risks of systemic collapse are real, as they have been at other times in U.S. history. Gerrymandering enabled by computers and encouraged by polarization undermines the democratic process—but so has gerrymandering done from the very beginning of the republic. Our free speech tradition is undergoing one of its periodic re-centerings in the light of new communications technologies. Capitalism, the social force unmentioned in the Declaration or the Constitution but central to the American way of life from the start, continues on its unparalleled path, at once juggernaut and roller coaster. The United States is much more like an empire today than republican Founders like Jefferson and Madison would have liked. But others, like Hamilton and Washington, also present at the start, would be glad of our imperial reach, still unparalleled on the globe, despite the forebodings of the decline that eventually meets all human creations.

The upshot is that the dialectic between the revolutionary impulses of 1776 and the more ordered, law-like processes of 1787–89 persists. The Constitution of the United States is still functioning despite being threatened by powerful populist and popular forces. As Justice Oliver Wendell Holmes wrote a little more than a hundred years ago, the Constitution

> called into life a being the development of which could not have been foreseen completely by the most gifted of its begetters. It was enough for them to realize or to hope that they had created an organism; it

has taken a century and has cost their successors much sweat and blood to prove that they created a nation.

In other words, the whole operation takes unending work to maintain. That's true of every state, every nation, every form of government.

Here we still are, pursuing a happiness we haven't achieved and (happily) never will.

2

Making Americans: A History

Annette Gordon-Reed

Who can lay claim to being an American? A common view holds that one born in the United States of America, or one who comes to live in the country, accepts American values, and gains formal citizenship, *is* an American. President Ronald Reagan often reflected on the way the United States differed from other countries on this point. He endorsed a passage in a letter that stated it was possible for a person to live in France, but never really be considered French. The same holds true for other countries around the globe because the people in those countries believe that their identity as citizens is firmly tied to ancestry and ethnicity.

The United States, Reagan claimed, stood alone in its approach to national identity. Being an American was not a matter of ancestry. It was about one's beliefs that were bound to a set of ideals and principles set forth in the founding documents of the United States of America, principally, the Declaration of Independence and the Constitution of the United States. America was a nation based upon a creed rather than notions of blood. The Declaration's statement of the "self-evident" truth that "all men are created equal," and basing the right to create a new country on that concept, opened the door to a new way to think about how nations are constituted. Reagan certainly was not the first person to depict the United States as a nation based upon ideals. That claim has been made over the course of 250 years, and it has been made with great insistence and pride by people of all races, creeds, colors, and political persuasions.

Of course, there have always been Americans who have sharply dissented from the United States-as-a-creedal-nation construction, denying that there can ever be such a thing. Nations, in their view, are built through the process of making and living in communities over a long period of time; communities that share a common ancestry, language, traditions, and culture. Proponents of what is often called the "blood and soil" or the "heritage American" perspective note that it was people of European descent who, by their numbers, were primarily responsible for creating the United States. Even more specifically, they argue that because those people were mainly Anglo-Protestant, the United States of America should be recognized and—this is critical, particularly for the development of law—*preserved as* an Anglo-Protestant nation. People of color, Catholics, Jewish people, Indigenous people, could live in America, but could never be considered as real Americans. The word Anglo, as does the word "ancestry", creates an explicitly racial understanding of American identity and represents the primary challenge to the idea that Americanness is based upon a belief in a set of ideas. After all, people who were not born Protestant can become Protestant. People who are not Anglo, according to the definition that those who focus on ancestry would apply, cannot "become" Anglo.

These warring viewpoints on American identity have shaped arguments and understandings about the substance and possibilities of American law. Americans profess to have created "a government of law and not of men," under a written Constitution that safeguards and details the powers and rights of citizenship. If the Anglo-Protestant character of American identity is foundational and has to be preserved, can any steps be taken to alter that commitment? Many Americans would answer "no" to that question.

Perhaps no more salient discussion of this question can be found than in Chief Justice Roger Taney's infamous majority opinion in *Dred Scott v. Sandford* (1857). Taney explained why people of African descent—whether enslaved or free—could not be American citizens, employing an ancestry-based and racialized view American identity. No matter what a Black person believed, no matter that Black men had served in the Continental Army of the United States—and in the militia in some states—in the struggle against Great Britain, they were forever disqualified from being real Americans. This was not about their civic status as enslaved people. Blacks who had been born free were equally foreclosed. Justice Benjamin R. Curtis's strong dissent corrected Taney's faulty history on the question of Blacks' place in early America to no avail. Later, in his

Gettysburg address, Abraham Lincoln laid the philosophical groundwork to prepare the nation to formally move beyond Taney and embrace what Lincoln called a "new birth of freedom." He used the Declaration of Independence's statement about equality to justify bringing African American people into the polity and cementing their identity as full Americans. It would take the United States Army's successful prosecution of the Civil War (with the aid of nearly 200,000 Black soldiers) to create the conditions that allowed for the legal settlement of Blacks' place in American civic life. The Thirteenth, Fourteenth, and Fifteenth Amendments ended racially-based legalized slavery, made Black people full citizens, and prohibited interference with their right to vote.

We know the sad story of how the promise of equality through law was thwarted in the decades immediately following the end of the War, largely by people who adhered to the blood and soil view of American identity. Indeed, as a result of the failure to fully implement the post-War legal measures to ensure Blacks' rights, W.E.B. Dubois could confidently state in *The Souls of Black Folk* (1903) that "the problem of the 20th Century is the problem of the color line." In his native United States, Blacks and their White allies, turned to law to solve that problem, instituting a movement that is often referred to as a Second American Revolution that was, in many respects, successful.

There was then, and there is now, ferocious opposition to using law to help the nation live up to the Declaration's creed. One hears blood and soil rhetoric at the very highest level of government. The frenzy of the effort to deport immigrants, particularly brown-skinned immigrants, hints at a not too far below the surface desire to rid the nation of non-White people, to live the fantasy of a White Christian nation. This is all very far away from the lofty aspirations of the Declaration and its belief in the power of ideas. It is also far from the words of the Declaration's author, written fifty years after 1776, when he predicted that the Declaration would one day apply to people the world over. Now more than ever, we need our legal traditions of idealism, equality, and inclusion to resist the current tide of racism and reactionaryism.

3

CONSTITUTING DEMOCRACY: INVESTING IN A VIRTUOUS CIRCLE

MARTHA MINOW

William Hastie, a U.S. civil rights advocate and later federal judge, once explained, "Democracy is a process, not a static condition. It is becoming rather than being. It can be easily lost, but never is fully won. Its essence is eternal struggle." The project of self-governance requires setting up and maintaining institutions and also cultivating and sustaining individual capacities—attitudes and behaviors connected with participating in the political order while preserving its values. Institutions such as election boards, city councils, legislatures, courts, and administrative agencies alone do not work without the participation of people bringing their commitments and skills. Conversely, individuals' virtues and qualities cannot produce stable practices to persist through daily tumult and periods of strain. The qualities of thinking, listening, cooperating, and tolerating needed to support and sustain democratic institutions themselves need laws and organizations, such as schools and media organizations, for cultivating and renewing the capacities of individuals.

Democracy—rule by the people—is a government system with goals that are also its preconditions. Respect for individual freedoms of speech and association; political participation and rights to vote in fair elections for all adults; and elected governmental representatives accountable to the electorate for their decisions comprise the "procedural minimum" that Robert Dahl in his *A Preface to Democratic Theory* defined as preconditions for democracy. Constitutional democracy aims to produce what it also presumes: equal respect for self-governing members of society. Such a virtuous cycle does not start and nor does it continue without genuine investments. Meaningful education regardless of family resources, reliable news sources amid shifting technologies and competition for attention, day-to-day security, and norms of reciprocity each demand not only initial but ongoing contributions of time and money to serve as sustaining ingredients for constitutional democracy. Civic virtues require infrastructures of education, information, personal safety, and political and economic fair play, as well as the mechanisms of constitutional democracy, such as voting rights and checks and balances of governmental institutions.

Even ardent supporters of constitutional democracy emphasize the daunting obstacles to make it work at any time and any place. To engage and equip large numbers of people to govern themselves, to cultivate leaders who can earn and keep respect, to manage conflicts without violence, and to cultivate respect for the rights of others may be simply too hard to sustain, even if a system with such claims can get off the ground. Framers of the U.S. Constitution knew that popular sovereignty would not always serve long-term interests of the nation much less rights for individuals. Top of mind for them were prior republics that had not endured. They devised a structure to tackle the challenges they anticipated. The project of constitutional democracy can inscribe expectations through fragile ideals, captured in words of fallible human beings that at least set standards for judging failures of underlying commitments.

This already fragile arrangement is under attack. Increasingly in constitutional democracies across the globe, a kind of "playbook for authoritarians" appears to guide leaders: blame others, attack, foment social divisions, undermine trust in institutions, and demonize any source of authority other than themselves. Rising generations express the most profound disaffection about democracy. Among 18- to 29-year-olds in the United States, only 57 percent told a prominent pollster that keeping the nation a democracy is very important. Those coming of age in recent years have witnessed democracies roiled by economic instability and record-breaking inequality, refugee and immigration crises and violent government actors claiming to address them, environmental catastrophes, fumbling responses to the COVID-19 pandemic, global wars, and elections flooded with dark money and allegations of corruption. People of varied views and backgrounds—people who disagree about many matters—converge in seeing political and economic systems of the United States as rigged and expressing high levels of distrust of institutions, neighbors, and one another. As individual leaders and their supporters accumulate personal power and wealth, they hollow out democratic institutions, constitutional values, and trust essential to both.

Irony reigns as major anniversaries of the U.S. Declaration of Independence, Constitution, and Bill of Rights unfold now amid the apparent fragility of freedom, law, and rights. Leading U.S. officials attack elections, education, and journalists. Masked and armed government employees unleash violence and fear in the name of immigration law enforcement. Officials dismantle historic markers of both racial injustice and legal commitments to overcome it. Government threats and corporate consolidations shrink independent news reporting. Debates over whether the nation has a constitutional crisis seem clueless. Law firms, universities, businesses, and their leaders compromise their values, suppress their criticisms, and try to lay low. The rights and structures imagined by the U.S. Constitution in the eyes of many do not guard against entrenched power and do not attain effective self-government.

The Constitution enables judicial enforcement, authorizes elections, and divides governmental power to check tyranny. It imagines a virtuous circle, checking power while enabling self-government and individual rights. The rights and structures of constitutional democracy presuppose capacities among leaders and groups in society, including the attitudes, beliefs, and practices enabling voting, compromising, turn-taking, and tolerating differences and disagreements.

Today, those capacities are strained and the ideals of constitutional democracy seem remote. But the same was true during past vehement social conflicts, periods of corruption, a brutal civil war, and slavery. The seeds of freedom and core values of both self-governance and power-checking institutions remain inspiring.

Struggles for constitutional democracy in the United States are still worth it, even as any serious effort requires new and continuing investments of considerable resources, time, and hope. Those struggles cannot be confined to political parties or elections. They also must involve people pursuing the public good as they see it. Discussion of preconditions for constitutional democracy is an invitation to participate in those struggles.

<h1 style="text-align:center">4</h1>

DEMOCRACY IS A NEGOTIATION

SHEILA HEEN

American democracy is designed to operate on persuasive power. Congress and the president must persuade one another to pass bills and budgets. If challenged, they must persuade courts that their actions do not overstep constitutional bounds. Litigants must persuade judges or juries; jurors must persuade one another to reach a verdict. Judges write opinions to explain—and persuade others of—their reasoning. The electoral process itself is one big negotiation. Voters cast their own ballots—an act of unilateral power—but must persuade others if their candidate is to prevail. State governments, town councils, school committees—at every level of governance our system depends on our ability to negotiate with one another to address problems and reach outcomes we can live with, together.

Our collective ability to negotiate—and thus sustain our democracy—is breaking down. Negotiation scholars point to at least three conditions for effective, durable outcomes. All three are being undermined.

First: successful negotiation requires knowing who is in "the room where it happens."

Negotiated outcomes tend to serve the interests of those at the table, able to voice their perspectives and sway others' views.

Today, it is almost impossible to know who all those actors are. While special interests have long influenced lawmakers, we now face an expanding number of hard-to-identify actors: Super PACs, billionaire funders, unverified social media accounts, and bots—domestic and foreign alike. They masquerade as Americans or "pro-democracy" organizations while supporting or attacking candidates, pushing their pet issues, and spreading disinformation. When we cannot identify who is speaking, we cannot hold them accountable for the information they provide or determine whether they should have a seat at our democratic table at all. Instead, we face a cacophony of voices, many of whom are hiding their identities while aggressively working to influence America's future.

Without clarity about who is speaking, whose interests are being served, and whether information is reliable, it becomes harder for Americans to engage and negotiate.

Second: successful negotiation requires a willingness to engage.

Our divisive public conversation is eroding our belief that good-faith negotiation is possible—and with it, the desire to try. Informational and ideological segregation—separate news sources and narratives—is a serious and growing problem, amplified by algorithms that reinforce existing views. We are exposed less and less often to perspectives different from our own.

When we do encounter opposing views, they are often filtered through commentators intent on discrediting them. Parody, exaggeration, and dismissiveness delight; the "other side" is portrayed as idiots or evil. As a result, each side's perception of the other is increasingly inaccurate—a caricature. Engaging with people like that—even family, friends, or neighbors—can feel pointless, even foolhardy.

In reality, *ideological* polarization—the extent to which Americans actually hold views at the extreme poles of left or right—has grown only modestly. Most individuals hold a range of views, tempered by mixed feelings and an appreciation of complexity. Americans agree on more than the public narrative admits. Yet *affective* polarization—the extent to which we distrust and dislike one another and see the other as a threat to the nation's well-being—has grown dramatically. Misperceptions are greatest among the most politically engaged—those most immersed in the ideologically reinforcing storylines we are fed.

Third: successful negotiation requires space to acknowledge what is legitimate about the other side's concerns.

This antipathy is especially dangerous in a democratic republic, where representatives must understand problems, set priorities, and work out solutions. Today's winner-take-all narratives make open negotiation politically risky. Candid conversation can look like betrayal—especially in a world of leaked emails and smartphone recordings.

Yet candid exchange about interests and views is the bedrock of a functional democracy. It is what representatives are charged to do. The spaces negotiators need—where they can move beyond posturing, listen to understand, acknowledge legitimate concerns, and explore solutions—have largely disappeared. Public backlash deters engagement across divides, even though those "opponents" represent the concerns of our friends and neighbors.

None of this is surprising. But it matters.

Negotiation protects us from unchecked unilateral power.

All governance relies on two forms of power: unilateral and persuasive. Unilateral power enables one to dictate outcomes; persuasive power requires you to influence others toward your preferred outcome. When persuasion breaks down and an "us versus them" mindset takes hold, unilateral action becomes more attractive. One side imposes its will on the country; the other side feels justified in retaliating in turn. This zero-sum fight is cast as justification of each side's right to use might. A functioning system of persuasion is vital to protect us from the unchecked and illegitimate exercise of unilateral power.

The Framers understood this interplay. The Constitution was crafted by men writing their way out from under a regime of concentrated unilateral power. Accordingly, they distributed unilateral power sparingly and embedded checks across branches. The Bill of Rights added further safeguards, including freedom of speech and of the press, ensuring scrutiny of how governmental power is exercised. Their design positioned negotiation as the primary engine of all levels of our democracy.

Negotiation is an antidote to tyranny. Those who seek unchecked power must thwart negotiation—by dividing Americans, obscuring our shared interests, and preventing our collective response. Negotiation is messy and imperfect, but it is also fragile: vulnerable to misinformation, mistrust, and silence.

We must rebuild the conditions for successful negotiation if our democratic values are to endure. Americans across the political spectrum still share core commitments: that our government answers to its people, and that our leaders must persuade rather than impose as they work to serve our collective interests.

America's problems can never be solved through force. Democracy must include each side's interests with full participation in joint problem-solving. Understanding, hearing, and caring about each other is the only path to a stable and viable democracy.

Negotiation is the engine of that healthy democracy—and essential to our ongoing quest to form a more perfect union.

5

From Independence to Interdependence: The Evolution of the American Project

Rachel A. Viscomi

In 1776, the most important task facing the American colonies was to secure autonomy from British rule. The Declaration of Independence met the moment perfectly: It framed self-governance as the only reasonable alternative to subjection, grounded its authority in natural rights, and recast colonial grievances as a clear moral mandate. It was a document suited to a revolutionary age: linear in its logic, unambiguous in its story of tyranny and resistance, and deeply galvanizing.

Two hundred and fifty years later, we face a different world and a new challenge. If embodying the ideals of the American project in 1776 required that we establish our independence, then embodying those ideals in 2026 requires that we instead embrace our interdependence. Over the last two and a half centuries our world has become increasingly interconnected. Then, information traveled on horseback; today, it circulates globally in real time. We can stream films from across the globe, listen to radio stations broadcast on another continent, translate between languages, and coordinate across time zones instantaneously.

Our universities and research institutions draw talent from every continent. Our security is dependent on the strength of our alliances, international law, and multilateral institutions. Our economy relies on international supply chains and migrant labor. Our media environment spills across borders in seconds. Climate disruption, pandemics, cyber threats, and financial contagion all ignore national lines. For the United States to thrive for the next 250 years, we must cultivate our ability as citizens to understand our agency and interconnection, to see how our choices interact with institutions, narratives, and global systems.

Unfortunately, much of American political culture still echoes the revolutionary frame, approaching complex issues through an overly simplistic lens that assumes every problem can be traced to a discrete event or direct cause. The zero-sum orientation that helped catalyze our founding turns every conflict into a test of domination. Systems thinking, by contrast, looks for the patterns that connect these events. What recurring dynamics—economic concentration, racial hierarchy, institutional mistrust, media amplification, technological acceleration—are interacting to produce our current crises, and where might we find leverage to change them?

A linear paradigm casts problems as disputes between opposing actors; causes are reduced to the bad decisions of individuals or parties; solutions are imagined as better deals, tougher stances, or clearer victories. Elections become stories of who is to blame and who will fix things, pitting us against each other and obscuring attention to the institutional and economic systems that continue to generate the same outcomes. We see poverty and crime through the lens of bad people and bad choices rather than in relation to the many interacting forces—housing, education, labor, and policing systems—that shape people's options over time. Immigration is framed as a border "invasion" to be stopped, not as the downstream expression of foreign policy, trade decisions, climate disruption, violence, and demographic shifts in which the United States is deeply implicated.

Social media algorithms and profit-driven news cycles amplify and entrench this mindset. As local news and on-the-ground reporting have been decimated, the space for nuanced, context-rich coverage has shrunk, rewarding easy outrage while sidelining the slower, more complex analysis of structural forces and interdependencies that actually drive our conflicts. Across the board, we see an outdated playbook: identify a culprit, assign blame, demand retribution.

In a hyperconnected world, treating every domain—trade, immigration, foreign aid, global media—as an arena for zero-sum domination is not strength; it is self-defeating folly. Tariffs justified as punishing rivals ricochet through supply chains, hurting American workers and consumers. A "tough" immigration stance that criminalizes asylum seekers and demonizes newcomers and American citizens alike undercuts the very sources of dynamism and renewal that have defined the American story. Politicizing public diplomacy and weaponizing foreign aid for short-term leverage corrode the soft power and moral credibility on which our long-term legitimacy depends.

This reductive approach cannot help but fail. It offers a one-dimensional solution to a three-dimensional problem. It not only fails to resolve the challenges it identifies, it embeds them more deeply.

Until we can see the role that we as a nation are playing in co-creating the dynamics we are experiencing, it will be hard to find a path forward. As long as our public imagination remains confined to simple stories of heroes and villains, we will remain bound in cycles of polarity and polarization.

What we need is not more outrage, but more capacity. Reenvisioning democracy as a practice rather than an inheritance can reshape what we ask of ourselves as citizens. Instead of consumers of democracy—people who complain about what "they" are doing in Washington while waiting for the next election—we need to see ourselves as co-creators of democracy. We must become citizens who ask: How is my community organized? Who is excluded? What stories are we telling about each other? How do corporate power, campaign finance, and ownership structures shape whose voices are heard and whose are silenced? Where are the leverage points that will enable us to change the conditions that keep generating the same conflicts?

Reimagining citizenship in an interdependent order also requires renewing the institutions that make honest systems analysis possible. Free speech, independent journalism, and academic freedom are not simply shields for individual expression; they are shared responsibilities to keep our informational ecosystem open to challenge and correction, vital to naming how concentrated power and structural inequities actually work.

Making these shifts—from linear myopia to systemic vision, from individualistic gain to holistic thriving, from external blame to self-reflection and awareness of interconnection—will not be easy. It will require us to give up the comfort of easy stories that sort the world into good guys and bad guys. It invites us to stop imagining that "the problem" is entirely out there, in some other party, ideology, or group that must be defeated or eradicated. Instead of fighting against enemies, we are called to cultivate and nurture systems that support our collective wellbeing.

The Founding era was about declaring independence. Our era asks us to meet the realities of interdependence grounded in collective care and responsibility. The question before us is no longer how to stand apart, but how to stand together. The next chapter of the American project will not be written for us. It can only be written by us, together, as we embrace our responsibilities with wisdom and courage and learn to live up to the promise of our nation.

PART II

FREE SPEECH AND DISSENT

Free speech and the right to dissent are cornerstones of democracy. Cass Sunstein opens with the argument that the "crown jewel" of American law is the First Amendment ban on viewpoint discrimination: the simple idea that the government may never regulate speech because it does not like the point of view being expressed. For Rebecca Tushnet, the central preoccupation of the First Amendment is distrust of government authority, a distrust that demands strong restrictions on the government's ability to restrain all sorts of expression. Laura Weinrib surveys the rich history of the right to dissent, arguing that the right should be understood not merely as a formal liberty but rather as the meaningful ability to make speech consequential in order to effectuate political change. In a similar vein, Sharon Block proposes a reinvigoration of the First Amendment "right of the people . . . to petition the Government for a redress of grievances." This right is not "merely the right to complain into the void," but to do so in a way that obligates those in power to listen and respond. Finally, Tomiko Brown-Nagin connects the power of dissent to American exceptionalism, arguing that American democracy is exceptional precisely because those who have been wronged by the state have themselves been engines of democratic change. Academic freedom, she maintains, requires the ability to teach about that history of dissent and exceptionalism. In each of these ways, these authors show how arguments over the scope and strength of free speech turn out to be arguments about the very nature of our polity.

6

THE BAN ON VIEWPOINT DISCRIMINATION

CASS R. SUNSTEIN

There is a lot to celebrate in American law, but if we are seeking its crown jewel, it might be the constitutional ban on viewpoint discrimination. The idea is simple: The government cannot ever regulate speech because it does not like the point of view that is being expressed. In *West Virginia State Board of Education v. Barnette*, decided in 1943 and hence in the midst of World War II, the Court helped give birth to the idea with this unforgettable warning: "Compulsory unification of opinion achieves only the unanimity of the graveyard."

To see how the ban on viewpoint discrimination works, suppose that the government enacts a law forbidding people from making or spreading negative statements about the president. Suppose further that positive statements and neutral statements are permitted. That law would clearly be directed against one point of view, and it would be unconstitutional for that reason. Here too, *West Virginia State Board of Education v. Barnette* offers memorable words: "If there is any fixed star in our constitutional constellation, it is that no official, high or petty, can prescribe what shall be orthodox in politics, nationalism, religion, or other matters of opinion or force citizens to confess by word or act their faith therein." We should pause over the starkness, and the drama, of those words. Until 1943, that principle had not been understood to be a fixed star in our constitutional constellation. But by saying that it is, the Supreme Court made it so.

The ban on viewpoint discrimination was presaged in *Barnette*, but it was not clearly stated there. Notwithstanding the Court's sonorous words, the case did not announce that ban in plain terms. Indeed, it did not fully emerge until decades later. The earliest announcement came in 1972, from *Police Department v. Mosley*: "[A]bove all else, the First Amendment means that government has no power to restrict expression because of its message, its ideas, its subject matter, or its content." That sentence is declarative, but it is also a bit loose. It conflates various kinds of restrictions, including viewpoint discrimination, subject matter discrimination, and content discrimination. (A prohibition on discussion of abortion, or of the Civil War, would be viewpoint-neutral but content-based.) Remarkably, it was not until the 1990s that the "above all else" claim was transmuted into something close to a flat prohibition on viewpoint discrimination. Consider these unambiguous words from *Rosenberger v. Rector and Visitors of the University of Virginia*: "When the government targets not subject matter, but particular views taken by speakers on a subject, the violation of the First Amendment is all the more blatant. Viewpoint discrimination is thus an egregious form of content discrimination." So there we are; here we are, with the clear announcement of the prohibited category in *Rosenberger*.

The presumption against viewpoint discrimination is now close to irrebuttable. Under current law, a ban on negative statements about the president would unquestionably be invalid. But that is just one example. The prohibition on viewpoint discrimination reaches far and wide. A state could not forbid people from criticizing an ongoing war effort. It could not ban people from speaking in favor of critical race theory. It could not forbid people from arguing that abortion is a form of murder—or that restrictions on abortion are a way of enslaving women. The ban on viewpoint discrimination plays a large role in universities and colleges as well, at least if they are public (and so bound by the First Amendment). A public university cannot ban students from saying that Israel has engaged in genocide, that the civil rights laws should be repealed, that the United States is a racist country, or that Taylor Swift is a terrible singer.

What is remarkable, and worth underlining (and shouting from the rooftops), is the novelty of the ban on viewpoint discrimination. Before the second half of the twentieth century, the First Amendment was not clearly understood to forbid viewpoint discrimination (notwithstanding the seeds planted in *Barnette*). You could trace the ban to *Mosley* in 1972, or to *Rosenberger* in 1995. The ban should be understood as a specification, or a flowering, of the First Amendment's simple, vague, ambiguous statement: "Congress shall make no law . . . abridging the freedom of speech, or of the press." The ban on viewpoint discrimination cannot, of course, be found in the text itself, or in anything that James Madison or Alexander Hamilton wrote. It is a product of national learning over time—not only in the Founding period, and not only in the Civil War, but also in World War I, World War II, the Vietnam War, the civil rights movement, the women's movement, and more.

Above all, the ban on viewpoint discrimination reflects hard-won wisdom: We are allowed to rule ourselves. When the government forbids its disfavored point of view, it is likely to be attempting to entrench its preferred point of view—and thus to obliterate the processes of discussion and deliberation that are fundamental to a free society. It is seeking to shatter a system that allows for both continuity and change. It is seeking to load the dice. By banning viewpoint discrimination, the First Amendment, as it is now understood, is taken to say that here, We the People rule. Of all the commitments of constitutional law, that one might be the most fundamental.

7

Fear of Witches: Free Speech and Distrust of Government Speech Restrictions

Rebecca Tushnet

I have always taught First Amendment doctrine as centrally concerned with distrust of government authority. Americans have a variety of reasons—many of them quite good—to distrust that lawmakers will be correct when they attribute harm to speech. We reasonably believe that, whatever problems plague lawmaking about tangible products or general economic activity, the problems with laws that target speech are greater. As one famous caution goes, "[f]ear . . . cannot alone justify suppression of free speech and assembly. Men feared witches and burnt women. It is the function of speech to free [people] from the bondage of irrational fears." That is, men feared that witches' (spoken and written) curses were real, and so did real, irreparable harm to women because they feared the mirage of harm they imagined from witches' speech. To avoid those mistakes, we must be extremely hesitant to regulate speech alone.

The principle of distrust of government speech suppression has never been more important. Given the deep fissures in American society, we will need to tolerate much speech that we despise because we ourselves will regularly need that same reciprocity.

Rules requiring a clear showing of harm from speech function to protect unpopular people from punishment for being unpopular. The free speech jurisprudence of the second half of the twentieth century largely focused on this insight. That's what led the Supreme Court to invalidate bans on flag-burning and on non-obscene sexual images of fictional children, and to reject mandatory labeling of violent videogames, a policy supported by the theory that children who play such videogames might become violent themselves.

But speech protections are not free. The negative consequence of this distrust of speech regulation is to undermine all sorts of other salutary regulatory regimes, often called "First Amendment Lochnerism." That is, after the New Deal prevailed over challenges to its constitutional legitimacy, it became much harder to invalidate laws that regulated economic activity than to invalidate laws regulating speech. This created an incentive to reframe economic regulation as speech regulation—and powerful institutions could afford very good lawyers who were able to do so. The death of real campaign finance regulation was perhaps the worst result, though First Amendment Lochnerism has also taken down things like restrictions on credit card surcharges, bans on selling "flushable" wipes that clog and destroy municipal sewer systems, and mandatory labels for calorie-dense soda.

More recently, Justices on the Supreme Court have led the charge to allow speech regulation merely because it is customary. We are supposed to understand that speech banned by the Founding generation may be banned today, but no other speech, unless it's sufficiently analogous to speech that was banned in the past. The idea is that no present assessment of harms and benefits should count, at least in the absence of a constitutional amendment. This approach loses the real protective force of distrust, because it turns out that today's unpopular speech looks a lot like the banned speech of the past, at least to many judges of this "historical" persuasion.

So websites that host adult content may have to employ intrusive, insecure age verification services for every visitor because physical businesses have long had to check IDs when a patron seeks to buy adult content. Meanwhile, harmful speech that is part of old-school discriminatory behavior, such as denying service to LGBTQ+ patrons or conversion therapy that seeks to create heterosexuality where it doesn't exist, looks to those same judges like business as usual, and thus historically protected by the First Amendment. It is particularly striking to see the Court's supposedly historical reasoning used to strike down modern gun regulations but uphold modern speech restrictions; history and tradition analysis turns out to be quite flexible rather than, as its proponents claim, a better way of preventing judges from imposing their preferences on the rest of us.

Using history instead of harm evidence freezes the distrust principle. Blind to the actual harms inflicted on unpopular people, this revamped First Amendment won't protect today's women from the stake. This problem is worsened by the larger authoritarian turn in American politics and the destruction of governing capacity caused by the hollowing out of existing institutions, especially trained administrators with some independence.

A government with less capacity for governing has more incentives to suppress speech, speech that might consolidate consensus against it and move the conversation in favor of change. It also has incentives, because of that lack of governing capacity, to strong-arm social institutions and intermediaries to do its speech-suppressive work for it. The destruction of positive state capacity thus encourages a democratically declining state to make it harder to criticize or to publicly imagine different possibilities. Texas and Florida have been at the forefront of such official suppression, attempting to prevent schools and even private entities from acknowledging the existence of LGBTQ+ people, the history and continuation of racial discrimination, and other inconvenient truths. While courts have struck some of these restrictions down as violations of the First Amendment, others remain in place.

This speech suppression is made worse by the media consolidation enabled by decades of antitrust inaction—which eroded restrictions on media ownership designed to keep a variety of voices in the public sphere. It's much easier to intimidate a few big businesses than a thousand local papers. Consolidation has allowed the federal government to effectively threaten major media with significant economic penalties for disagreeing with it. A conglomerate that operates a news division offers many more attack surfaces for regulators than a local newspaper; the conglomerate's theoretically bigger resources thus are less likely to be deployed in defense of free speech. A billionaire might deem it in his interest to buy and gut the Washington Post in order to keep in favor with the ruling party. These threats are not limited to news media. Government funding for research and development turns out to be a potential chokehold on universities' speech and academic freedom to choose professors, courses, and students.

The twentieth century's distrust of speech regulation was not enough to prevent this democratic backsliding. Our prior First Amendment jurisprudence lacked, among other things, a strong public right to know. Without robust public knowledge in the first place, it is harder to show the harm of suppressing it. Thus, it is hard to make a traditional First Amendment argument against the disappearance of evidence about vaccine-preventable illnesses or cover-ups of sexual abuse by powerful men.

Restoring American democracy will require many things. One of them should be a return to the idea that evidence of harm matters to speech regulation. Evidence of what the Founding generation saw as harmful is not the same thing. As Oliver Wendell Holmes, one of our greatest legal scholars and judges, said, "[i]t is revolting to have no better reason for a rule of law than that so it was laid down in the time of Henry IV. It is still more revolting if the grounds upon which it was laid down have vanished long since, and the rule simply persists from blind imitation of the past."

8

EFFECTIVE DISSENT

LAURA WEINRIB

On its 250th anniversary, the Declaration of Independence calls for more than commemoration; it invites a renewed reckoning with the terms of democratic self-government. Much debate has centered on the depth of the document's commitment to equality: who exactly its drafters believed were "created equal" and how far that promise was meant to reach. But the Declaration also bears on a related question, one just as central to American struggles over rights: what is the scope of the liberty to dissent in the nation's political tradition? On this question, many readers have found in the Declaration's own logic a basis for a more demanding claim. In urging resistance to tyranny, the Declaration did not cast dissent as a matter of formal liberty alone. It was at once a catalog of grievances, a mobilizing tract, and a blueprint for remaking authority. It was structural as much as expressive. Generations of Americans have turned to its language not simply to defend the right to dissent, but to argue that a legitimate political order must make dissent effective.

The document itself suggests why. "In every stage of these Oppressions We have Petitioned for Redress in the most humble terms," it declares, but "Our repeated Petitions have been answered only by repeated injury." The force of that passage lies in the sequence it describes. The colonists treated petition as a course they had already pursued, only to find it futile; it was the failure to provide relief that rendered the sovereign "unfit to be the ruler of a free people." Read this way, the Declaration presents protected avenues of dissent as insufficient. Petition mattered. But it was not enough.

At some point, the argument runs, justice requires not only the freedom to voice opposition but the reconstitution of power. That dual character has marked the Declaration's afterlife. For many, the Declaration both justified dissent and supplied a standard for judging whether dissent had actually secured equal citizenship, understood not merely as formal inclusion but as the practical independence necessary for people to participate on equal terms. Activists who invoked the Declaration against the nation's exclusions—exclusions that many of the document's drafters, despite their lofty language, helped to entrench—used it to authorize resistance. They also used it to measure whether political struggle had transformed the circumstances under which people lived.

Frederick Douglass did this in attacking slavery, wielding the Declaration as an indictment of a regime that proclaimed equality while denying Black Americans any real standing in the political community. The Seneca Falls Declaration of Sentiments borrowed the Declaration's cadence and structure almost verbatim while insisting that liberty and consent were hollow so long as women remained legally and politically subordinate. Nineteenth-century labor movements appealed to the Declaration to defend worker independence and dignity against new forms of economic subordination. And in the free-speech fights of the early twentieth century, Wobblies and other labor radicals pushed the point further: by reading aloud from the Declaration to provoke arrest and prosecution, they dramatized the gap between paper rights and the social basis required to exercise them. Workers, they urged, needed the collective power and protection of organization; otherwise, free speech belonged chiefly to those who could afford it.

These movements did not speak in a single idiom. Yet in their appeals to the Declaration, a revealing argument recurs. Effective dissent requires more than formal liberty. It requires the material independence and political standing necessary to make speech consequential. Those who fought over the scope of the Declaration's promise of equality also repeatedly treated expressive freedom as something more than a right exercised in the abstract. The Declaration's authority has therefore lain not only in defending dissent, but in asking whether the social order gives people the capacity to make dissent matter.

On occasion, American law has gestured toward this broader understanding. In *Yick Wo v. Hopkins* (1886), the Supreme Court linked the "fundamental rights to life, liberty, and the pursuit of happiness" to "just and equal laws," adding that no person should be "compelled to hold his life, or the means of living, or any material right essential to the enjoyment of life, at the mere will of another." It is an extraordinary passage. It can be read to suggest that the promises associated with the Declaration are not satisfied by noninterference alone. They require freedom from arbitrary domination, including control by others over the conditions of independent life.

That insight, however, has never been fully absorbed into American constitutionalism. Again and again, our law has recognized protest while disclaiming responsibility for the infrastructure that makes it effective. To be sure, the twentieth-century constitutional order produced genuine and indispensable gains. The retreat from the *Lochner* era's aggressive protection of property rights and "liberty of contract," together with a new willingness to protect speech, political dissent, and vulnerable minorities, mattered concretely to people's lives. But that settlement also helped institutionalize a damaging separation. It encouraged lawyers and judges to imagine that democracy could be preserved by protecting the channels of speech and dissent while leaving the underlying distribution of wealth and power largely untouched. Rights, in this form, could obscure deeper struggles over social and economic organization and divert energy from more thoroughgoing reform.

The result was to make expressive liberty foundational, but insufficient. Speech could be protected while the underpinnings of equal citizenship remained fragile. Protest could be recognized while redistributive demands were deflected. The recognition of rights could function not as a pressure pump for democratic transformation, but as a release valve for democratic unrest.

Some contemporaries saw the problem clearly. Just days after the Supreme Court upheld the National Labor Relations Act, the radical labor lawyer Maurice Sugar argued that rights do not exist "in a political or economic vacuum." They become real through conflict, through their assertion against those who would withhold them. His example was telling: "The rights of life, liberty and the pursuit of happiness referred to in our Declaration of Independence sprang out of the denial of those rights by others."

Yet that broader understanding competed with another, more influential twentieth-century tendency: to equate democratic legitimacy with free expression alone. In its starkest form, that view holds that constitutional law need not concern itself with substantive justice so long as it keeps open the avenues through which democratic majorities may pursue it. Take Justice Holmes's famous pronouncement, dissenting in *Gitlow v. New York*: "If in the long run the beliefs expressed in proletarian dictatorship are destined to be accepted by the dominant forces of the community, the only meaning of free speech is that they should be given their chance and have their way." That statement was strikingly responsive to the radical claim pressed by Gitlow's ACLU lawyers that the Constitution had incorporated a "right asserted in the Declaration of Independence to alter or abolish a system of government." But Holmes's formulation has also been read to support a converse implication: If transformative demands have not prevailed, the existence of robust protection for speech and minority rights is taken to mean that the polity is satisfied with the world as it is. Provided the channels of representation remain nominally open, the failure of structural change is recast as tacit endorsement of the status quo, or at least as the valid outcome of democratic contestation.

That inference, however, does not follow. A society may preserve opportunities for participation while making effective political challenge exceedingly difficult. It may protect dissent in law while neutralizing it in practice through inequality, dependency, fragmentation, and fear. One need only think of workers who are legally free to criticize an employer but know that doing so may cost them their jobs; tenants who may organize in principle but fear eviction or blacklisting; or students and faculty whose speech is formally protected yet constrained by donor pressure, administrative surveillance, or professional reprisal. The danger, then, is not only that rights become too thin. It is that thin rights become justificatory: evidence not just that dissent is permitted, but that existing arrangements have earned their legitimacy.

These observations bear directly on the present moment. Our danger is not merely the silencing of protest by direct censorship, though that danger is real enough and newly resurgent. It is also the conversion of protest into a bare right of expression while government and aligned private actors narrow the terrain of meaningful dissent through economic dependency, institutional intimidation, and diffuse coercion. Today, this often works not through overt prohibition but through funding threats, contractual leverage, accreditation fears, selective investigations, and other pressures to which institutions preemptively yield. In those moments, ostensibly private actors become instruments of state suppression; a person may remain technically free to speak while lacking the institutional protection, economic independence, or collective strength that would make speech matter. Protest may still occur even as the social basis for effective dissent is steadily withdrawn.

The Declaration remains useful at 250 only if we resist reducing it to a civic hymn to patriotic disagreement. Its language emerged from the breakdown of a political order that had rendered petition futile. Later generations repeatedly returned to it to name conditions in which equal standing remained out of reach. Its lasting force lies in the connection it has nourished between dissent and self-government, between grievance and institutional transformation.

Seen in that light, today's democratic crisis is far more urgent than a doctrinal puzzle about the scope of the First Amendment. It is a crisis of democratic agency. A polity in which dissent is formally permitted but institutionally penalized, economically precarious, and practically curtailed has not fulfilled the Declaration's promise. It has hollowed it out.

To honor the Declaration now is therefore to do more than defend the right to speak. It is to rebuild the conditions under which speaking can matter: institutions resilient enough to withstand political retaliation, workplaces and universities less governed by fear, and forms of collective power strong enough to make dissent more than a matter of personal risk. Only then can dissent become not simply an outlet for grievance, but an instrument of democratic change.

9

REINVIGORATING THE RIGHT TO PETITION

SHARON BLOCK

Public confidence in American democracy is in crisis. At the heart of the crisis is a failure of a basic democratic promise: that people can petition their government for a redress of grievances in a way that obligates those in power to listen and respond. Large numbers of people believe, with good reason, that government is unresponsive, captured by special interests and fundamentally out of touch with their lives. They see lawmakers, agency officials, and the President surrounded by lobbyists and donors who enjoy direct access to communicate their own desires and demands. At the same time, ordinary people without such access perceive that their own experiences of precarious work, scarce housing, racialized policing and environmental peril rarely shape public policy.

A solution to this crisis is already at our fingertips. The First Amendment declares that "Congress shall make no law . . . abridging . . . the right of the people . . . to petition the Government for a redress of grievances." Read literally, this promise means only that the government cannot retaliate against members of the public for speaking up. But for democracy to function as it should, the right to petition must be more robust and more dynamic. It cannot merely be the right to complain into the void. It should be an open, two-way bridge between ordinary people and official power. Absent a meaningful right to petition, the bridge between the governed and the governing opens too infrequently—only on Election Day.

Earlier in our country's history, the right to petition the government was taken very seriously. We should remember that the Declaration of Independence itself is, in part, a complaint that petitions had gone unheeded: "Our repeated Petitions have been answered only by repeated injury." This failure by the King and British Parliament to answer the colonists' petitions was considered a justification for the American Revolution itself.

Decades later, abolitionists used the now long-abandoned congressional practice of devoting time at the beginning of each legislative session to reading constituent petitions as an organizing and publicity tool. The tool was so effective, with hundreds of thousands of anti-slavery petitions being delivered to Congress in the years leading up to the Civil War, that pro-slavery representatives pushed through the Pinckney Resolutions, which barred the House from considering any anti-slavery petitions at all. John Quincy Adams viewed the right to directly petition the House as so important that he regularly read petitions out loud in violation of the Pinckney gag rule and worked strenuously to get it repealed. Historically, then, petitioning has been an important and effective mechanism for those without direct power to force their concerns onto the political agenda of those more powerful.

Today, that right has effectively disappeared. The right to petition must mean more than the right to send a message to an unmonitored inbox or to tag an elected official in a social media post. A meaningful right to petition should encompass three elements: accessible channels to reach those in power; an obligation for those in power to substantively respond; and a guarantee that all petitions are treated equitably, regardless of the petitioner's status.

These principles of meaningful petitioning have found their way into various regulatory regimes, with more or less success. For example, they bear a resemblance to the system created by the Administrative Procedure Act—the statute passed in 1946 for the ostensible purpose of giving the public an opportunity to weigh in on federal regulations and significant executive actions. The APA requires federal agencies to make public their intent to issue regulations, to receive comments from any member of the public on those proposed regulations, and to respond to "significant comments" and public petitions for rulemakings.

In practice, however, the APA's process has not actually produced a meaningful petitioning right. The APA's process fails to deliver as a truly democracy-affirming exercise because it has been captured by the same moneyed interests that have captured so much of our democracy. Corporate interests, the wealthy and the well-connected can hire lawyers and experts to draft lengthy technical submissions, meet with agency and White House officials, and litigate in support of their positions before a judiciary that reports up to a Supreme Court aligned with their interests.

In contrast, the rest of the population likely does not even know when agencies are considering rules that may have a profound impact on their lives or that they can submit petitions to ask an agency to take action—most people are too busy working just to make ends meet. If they do know and find the time to engage with the system, their comments must compete with comments submitted by corporate interests. Where comments and petitions on behalf of corporate interests are lengthy and technical, regular people often submit comments that share personal details about their lives or short "postcard" messages that are part of mass campaigns. Formally, everyone's submissions are in the agency's record, but practically, the corporate comments carry more weight.

This same dynamic plays out in an even more extreme manner in the legislative sphere. Lobbyists draft bills, wage public campaigns to frame the issues in a manner favorable to their corporate clients, and negotiate access to members of Congress. These activities take place in the shadow of maxed out campaign donations and unlimited independent expenditures. The wealthy and well-connected enjoy a premium channel of petitioning while everyone else gets the equivalent of a public comment box.

We know how to make the process work well for people. In particular, the Consumer Financial Protection Bureau had done more than most agencies to create a feedback loop for members of the public who raise their concerns to the agency. The CFPB keeps a public docket of all rule-making petitions filed and reports out publicly on the disposition of the petitions. It also has created a public database of complaints filed by consumers about financial products. The Bureau had attempted to get responses for consumers to their complaints within fifteen days. And, at least during the Biden Administration, the CFPB devoted significant resources to reaching out to consumers to create channels of communication outside of the Beltway. Unfortunately, the Trump Administration has attempted to shut down the CFPB.

How could we create a meaningful right to petition for everyone? First, we have to reform the failed campaign finance system. As long as elected officials are dependent on donors to fuel their campaigns, petitions from the general public and from big fundraisers are never going to receive equal consideration. Second, we need a system that does not just passively accept input. Instead, lawmakers and agencies should be required to reach out to solicit input from a broad range of stakeholders. One way to maximize outreach is for lawmakers and agencies to work through the kinds of organizations that most of the public engages with already on a regular basis—unions, local governments, schools, and other kinds of community-based organizations. Finally, we need a system with greater transparency so that members of the public know what happened to their grievances. There should be an obligation for lawmakers and agencies to provide feedback in a timely manner so that members of the public can hold them accountable for how they respond.

It is naïve to think that a public that engages with its government only once a year or every other year at the ballot box will feel a strong attachment to democratic institutions. But a *meaningful* right to petition could be the antidote to our nation's democratic malaise. Until we reshape our political institutions to honor the value of everyone's petitions, the public's crisis of confidence in democracy will remain understandable and justified.

10

On American Exceptionalism and the Academic Freedom to Learn about History's "Bad" Parts

Tomiko Brown-Nagin

The idea that the United States is superior to other countries because of its founding ideals—a cornerstone of American exceptionalism—will animate many commemorations of the Declaration of Independence's 250th anniversary. Yet some of the most ardent champions of American exceptionalism do not seem to recognize what actually makes America exceptional.

What is exceptional about American history is not the absence of injustice. It is the extent to which some of the very people who endured this injustice—and their descendants—drove the country's transformation toward its founding ideals of liberty, equality, and the pursuit of happiness for all.

Part of that exceptionalism depends on our ability to teach and learn about the most difficult aspects of American history. Yet, many recent critiques of educational institutions target the discipline of history. Research and teaching about slavery and the experience of marginalized groups have been denigrated and proscribed. Critics claim that focusing on the "bad" parts of American history tarnishes the nation's image, is unpatriotic, and therefore impermissible.

This view shortchanges the nation's legal history and conflicts with academic freedoms long protected by law. The freedom to teach and learn how the United States became a multiracial democracy with equal rights—including for descendants of the enslaved—is fundamental to its claim to greatness.

Reconstruction offers a paradigmatic example. Formerly enslaved people and their allies reshaped the Constitution itself: the Fourteenth and Fifteenth Amendments, drafted and ratified in a polity shaped by Black political agitation, redefined citizenship, equal protection, and suffrage—an unprecedented expansion for a former slave society.

Consider the remarkable impact of two men of color: Hiram Rhodes Revels and Robert Smalls. Hiram Rhodes Revels, born free, became the first Black U.S. senator, occupying the seat once held by Jefferson Davis, president of the Confederacy. His seating, over objections that echoed *Dred Scott v. Sandford* (1857), gave concrete effect to the Reconstruction Amendments' new understanding of national citizenship. A Senate once dominated by slaveholders now included a Black senator from the Deep South. Robert Smalls, a former slave who served in Congress and the South Carolina legislature, helped turn a bastion of pro-slavery sentiment into a laboratory of Black political power. He championed universal public education, land and labor reforms, and federal protections for Black suffrage, resisting efforts to abandon them to hostile state and local politics. Central to American exceptionalism is this extraordinary ability of the dispossessed not only to alter but to become an active and meaningful part of our system of governance.

The former Confederate states' rollback of these strides toward equal rights, through segregation statutes, racially unequal enforcement of facially neutral laws, and violence, demanded a Second Reconstruction. Descendants of enslaved people once again led the legal fight to reinterpret the Reconstruction Amendments to secure equal citizenship and voting rights. Thurgood Marshall and Charles Hamilton Houston, with assistance from the likes of Jack Greenberg and Constance Baker Motley, crafted and implemented the strategy that culminated in *Brown v. Board of Education* (1954). That landmark case struck down state-mandated school segregation by reinterpreting the Fourteenth Amendment. Often hailed as a repudiation of America's "original sin" and a great triumph, *Brown* cannot be appreciated apart from the "bad" history—discriminatory assumptions about citizenship and racial exclusion—that it repudiated.

In his now widely hailed "I Have a Dream" speech at the March on Washington in 1963, the Reverend Dr. Martin Luther King, Jr. called the Declaration "a promissory note" that was redeemable for the descendants of slaves and slaveholders alike. And he famously hoped that "the sons of former slaves and the sons of former slave owners will be able to sit down together at the table of brotherhood." The civil rights and voting rights statutes that resulted from advocacy by Dr. King and the student movement in campaigns at Birmingham and Selma transformed the United States into a multiracial democracy, now celebrated by most Americans as one of its greatest achievements. This movement gave fuller meaning to the Declaration's lofty promises.

All to say: formerly enslaved people and their descendants were central agents in the constitutional and political changes now hailed as the fulfillment of American ideals. This pattern—enslavement and exclusion followed by structural democratic enlargement led by those excluded—is historically distinctive.

In most former slave societies, formerly enslaved people did not so quickly reshape constitutional law, federal legislation, and national political identity. In Brazil (which abolished slavery only in 1888) and Britain's Caribbean colonies, emancipated people were not quickly incorporated into the polity; in many cases, universal suffrage initially arrived only in the mid-twentieth century, when the United States began its second Reconstruction.

The United States is also distinctive in fighting a brutal civil war over the Confederate states' bid to preserve slavery, but no account of its exceptionalism can ignore Black leadership in a centuries-long, cross-racial struggle against slavery and its legacies, and in the transformation of American law and society.

It would be particularly perverse to suppress this exceptional history in the name of American exceptionalism, given the Constitution's protection for academic freedom. It is a core concept rooted in the First Amendment's protection of expressive and associational freedoms and the Fourteenth Amendment's protection of due process and equal protection of the laws. In cases such as *Meyer v. Nebraska* (1923), *Sweezy v. New Hampshire* (1957), and *Keyishian v. Board of Regents* (1967), the U.S. Supreme Court affirmed the rights to research, teach, and learn free from censorship. This is a modern legal expression of the commitment to "useful knowledge" that Thomas Jefferson, the architect of the Declaration, saw as vital to democracy.

We should learn from our history, especially the painful parts. Studying the nation's full story shows how a republic committed at its founding to both slavery and equality has struggled to extend rights to the descendants of slaves and slaveowners, to voluntary and involuntary immigrants, and to men and women alike—threads in a single, if frayed, democratic fabric.

The freedom to study how a society built on both slavery and equality moved, however unevenly, toward broader rights is not a luxury. It is part of what makes the United States worth celebrating. Attempts to ban or sanitize honest teaching about slavery, Reconstruction, and civil rights do not defend American exceptionalism; they undermine it. They deny access to the very history that shows how profoundly Americans—including descendants of the enslaved—have worked to bring the nation closer to its founding promises.

PART III
AMERICAN IDENTITY, CITIZENSHIP, AND RACE

Who gets to be American? The question is as old and conflicted as the Declaration itself. Guy Charles reminds us that "America has been multicultural, multiethnic, multireligious, and multiracial from the beginning," even though we have never come to an agreement on what our political identity should look like. The audacious promise of the Declaration, as he sees it, is the assertion that the United States is "one people" bound together politically under law, notwithstanding the country's enormous racial, religious, and cultural heterogeneity. He concludes that "[b]ecause of our differences, we must recognize that our fates are linked," a recognition that "is the gateway to building and preserving the nation." Ken Mack charts the fraught legal history of two dominant responses to the citizenship question: one that permits the governmental exclusion and repression of "outsiders," and a competing, open-ended tradition that welcomes all groups into the polity on equal terms. Randall Kennedy grapples with those conflicting traditions in a pessimistic vein: admiration for America's traditions of prosperity and freedom, alongside disgust for its history of violent exclusion. John Coates argues that the equality battle is far from over, and that the legacy of slavery accepted by the Founders can be glimpsed in every major aspect of our modern polity. And Michael Klarman closes the section with a sweeping analysis of the recent renaissance of white supremacy, reminding us that U.S. history has always involved heated battles over our racial identity and past. The Declaration may have asserted that "all men are created equal," but as these authors describe in sobering detail, 250 years later we are still grappling with what that actually means.

11

ONE PEOPLE: THE AUDACIOUS PROVOCATION OF AMERICA

GUY-URIEL E. CHARLES

The Declaration of Independence begins with an arresting, audacious assumption about nationhood. Before it proclaims self-evident truths, identifies inalienable rights, and catalogs grievances against the Crown, it advances an implicit claim—that the new nation emerging from political separation from Britain comprises "one people." This emergent nation was and would continue to be united in a common cause. It would be a single "people" entitled by the "Laws of Nature and Nature's God" to a new conception of equality. Two hundred and fifty years later, Americans are still asking themselves what it means to be a people and what is it, exactly, that makes them one.

The phrase–*one people*–hazards an audacious provocation. The Declaration was, in every respect, a bold and risky enterprise. A disparate collection of people pledged to pursue a political and, eventually, constitutional project not merely for themselves but for one another, an assertion not just of individual rights, but an interdependent "Right of the People" to institute a new republic. The American constitutional republic is a collective undertaking that promises mutual benefit across differences.

Human flourishing is a collective enterprise.

The "one people" of the Declaration is not a demographic claim or an appeal to heritage. As a matter of description, America has been multicultural, multiethnic, multireligious, and multiracial from the beginning. Consider who was present at the founding. The men who signed the Declaration were part of a continent home to scores of Indigenous nations with sovereign histories etched into the land over millennia. That same continent, in 1776, was inhabited by both free and enslaved people from Africa, whose labor made possible the material wealth that would help build an American empire. Spanish and French communities occupied vast stretches of the coasts and the interior. Irish Catholic immigrants, German Pietists, and Sephardic Jews were familiar presences on the colonial landscape. And though we often talk about the founding fathers, the American constitutional project would have been impossible without the often-unacknowledged contributions of the founding mothers.

"One people," then, cannot mean cultural, racial, or demographic homogeneity. America has never been a single, homogeneous nation. It was not in 1776, it is not in the twenty-first century, and it will not be so when the republic marks its 500th anniversary.

The unity the Declaration implies is not that of blood or even of custom. It is the unity of shared political obligation, sustained by law. It is the audacious idea that people of different languages, races, faiths, genders, classes, regions, or circumstances can nonetheless covenant together for mutual benefit. The Declaration, the Constitution, and our credal documents—such as the Preamble to the Constitution, the Pledge of Allegiance, the Star-Spangled Banner, and *e pluribus unum*, our de facto motto—represent a wager. People who may not be alike in any tribal sense could become a single political community through the advantage of mutual reliance. Mutual dependence because we are different is the basis of our nationhood.

We often evaluate the American project by its deficiencies. The monuments of exclusion are familiar and readily recognizable. Our Constitution, designed to protect individual liberty, made an exception for chattel slavery, which was not officially abolished until 1865 by the Thirteenth Amendment. Women were not officially incorporated into the political community until 1920 with the Nineteenth Amendment. We continue to live with the legacies of the dispossessing of Indigenous peoples, the internment of Japanese Americans, and the exclusion of people of Chinese descent, to name only the most visible blemishes. The enterprise of including excluded groups within the constitutional compact is an important and necessary project, and the republic is rightly evaluated by its ability to carry it out.

However, extending America's constitutional ideals to the excluded and marginalized, though vital, is not the only thing that makes the American promise audacious. It should not be the sole or even most consequential measure of the American constitutional experiment's success or failure. Rather, it is part of an even larger ambition. Mutual and collective flourishing is the metric for assessing national and constitutional success.

The American promise is audacious because it presumes a unitary peoplehood that embraces differences–race, ethnicity, national origin, religion, gender, class, region–and anchors a commitment to mutual prosperity. Mutual prosperity is the incentive for investing in the enterprise of making *unum*, one, out of *pluribus*. The Preamble to the Constitution does not propose to secure the blessings of liberty for some of the people, or for the people of a certain race, ethnicity, or religion, or for the people whose ancestors were part of the founding. The Declaration–eventually the Constitution–commits the nation to shared governance, shared rights, and shared accountability under the law for "one people."

The audacity of America, both asserted by its credal documents and reflected in its history, is the promise that profound human diversity can animate the constitutional project. A constitutional republic composed of drastically different peoples requires a functioning constitutional order that extends the blessings of liberty collectively to "ourselves and our Posterity." Faced with the reality of a heterogenous multicultural community, the drafters of the Declaration and the Constitution offered a basis for a unified project.

When schoolchildren declare and when we as schoolchildren declared that we are one nation with liberty and justice for all, we were at once describing what is only partially true of our republic, foretelling what will be true of our republic, and arguing what needs to be true if we are to be a constitutional republic. We find many things in our credal documents: what is actually there, what we hope will be there, and what we think should be there. The conception of nationhood is at once descriptive, predictive, and prescriptive. Even so, the Declaration, and eventually the Constitution, made an audacious wager on the idea that we are "one people."

Two hundred and fifty years after the founding of this constitutional republic, Americans are still debating the nature of their political identity. They are still determining who counts, who belongs, and what Americans owe to one another. The founding era reminds us that we need not crash against those rocks. A collection of unlike people could bind themselves together, cast their lot together, and entrust their fate to others very different from themselves. They could form one nation. When some are left out, the republic fails those left out, but more importantly, the republic fails the constitutional order itself. The tie that binds, that makes one people, frays.

Nationhood is a continual process. Because of our differences, we must recognize that our fates are linked. This recognition is the gateway to building and preserving the nation. As the Star-Spangled Banner declares: "Praise the Power that hath made and preserv'd us a nation!" To forge a single nation among people who are profoundly different, America offers the promise of mutual obligation, of collective flourishing. If, 250 years hence, we keep the pledge to mutual flourishing that is America's audacious provocation, we will, bound by our differences, remain one people.

12

What Is America?: The Presumptions that Law Makes

Kenneth W. Mack

Thurgood Marshall—the first Black Supreme Court Justice and an architect of the *Brown v. Board of Education* litigation—marked the American Constitution's bicentennial by dissenting from that year's celebrations. In a speech for the occasion, Marshall underscored the document's original defects and noted that it took two centuries of struggle after the Founding to more fully enshrine liberty and equality in our basic law. Marshall worried about the constitutional compromise over slavery, but he might also have pointed to the deeply ambivalent answers that the founding moment gave to the question of what, exactly, was America.

Since the nation's founding, the United States has grappled with the definitional question of who can lay claim to being American. In 1776, American law contained multiple traditions that could have defined the new republic's experiment in self-government. Benjamin Franklin famously invoked one of these traditions when, during the 1750s, he wrote of his worry that white English people and their culture would be swamped by waves of "swarthy" Germans, as well as "tawny" French, Italians, Swedes, others—and Black people. America, at its independence two decades later, might have embraced these sentiments: a tradition of insularity, of a bounded community vigilant in defending its borders of belonging. Or it might have embraced a different tradition: an open-ended society that left room for outsiders—defined by ethnicity, religion, race, sex, foreign birth, or some other category—to join as full members. American law remained unsettled on such questions, as it often has to this day. The original Constitution, for instance, said very little about who was, or might become, a citizen. The Indigenous inhabitants of

North America, it assumed, were mostly citizens of quasi foreign nations, but it otherwise left American citizenship itself largely undefined.

Americans have repeatedly confronted two competing ways of reading the nation's core principles—and two competing ways of interpreting the federal government's power to repress disfavored groups with ties to foreign nations: one that treats such repression as presumptively valid, and another that treats it as presumptively invalid. Those presumptions have mattered, sometimes enormously, because they are answers—implicit or explicit—to the question of what kind of nation America is. It was through those presumptions that the most fundamental questions of membership were contested and, over time, partially answered.

Take, for instance, the question of whether free African Americans (as opposed to those who were enslaved) were full citizens. American basic law left that issue, like so many others, strikingly unresolved. The swarthy Germans who had once worried Franklin, and their successors, did in fact exercise basic citizenship rights in the new American republic, even though formal law offered little clarity on Franklin's deeper anxiety about whether white English culture should be preserved inviolate.

One presumption, most famously stated in the Declaration of Independence, held that free men were equal. In the decades after the Founding, free Black people began to invoke that presumption to challenge the justifications for the "black laws"—laws in states such as Ohio, Michigan, and Illinois—that barred African Americans from traveling, serving on juries, and exercising other core incidents of citizenship. Free Black communities would eventually press American courts with arguments for what became known as birthright citizenship, and their views were ultimately written into the Fourteenth Amendment, as the historian Martha Jones has shown.

Even then, the Amendment's promise remained, in one respect, slightly open-ended. Its birthright guarantee was limited to those born here who were "subject to the jurisdiction" of the United States. Over time, the consensus developed that this exception should be read narrowly, with a few exceptions such as Native Americans who didn't fully gain citizenship as a group until 1924. The presumption has long favored citizenship for nearly everyone born on U.S. soil, even though there have been periodic efforts to expand the exceptions to that rule. And the presumption mattered.

America could have become a nation whose laws explicitly authorized the creation of a permanent category of second-class, unequal members. Other nations have moved in that direction in recent years, and that choice may yet split those societies apart. But, propelled by the claims of free Black people—and many others—Americans made a different choice.

There was also the question of whether the foreign-born, and their immediate descendants, should be treated as full members of American society. Congress quickly established in the 1790 Naturalization Act that any "free white person" born abroad could become a citizen within two years. That built on a 1740 Parliamentary Act that allowed Protestant aliens who lived in America for seven years to become British subjects. At first glance, the presumption seemed plain: America was a white Protestant country. Yet even that presumption proved more malleable than it appeared. Free Black people challenged it, and so did a century and a half of litigation under the naturalization laws over whether people born in various parts of the world, from the Middle East to Asia, and people of various religious beliefs, were "white." What, exactly, was America's racial and religious character? The initial answer seemed straightforward, but in practice it was far more ambiguous, and through that ambiguity flowed the claims of many kinds of people to belonging.

From the beginning, too, the nation confronted the question of whether it would tolerate or be hostile to the entry and presence of those born elsewhere. The Federalist Party of President John Adams, for example, singled out the foreign-born in the 1798 Alien and Sedition Acts, which, among other things, allowed the president to expel any alien who might be disloyal, and during times of war or threatened invasion to detain and deport alien males born in hostile nations. Three of the four Acts were repealed or allowed to expire and not renewed when the Jeffersonians won the presidency in 1800. But the Alien Enemies Act remained on the books and has been invoked periodically throughout American history—including during World War II in the detention of "alien enemies," alongside the broader mass removal and incarceration of Japanese Americans, many of whom were U.S. citizens. In more recent years, it has also been cited amid efforts to expel other disfavored groups.

In addition to citizenship, Americans have also debated the question of which immigrant groups the country would welcome. In the early decades after the Founding there was little sustained effort to prevent the foreign-born from entering or leaving the country. That changed decisively with the 1875 Page Act and the 1882 Chinese Exclusion Act, which targeted Asian women and Chinese laborers, respectively. These were followed by additional laws and federal actions that eventually banned immigration from much of Asia and sought to reduce Catholic and Jewish immigration from Eastern and Southern Europe in favor of Northern European Protestants. That restrictionist project was, in turn, substantially reversed by the 1965 Immigration and Nationality Act, which removed most vestiges of that regime and helped make America a country increasingly populated by people of varied faiths, colors, and ethnicities from across the world. In that sense, we are still answering Franklin's old question about what America would be. Americans have answered it differently at different times, and those answers have shaped the nation we have inherited after 250 years.

Finally, there was the question of what equality meant for those born free on American soil. In the decades after the Founding, women's rights activists pressed this question by pointing out that women were ostensibly full American citizens but could not vote—and that married women had limited rights to work, to keep their wages, and to control their own property. As late as the 1950s and 1960s, Americans debated whether women could be barred from serving on juries or excluded from certain lines of work simply because "the paramount destiny and mission of woman are to fulfill the noble and benign offices of wife and mother," as a famous Supreme Court concurring opinion had once put it. Here, too, presumptions mattered. At the Founding, the law often presumed that a woman was represented in public life by her father or husband. Yet enough ambiguity remained to sustain nearly two centuries of activism. By the 1970s, a different assumption took firmer hold: that basic citizenship rights—to work, to participate in court, to receive equal government benefits—should not be circumscribed by sex.

At the Founding, basic questions about what, exactly, was America remained unresolved, and neither law nor tradition settled them. But presumptions did exist, sometimes written into law and at other times simply taken for granted. And those presumptions have mattered, sometimes a great deal. The British North America that Franklin imagined in his early essay would likely have produced a United States that was far smaller, far less influential in the world, far less prosperous, more homogeneous, more intolerant and insular, and more dangerously divided than the America we have inherited. Franklin himself seemed to change his mind after the revolution. "Strangers are welcome," he wrote of the newly independent America, "because there is room enough for them all." He'd made a choice, as did the dreamers, activists and ordinary citizens of whom Thurgood Marshall spoke. It is they who shaped the America we have inherited.

We are once again at a moment of choosing, and we are not alone: America is not the only democratic nation facing such choices about its past traditions and its future. We are unlikely to put fully to rest the ongoing debate over what kind of community we inhabit—but the choices made now will matter enormously for America and for the wider world we share.

13

BICENTENNIAL MELANCHOLIA

RANDALL KENNEDY

I am grateful that I am the beneficiary of a society, undergirded by the government of the United States of America, that has afforded me a splendid life. I am keenly aware that I enjoy life-enhancing conditions, opportunities, and freedoms that others around the world are denied and that have been denied to earlier generations of Americans on account of various prejudices.

A beautiful feature of the United States is the space given to dissidents to challenge social wrongs. Protest has always been menaced by repression. But a tradition of civil liberties has permitted Americans to talk to their government and to one another with an openness that is striking. Lawyers and judges have played a major role in the development of that tradition. I have been privileged to know some of them, including Thurgood Marshall, J. Skelly Wright, Jack Greenberg, Matthew Perry, Julius Chambers, Michael Meltsner, Morton Stavis, Owen Fiss, Thomas I. Emerson, Burke Marshall, Martha Minow, Margaret Burnham, David Cole, Charles Ogletree, Derrick Bell, Norman Dorsen, Drew Days, Lani Guinier, Laurence Tribe, Nadine Strossen, Margaret Marshall, Mary Bonauto.

I am simultaneously disgusted by the United States. It has never come close to atoning for its ethnic cleansing on a continental scale, preferring instead to indulge mythologies about "empty" wilderness. It has never suitably faced the enormity of the crime of slavery, preferring instead to portray the civil war as reparations. The fight over slavery was indeed the ultimate cause of the civil war. But the United States pursued the war to preserve its fullness, not to abolish slavery; the destruction of racial bondage was a beneficent but collateral consequence of war for union. Nor has the United States faced up to the ugly legacies of its predations abroad, injuring, among others, Mexico, the Philippines, Haiti, Nicaragua, Iran, Guatemala, and Vietnam.

One might derive solace from believing that America's encounters with evils had enlightened its leaders and people making it less susceptible to wickedness in the future. But such a belief would be naive. Consider the federal Supreme Court, a branch of government that many view as more thoughtful and humane than the legislative and executive branches. Given its record over the past several decades, can one be at all confident that, confronted with analogous conflicts, the current Supreme Court would approach things differently than predecessors that bequeathed such awful rulings as *Plessy v. Ferguson*, *Giles v. Harris*, *Chae Chan Ping v. United States*, or *Korematsu v. United States*?

There is a related but more recent and urgent reason for disgust. In 2024, the American electorate elevated to the presidency a man who had shown contempt for the most elementary decencies. He denied the outcome of a previous election that he lost. He sought to undermine the legitimacy of the electoral process by disseminating falsehoods and soliciting votes from state officials who, to their credit, rejected his entreaties. In 2025, after that man was sworn in as the country's 47th president, he pardoned rioters who had, on January 6, 2021, overrun the Capitol in an effort to prevent congressional ratification of the 2020 election. He has acted in a manner that reasonably raises fears that he and his allies might seize upon pretexts to interfere with, or indeed cancel, elections.

Across a variety of fields, he has foreseeably exacerbated misery and deployed unnecessary violence. He has put public health in jeopardy by promoting to influential positions people who have exhibited animus toward environmentalism and medical science. He has cavalierly destroyed programs that ministered to the elemental needs of people around the world, a callous act that will lead to the expedited deaths of millions. To combat illegal immigration, he has ordered or tolerated the cruel separation of children from parents, leading to situations in which boys and girls have become perhaps permanently lost to their mothers and fathers. He has dispatched paramilitary forces throughout the land in order to hunt down the undocumented in a fashion reminiscent of the 1850s when, empowered by federal law, slaveholders chased their human property.

He has overseen the killing of hundreds on the high seas, purportedly for drug smuggling, thereby likely violating international law and, in any event, exacting a punishment disproportionate to the alleged offense. The incumbent president disseminated on social media depictions of African Americans as apes—people who happened to be a former president and his wife. While one might have thought that such an egregiously racist act would provoke a broad-based congressional rebuke, in fact, it elicited distressingly few vocal objections. The incumbent president, who has been credibly accused of sexual assault, routinely makes sexist comments. One could easily list many more outrages; they surface almost daily. And they are not secret; they are notorious. Yet Donald J. Trump remains in power with substantial public backing.

On July 4, 2026, I will try to maintain emotional and intellectual poise in the presence of an event so full of contradiction. I suspect, though, that my sentiments will tend in a heavily negative direction. I would surely prefer to feel admiration. Instead, I will feel anger. Celebration is out of the question. Bring on melancholy.

14

The Founders' Choice Is Not Yet in the Past

John Coates

The Founders made choices in 1776 (for cites, see tinyurl.com/4hxmsakk). One choice was not only to continue a system of oppression by which whites profited from the forced labor of blacks, but also to suppress any mention of it. That choice opened a tragedy in three acts, and left a legacy of harm and willful blindness that continues to this day. Slavery was mentioned repeatedly in the Continental Congress—not the race-based slavery imposed by many of the delegates, but the slavery they feared was being imposed on them in a sustained regression of liberty. Already proclaimed traitorous by their king, they declared independence. Not all colonists were convinced. War has ever-uncertain ends. They needed foreign support. To persuade, as lawyers will, they set out a list of complaints to cast an act of dubious legality in the legal form of a bill of particulars.

Beyond colonial unity and French cannon, the document had two other goals: to inspire and divide. Explicitly, it addressed "mankind" (posterity, the world), and implicitly, potential English allies, Whig oligarchs whose grandfathers had published the Declaration of Right in 1689. Divided over how divided government should be, English elites might (and did) sap the will of the mother country to wage war. For these audiences, Jefferson penned a second paragraph, the one for which the Declaration is still best remembered: a sweeping and (as he later put it) "pregnant" statement of nothing less than the rights of men—equality, life, liberty, and the pursuit of happiness.

At the Declaration's heart—opening of the first act of the tragedy—was a self-evident contradiction. It declared equal liberty for all and passed in silence over slavery. This was not oversight. Jefferson's original draft condemned the colonies' existing system of slavery as an "assemblage of horrors," a "cruel war" waged by King George "against human nature itself." This language was removed by the wealthy white men in Philadelphia to avoid offending enslavers throughout the colonies, particularly South Carolina and Georgia.

The hypocrisy was obvious. Franklin had argued against slavery for decades. Jefferson wrote of his own degradation as an enslaver. A month's journey south, the coerced toil of a majority of the people of South Carolina produced rice and indigo for an elite to trade for English gilts or plows and boots made in Massachusetts. The hypocrisy was condemned immediately by Tories in America and lords in Britain, and soon by revolutionaries in France. It would have been obvious in Haiti, where, in part inspired by the ideals reflected in the document, the enslaved broke their own bonds (and for that reason went unrecognized as a state by Jefferson, as president).

The Founders' choice preserved the slave system itself—a "dual state" in which the rule of law was reserved for whites. For four score and seven years after 1776, whites stole children from parents, murdered those who pursued liberty and happiness, and traded honest lives for myth-ridden domination. Free labor of whites and blacks alike was devalued, and enslavers deepened their expertise in how to extract wealth from other humans, rather than create it. To weaken government, slavery's promoters embraced a harmful anti-tax ideology that persists today. Incentives to innovate, industrialize, and invest were distorted, delaying durable growth. Innovations that did occur were perverted. Whitney's gin cleaned slave-harvested cotton, gutting the potential value of mechanical harvesters, perpetuating slavery, and delaying development for half a century.

Millions were chained, malnourished, and raped. The man on our $20 bill enslaved a woman and brutalized her for "putting on airs." In the Deep South, half died as babies; none could expect to live beyond age 21. Survivors suffered "social death," aliens cut off from cultural roots and durable ties. In a simulacrum of legality, every judge was a tyrant, every law-abiding citizen a conspirator of pain. Slavery entrenched and deepened racism. Racists elaborated lies about biology and the Bible, implanting them in the minds of millions, free and enslaved, in a desperate effort to imprint rationalizations of the unprintable. Race cannot be found in DNA, as a third of Americans today still believe it can. Their racist belief that it can is proof that cultural, if metaphorical, DNA has a powerful persistence of its own.

In the Civil War, thirty times as many people died as in the Revolution. The bodies of the Founders' grandchildren—Paul Revere's grandson among them—littered fields and forests, the fire in their hearts snuffed out along with their fears and hates. Half went unidentified before burial. A quarter of Southern youth perished. Cruelty lived on amid two million traumatized combatants, in criminals such as Jesse James, who were celebrated for violence, and murderous organizations like the Red Shirts, the KKK, and the White League. As "Pitchfork Ben" Tillman bragged, "How did we recover our [i.e., white] liberty? By fraud and violence." Generational trauma endures. Among whites and blacks alike, violent crime and "zero-sum" (we/they) thinking in 2025 strongly correlate by geography with enslavement in 1860.

The concentration of power and capital needed to win the first modern war was too rich a soil to resist corruption, at all levels and in all branches of government, opening the second act of the tragedy. Public disgust with the politicians of the Gilded Age, together with collective exhaustion from the struggle to end slavery, produced the Great Betrayal of 1877. Reconstruction collapsed into Jim Crow, an apartheid system that daily called injustice "law." Constitutional amendments intended to remedy slavery were rendered dead letters by a racist Supreme Court. In a majority of states, not just the South, racist lynchings hung "strange fruit" (in Meeropol's nightmarish image, made famous by Holiday). American ideologues cast the seeds of eugenics into the world. In *Mein Kampf,* Hitler praised America as an inspiring model for racism.

Eight decades after the Civil War, starting in the 1950s, the Founders' choice led to marches, sit-ins, and lawsuits to defend equality, met by riots, massive resistance, and assassinations of civil rights leaders. A generation overthrew formal discrimination and gained a grudging recognition that "separate but equal" was but a formalist dodge. But—in this our third act of the Founders' tragedy—America is still failing the rule-of-law test. Our laws on the books are not congruent with the law in action, despite fitful bursts of unconvincing self-congratulation to the contrary.

Descendants of enslaved and other black Americans are significantly more likely to be arrested for minor drug possession than their white peers. They are more often charged with mandatory minimum crimes and get longer prison terms. Police routinely use force against them that would not be used against whites. Housing and schools remain segregated. Blacks suffer harmful effects on health, environmental quality, education, job opportunities, careers, and lifespan.

Yet Supreme Court justices and other politicians episodically assert that 400 years of harm are having no important ongoing or remediable effects. They deploy the rhetoric of anti-discrimination to perpetuate voter suppression and to limit equal opportunity. The Supreme Court has again perverted the Civil War amendments and the civil rights legislation that tried to remedy the Founders' choice. Starting in the 1960s, the Court turned a sensible proposition—courts should scrutinize laws intended to harm "discrete" minorities—into an effective bar against any law that attempts to aid such minorities, with ever-diminishing exceptions for remedying "specific" cases of injustice.

With sophistry and arrogance, a tiny group of unelected justices has decreed that remedying the legacy of slavery is not a "compelling" state interest. Setting aside federalism in this instance, they assert that all attempts to remedy slavery will only perpetuate its ills. They do so in face of contrary judgments of the Department of Justice (when it was working to uphold the rule of law), the military, business organizations, and educational institutions that must—unlike the Court—live with their consequences of their decisions. In doing so, they override legislative supermajorities who have studied the question far more seriously than the Court will ever be able to do.

How could anyone deny the past is not yet past? That institutions of immorality that could not be named in 1776 were preserved for one hundred years in form, for another one hundred in fact, and another fifty in enduring effect? When racist ideologies are alive and loud in 2026 on QAnon, 4chan, and X? When a president parrots racist claims about immigrants "poisoning the blood of our country," is re-elected, carves out white (and only white) South Africans from his immigration crackdown, and depicts the nation's only black president and his wife as apes? When the *Economist* can still publish (before pulling) an anonymous book review claiming the enslaved were well treated? When a country, rightly outraged by the murders of Renée Good and Alex Pretti, did not much seem to notice when an immigration enforcement agent killed Keith Porter a week earlier? Illusions are more harmful than ignorance. The Founders' choice to ignore slavery will not be in the past as long as we pretend that it is.

15

THE RENAISSANCE OF OPEN WHITE SUPREMACY

MICHAEL KLARMAN

One of the more surprising aspects of the second Trump administration has been the not-even-thinly-veiled renaissance of white supremacy. Let me first document the phenomenon, then briefly try to explain it, which involves connecting the administration's racism to the threat Trump poses to democracy and the rule of law.

Trump first came to public attention when he and his father refused to rent apartments to Black and Brown people in the early 1970s. In 1989, Trump bought full-page advertisements in New York newspapers calling for restoration of the death penalty for the Central Park Five—Black and Brown teenagers falsely accused of raping a white female jogger. Definitively cleared of the crime about fifteen years later, the five young men, wrongfully incarcerated for many years, received no apology from Trump. When Trump inaugurated his improbable 2016 run for the presidency, he called Mexican immigrants "rapists" and "criminals." Trump also insisted that a Mexican-American judge, born in the United States, could not fairly adjudicate a fraud lawsuit against Trump University. House Speaker Paul Ryan called Trump's statement the "textbook definition" of racism (while nonetheless continuing to back Trump's candidacy). In his first administration, President Trump reportedly disparaged Haiti as well as all of Africa as "shithole countries" and declared his preference for immigrants from Norway. He also suggested that Black football players protesting racial injustice during the national anthem should leave the United States and repeatedly disparaged the intelligence of Black reporters and congressional representatives.

Still, the white supremacist vitriol emanating from the second Trump administration has been stunning to behold. In February, 2026, Trump released a social media video characterizing the Obamas as apes. He has called Somali-Americans "garbage" and accused Haitian immigrants in Springfield, Ohio, of eating their neighbors' cats and dogs. The Trump administration has renamed military bases after Confederate generals who owned slaves. Juneteenth and the birthday of Martin Luther King, Jr., are no longer "free" days at national parks, while Trump's birthday is. The National Institutes of Health has terminated funding for hundreds of studies seeking to understand higher cancer and heart-disease rates among African Americans and significantly higher mortality rates among pregnant Black women—"woke science," the administration calls such studies.

The second Trump administration has reduced the annual number of refugees admitted into the United States from 125,000 to 7,500. The largest number of spots are reserved for white Afrikaners from South Africa—based on the lie that they have been subjected to a racial genocide. When a commercial jet and a military helicopter tragically crashed over the Potomac River just days into Trump's second term, killing sixty-seven persons, Trump immediately blamed the accident on "DEI" policies—implying that a Black or Brown pilot or air traffic controller must have been at fault.

The administration's National Security Strategy (NSS) turns Great Replacement Theory into U.S. foreign policy. According to the NSS, Europe faces the "stark prospect of civilizational erasure" with its lax controls on non-European immigration. Europe must "remain European." Moreover, U.S. policy should support "patriotic European Parties," such as the (neo-Nazi) Alternative for Germany.

The Trump administration seeks to rewrite American history to eliminate discussion of slavery, which Trump himself insists was not that bad. An executive order entitled "Restoring Truth and Sanity to American History" directs the Smithsonian Institution to comprehensively review its exhibits to ensure alignment with Trump's directive to celebrate American exceptionalism and remove "divisive" narratives. Trump clarifies that he does not wish to hear "how horrible our country is" and "how bad slavery was." The administration has ordered several National Park Service sites to remove materials related to slavery and Native Americans, including the infamous 1863 photograph of a formerly enslaved man bearing horrific scars on his back—one of most powerful images of the Civil War era.

Recruitment ads for Immigration and Customs Enforcement openly deploy white supremacist slogans and images, and they implicitly endorse a massive denaturalization of American citizens. Recruits are told that Trump's Department of Homeland Security will defend "American culture and identity" and the birthright of heritage Americans—messages that receive rave reviews from white supremacists online.

The second Trump administration does not even bother to hide its white supremacist leanings. "Blood and soil," at home and abroad, is its policy. Such an open embrace of white supremacy is stunning for anyone who has lived through the Obama presidency, the Black Lives Matter crusade, and the largest-ever mass demonstrations following the murder of George Floyd. What could possibly explain the resurgence of open white supremacy in the second Trump administration?

In assessing the variety of factors that have led tens of millions of Americans to lose faith in democracy and lend their support to an openly aspiring autocrat such as Trump, political scientists have generally identified racial resentment as the most important one. Put another way, Trump has been at least as much a symptom as a cause of the recent degradation of American democracy. Or, as Ezra Klein has put the point, "Trump didn't hijack the GOP. He understood it." Trump's presidency has accelerated the Republican Party's radicalization on race, but that presidency was also made possible by the racial resentment already coursing through Republican voters.

In the 1950s, the population of the United States was 90 percent white. In 1980, it remained 80 percent white. According to the 2020 census, however, the population of the nation is now only about 58 percent non-Hispanic white. Moreover, demographers predict that within the next twenty years, the United States will no longer have a white majority.

The coloring of the nation—as exemplified by the election of its first African-American president in 2008—has proved profoundly unsettling to many Americans, rendering them vulnerable to the appeals of a racist demagogue such as Trump. As late as the 1980s, the Democratic and Republican parties enjoyed the support of roughly equal percentages of those white voters who registered high levels of racial resentment. These are the voters who believe white Americans suffer more from race discrimination today than Black Americans; who still do not believe that Barack Obama was born in the United States; and who relish Trump's urging of Black and Brown Democratic congresswomen to return to the "shithole" nations from which they came (even though most of these women were born in the United States).

In more recent decades, however, these racially resentful Americans have overwhelmingly concentrated in the Republican Party. By the time of Obama's presidency, 64 percent of Republicans registered high levels of racial resentment. In the Republican presidential primaries of 2016, racial resentment highly correlated with support for Donald J. Trump.

Because "the fish rots from the head," the racism of Trump and his administration has seeped deeper into the ranks of the GOP. In a recent group chat, Young Republicans called Blacks "watermelon people" and "monkeys." One Michigander wrote, "I love Hitler." Some chat participants held elected public office and were positioned to become future party leaders. Rather than condemn such vile racism, Vice President J.D. Vance ridiculed the "pearl clutching" over the episode and defended the perpetrators as "young kids" (some in their 30s) doing something "stupid" for which their careers should not be ruined.

Around the same time, Tucker Carlson, who has more than twenty million followers on social media, (literally) embraced neo-Nazi Nick Fuentes, who has said, "I think the Holocaust is exaggerated. I don't hate Hitler. I think there's a Jewish conspiracy." In the face of widespread criticism of Carlson, Kevin Roberts, president of the Heritage Foundation, which supplied the blueprint for Trump's second administration, defended Carlson, "a close friend of the Heritage Foundation," for giving Fuentes a platform.

In Trump's first term, Darren Beattie, a White House speech writer, was fired when it became known that he had spoken at a conference of white nationalists. Beattie was rehired in the second term to an important diplomatic job at the State Department, despite a recent social media post asserting that "competent white men must be in charge if you want things to work." (Double bonus to the administration for hiring a white nationalist who also happens to be a misogynist).

The rot is spreading more deeply into society. In several recent incidents whites who have lost their jobs or faced legal consequences for directing the "n" word at Blacks, have been beneficiaries of hundreds of thousands of dollars contributed on crowd-sourced fundraising pages. Referring to a Cinnabon employee who proudly owned her racism, one contributor wrote, "No White person should lose their job for refusing to be harassed by Somalians." A recent survey from a conservative think tank reveals that nearly one-third of Republicans under the age of 50 openly express racist views.

*   *   *   *   *

In the early years of the twentieth century, the "Dunning School" offered a revisionist, white supremacist history of the Civil War and Reconstruction: The war was not about slavery but rather states' rights; the "Radical" Republicans who promoted racial equality were actually motivated by vengeance and partisanship; former slaves had not been well-equipped to participate in politics so soon after emancipation; and President Andrew Johnson was a hero for resisting Reconstruction, obstructing Black equality, and narrowly construing the postwar constitutional amendments. Not until the 1950s and 1960s did scholars writing during the civil rights movement invert that historical account.

Today, a white supremacist administration is, once again, suppressing or outright lying about America's racial history. Whether such efforts succeed will depend to a considerable degree on future developments—perhaps most importantly, whether this administration succeeds in its authoritarian and white-supremacist projects. The present necessarily shapes how we think about the past. And the future will determine whether the Trump administration's present efforts to distort our nation's racial history prove successful.

PART IV

THE SUPREME COURT

Is the Supreme Court the problem or the solution? In 1803, Chief Justice John Marshall declared in *Marbury v. Madison* that the United States is "a government of laws, and not of men," and at the same time, that "[i]t is emphatically the province and duty of the Judicial Department to say what the law is." That two-step sparked a centuries-long battle between the Supreme Court and the other political branches over the distribution of ultimate legal authority. Nikolas Bowie and Daphna Renan argue that when it comes to Congress and federal law, judicial supremacy is misplaced. As the most authentically democratic branch of the federal government, they maintain, Congress should be the final authority on the validity of federal law, not five unelected Justices of the Supreme Court. At the same time, the federal judiciary still has an important role to play as a check on the overreach and illegalities of the other branches. Richard Re worries that the current Supreme Court is hobbled by "two intersecting crises," one being the many aggressive claims to legal authority asserted by the Trump administration, and the other being the public perception that the conservative Supreme Court is making political and not judicially neutral decisions. Re argues that, notwithstanding these dual crises, weakening the Supreme Court might create an even deeper crisis of rule of law by undermining the judiciary's still-substantial checking function. These constitutional scholars offer far-ranging insights as well as substantive disagreements that illuminate some of the thorniest issues that have surrounded the Supreme Court since the Founding.

16

DECLARING INDEPENDENCE FROM JUDICIAL SUPREMACY

NIKOLAS BOWIE AND DAPHNA RENAN

Americans did not declare independence from a king only to submit to the supremacy of a different court. Yet 250 years after the Declaration of Independence, we have lost sight of what it means to govern ourselves as equal participants in the making, and remaking, of our American republic. Today, the Supreme Court has replaced our national representatives in Congress as the forum for resolving our most fundamental disagreements. If the United States is to survive another 250 years, we the people must reclaim our power to govern—and to set the terms of our governance—through federal lawmaking.

Abolitionists like Frederick Douglass and Charles Sumner once regarded the Declaration of Independence as the "soul" of the U.S. Constitution. They considered it the foundation on which the people could demand that Congress end slavery and extend the franchise. The Constitution requires Congress to "guarantee to every State in this Union a Republican Form of Government." They believed this guarantee was incompatible with a system of chattel slavery that denied the universal equality recognized by the Declaration.

The Declaration meant something quite different to the justices on the Supreme Court. In *Dred Scott v. Sandford*, in 1857, a majority of the Court denied that the authors of the Declaration could have imagined that black people would ever become U.S. citizens. Even though Thomas Jefferson himself participated in enacting an ordinance that abolished slavery in U.S. territory, the Court also denied that Congress had the power to do the same.

In the 1860s, American voters elected new members of Congress to reject the Court's conclusions and bring the Guarantee Clause to life.

Congress guided the Union through the Civil War, began the abolition of slavery over the Court's attempted veto, and employed the Guarantee Clause to reconstruct the country into a multiracial democracy. It also supplemented this guarantee with the Thirteenth, Fourteenth, and Fifteenth Amendments, each of which reiterated Congress's authority to bring equal citizenship to life.

In the years since then, however, the power of the people's representatives in Congress has been captured by the Court. Exercising the same contested power the justices wielded in *Dred Scott*, the Court undermined the project of Reconstruction by defying the voting rights and civil rights laws Congress enacted to enforce the new amendments. The Court has continued to threaten the foundations of multiracial democracy in the United States. It eviscerated federal campaign finance laws to unleash the might of millionaires on our politics. And, after gutting the Voting Rights Act a decade ago, the Court is expected to celebrate the 250th anniversary of the Declaration of Independence by burying the rest of the law this summer.

Even as the Court tears away the statutory safeguards of democracy, it is also emboldening an autocracy more dangerous than any this country has confronted since King George. In a progression of judicial opinions that will also crescendo this summer, the Court has invalidated Congress's efforts to prevent the federal government from being dominated by a corrupt and unaccountable one-man rule. For the first half of American history, when Congress and the president disagreed about the separation of powers, they codified their compromises in statutes. Many of these statutes granted power to the executive branch while including restrictions by which Congress, judges, and ordinary people could ensure that the law was being faithfully executed. But today's Court has preserved Congress's grant of power to the executive while eliminating the restrictions. It even handed the President a get-out-of-jail-free card in 2024, ensuring that much of the President's conduct, no matter how brazen or corrupt, could not be subject to federal criminal law.

This, then, is the republic that the Supreme Court has built—or the remnants of our republic that the Court has left standing.

Yet the Court's most destructive power—its ability to override the decisions of the people's representatives in federal lawmaking—is of its own making and nowhere settled by the Constitution. The Constitution recognizes federal legislation, and the Constitution itself, as supreme over the law of the states. But it says nothing about how to manage a conflict between the justices' interpretation of our founding document and an interpretation reflected in federal statutes. Today many take for granted horizontal review, or the power of the Court to reject federal legislation as incompatible with five justices' views on the Constitution. But those who signed the Declaration did not imagine that Americans were trading the control of the Crown for the control of the robe.

As the Declaration turns 250, we can learn from the ideas and ambition of the past how to reconstruct our democracy and more durably secure its guarantee of republican government. American history reveals a range of approaches suggested by reformers, from Douglass and Sumner to labor leaders, suffragists, and civil rights pioneers. These approaches to American constitutionalism remain available to us today. Congress could restructure the federal judiciary and change the size of the Court, as Democratic-Republicans in Congress chose to do at the dawn of the nineteenth century. Congress could adopt legislation rejecting interpretations of the Constitution that it disagrees with, as antislavery Republicans in Congress chose to do during the Civil War. Congress could limit the Court's power to invalidate federal legislation, as Republicans did during Reconstruction. Or Congress could once again create new institutions to enforce its legislation—as it has done throughout history—to ensure that the quality of our justice is not so dependent on the caliber of our justices.

Rejecting the Supreme Court's veto power over federal legislation does not mean rejecting the role of courts in American constitutional democracy. Federal courts would continue to play an important role as implementers of federal statutes. Indeed, eliminating judicial supremacy could make our democracy more law-abiding because it would make courts better able to enforce enacted law. If Congress required federal courts to enforce federal legislation, both institutions could work together to ensure that no person—whether a president or a federal agent—can ever again rise above the law. They could also engage in the vertical review of state laws, preventing them from depriving Americans of their federally protected rights.

Of course, reclaiming power for our national representatives is no guarantee they will use that power wisely. But in a democracy, the answer to a bad law is not a judge who refuses to enforce it. It is a citizenry that refuses to accept it. If the Declaration of Independence stands for anything, it is the idea that no Marble Palace can protect our rights and our government if we the people let down our guard.

This essay is an adaptation of our forthcoming book, *Supremacy: How Rule By The Court Replaced Government By The People* (W.W. Norton & Co., Sept. 2026).

17

A Court of Two Crises

Richard M. Re

The Supreme Court is presently ensnared in two intersecting crises.

The first is the "constitutional crisis" assertedly begun at the start of President Trump's second term. The newly elected, populist President advanced startlingly aggressive claims of authority, some of which were surely illegal. Federal courts struggled to respond. Compounding this challenge, executive officials called for impeaching resistant judges or defying their decrees—events that would likely have dealt the rule of law, already beleaguered, a mortal blow.

The second crisis pertains to the judiciary's own fraught claim to legitimacy in an era of political polarization. Because the Supreme Court now has such a strong ideological valence, it has become a natural target of partisan politics, with most criticisms coming from the left. And while many efforts at court reform respect the judiciary and aim to improve it, recent proposals often resemble deconstruction or capture. Most salient are partisan proposals that the Court itself be "expanded," a euphemism for what was once called court-packing.

The two crises may exacerbate one another. In responding to rule of law challenges, the Supreme Court has lately jeopardized its own public esteem. For example, the Justices issued terse orders allowing the President to remove myriad agency officials with statutory tenure, thereby inviting ferocious criticism on both political and legalistic grounds. What is more, federal jurisdiction does not extend to many important facets of government, such as the initiation of war abroad. So perhaps the courts, through a combination of failure and inevitability, have not done enough to protect the constitutional order, as many critics allege.

But if the critics respond by weakening the courts, they may only set the stage for even greater populism and attendant disregard for the rule of law. For it is hard to deny that the federal judiciary, overseen by the Supreme Court, has repeatedly checked the present administration. Sometimes the justices themselves have acted; other times, they have left lower court rulings intact. Examples have involved free speech, due process, deportations, national guard deployments, birthright citizenship, partisan impeachments, tariffs, the Federal Reserve, and still more measures not even attempted under the judiciary's watchful eye. So even if the courts could have done more, they have certainly done quite a bit.

For all its faults, then, the federal judiciary has come to play a critical counter-majoritarian role within an increasingly majoritarian government. At the Founding, the federal government was both limited in strength and insulated from populism. Congressional powers were few and limited, while the president was selected by an Electoral College, and Senators by state legislatures. Over time, however, that small-r republican regime eroded away. The federal legislative power became vast during the New Deal, the Electoral College became a ministerial body, and the direct election of Senators rendered even the upper house populist.

So, in a closely divided polity, small vote margins can and do yield outsized political consequences. To wit, four of the last five presidential elections (2008, 2016, 2020, and 2024) have ushered in unified governments, with the political branches controlled by a single party. The Senate filibuster still curbs majoritarian federal legislation—but for how much longer?

Despite this trend toward majoritarianism, the federal courts continue to reflect the Founding-era vision of republican government. Of course, federal judges are selected through a political process, so their decisions often have democratic legitimacy. But because its membership changes only gradually, and because its personnel are relatively insulated from electoral pressures, the federal judiciary is often out of step with the politics of the day. Frequent disagreements between President Trump and his own first-term judicial appointees offer only the latest illustration.

But if the federal judiciary is among the few counter-majoritarian forces remaining in the United States government, its fate is now in doubt. The same populist pressures that have worked on other components of the original United States government are now poised to iron out its courts, too. The danger here is long foretold. As Alexander Hamilton noted in *Federalist 78*, independent courts are "equally requisite to guard the Constitution and the rights of individuals from the effects of those ill humors, which" are fostered by "the arts of designing men."

On reflection, however, each crisis offers a way out of the other. If it can navigate our time of polarized populism, the judiciary may thereby solve its own legitimacy problem. Scholars have argued that judicial independence largely springs from the long-term incentives of partisan actors. Parties in power today anticipate relying on the judiciary once they are out of power tomorrow. And, again, courts have lately offered respite for the loyal opposition. If that pattern persists and political tides turn, the judiciary may emerge stronger than ever.

True, some critics oppose the Supreme Court on principle, regardless of how it rules. But other critics are not hostile so much as jealous, essentially lamenting that the justices are insufficiently on their side. Proposals regarding court reform could even be performative, in that their real goal may be to moderate the Third Branch or "work the ref." In all events, polls that measure Supreme Court approval suggest that many memories are short. If the judiciary would only re-prove its worth, it might be welcomed back with open arms.

History suggests much the same, as past moments of constitutional and judicial peril punctuate the long story of the Supreme Court. The partisan clash between Federalists and Jeffersonians gave rise to *Marbury v. Madison* (1803). Sectional strife over slavery set the stage for the disastrous ruling in *Dred Scott v. Sandford* (1857). And New Deal controversies yielded the "switch in time that saved nine" in *West Coast Hotel v. Parrish* (1937). Each time, the Supreme Court outlasted its own blunders as well as its critics—and soon was thriving again.

Two and a half centuries ago, the Declaration of Independence called for both expanded democracy and greater judicial power. History has followed that twin decree. Today, however, these trends are coming into conflict. Whether the Supreme Court can continue to check majoritarianism, including authoritarian populism, remains to be seen. But every time it succeeds, the odds increase that powerful courts, and the constitutional order, will ultimately endure. As H.L.A. Hart wrote in a related context, "Here all that succeeds is success."

PART V

THE FEDERAL GOVERNMENT

In 1776, there was no such place as "Washington, D.C.," and the idea of a centralized federal government was still theoretical. Today, the modern federal government sports a $7 trillion budget, hundreds of agencies, and over two million civilian employees, touching every aspect of American life. Jody Freeman describes the evolution and crucial democratic role of the federal regulatory apparatus that underlies this enormous governance undertaking—the modern administrative state—from 1789 through the New Deal to the close of the twentieth century. She details how that apparatus is currently being dismantled, and warns of the potentially irreversible long-term consequences for the polity. Howell Jackson unpacks the process for funding the federal behemoth—the federal budget process—through which Congress and the Executive negotiate over the size and terms of federal spending. Concerned about ballooning deficits and record public debt, Jackson predicts that we will soon see a substantial budgetary realignment of the kind that historically occurs approximately every fifty years. And Joseph Singer explores the ambivalent history of the relationship between the federal government and the 575 sovereign Indian nations with whom the United States has numerous treaties and agreements. Whatever "the United States" means, it cannot be understood without appreciating the powerful, conflicted, and complicated workings of our centralized federal government into which these scholars provide a tantalizing window.

18

A Federal Government Transformed

Jody Freeman

A new status quo has taken hold in Washington DC. The federal government is more partisan and less professional than at any time in the modern era. The administrative state on which we rely for the bulk of regulatory governance and protection is also weaker, having lost substantial expertise and capacity. The current administration has pushed longstanding legal boundaries and violated deep-rooted governance norms to exert unprecedented political control over the federal bureaucracy, prioritizing loyalty over competence. For the moment, the Supreme Court has largely allowed these monumental changes to the administrative apparatus to proceed. The federal government, as we have known it for decades, has thus been substantially transformed in ways that may be difficult if not impossible to reverse. At least for now, many agencies charged by Congress with protecting the public interest are less objective, less competent, less expert and less legally constrained than at any time in recent memory.

Federal administrative agencies have been a feature of the U.S. constitutional order since the Founding. In 1789, Congress established the first executive departments—War, State, and Treasury—followed by the Department of the Navy in 1798, the Department of the Interior in 1849, and the Department of Justice in 1870. In the latter half of the nineteenth century, Congress introduced a new agency form: multi-member commissions balanced along partisan lines, with appointees serving staggered terms and removable by the president only for cause. The rationale for this structure was that some insulation from plenary presidential control was necessary to bring dispassionate expertise to bear on problems of economic regulation. Such bodies became known as "independent" agencies to distinguish them from executive branch agencies whose heads serve at the president's pleasure.

Congress expanded the federal administrative state in successive waves: during the Progressive Era to regulate concentrations of monopoly power; during the 1930s in response to the exigencies of the Depression; and during the 1970s to address concerns spanning public health, environmental protection, consumer safety, and civil rights. By the close of the twentieth century, the federal government comprised more than a dozen cabinet departments containing several hundred sub-agencies, offices, and bureaus, along with over fifty independent agencies.

The legitimacy of the administrative state has long been contested. Critics argue that the independent agency structure violates Article II; that broad delegations of policymaking authority to administrative agencies contravene the Constitution's non-delegation doctrine; and that vesting agencies with both rulemaking and adjudicatory power offends the separation of powers. These structural objections have been matched by persistent ideological disagreement over the appropriate scope of federal regulation: conservatives resist agency interference in markets while progressives defend regulation as essential to the functioning of a modern economy and society.

Nevertheless, by the close of the twentieth century, the administrative state had become an entrenched feature of the American constitutional order, with the president, Congress, and the courts sharing oversight authority. Congress funds and authorizes agency action to implement statutory goals; the president, within certain constraints, hires and fires agency heads and supervises agency policymaking; and courts review agency decisions to ensure they are lawful. Unless Congress directs otherwise, federal agencies must adhere to the 1946 Administrative Procedure Act, which establishes procedures for notice and comment rulemaking and formal adjudication, and sets standards of judicial review, among other things.

A key feature of the federal government is its personnel. Agencies are powered by a permanent professional career staff, with an overlay of political appointees who come and go with successive administrations. The federal civil service evolved from a nineteenth century patronage system to one now largely based on merit, with career employees hired and promoted based primarily on professional qualifications, and protections in place against politically motivated dismissals. Career staff are expected to be non-partisan and serve administrations of both parties.

The tension between appropriate political accountability and inappropriate political pressure has long been an issue, but some insulation from plenary presidential control is a central feature of the modern federal workforce. Congress updated civil service protections most recently in the 1978 Civil Service Reform Act, as part of a broader set of sweeping reforms adopted in the wake of the Watergate scandal to strengthen ethics, transparency, and accountability in the federal government and reform the presidency to respond to the era's abuses. During this period, the Justice Department adopted new policies governing communication and contacts with the White House to ensure that prosecutorial discretion would not be improperly influenced by political considerations, a version of which have remained in place ever since. The goal was to place DOJ in a "neutral zone" of government, where independence and professionalism would prevail.

Modern presidents have largely accepted this legal edifice, even while pursuing political control. Presidents of both parties have layered political appointees over career staff and required central review of significant regulatory actions, for example, but kept their distance from independent agencies and respected the job protections of the civil service. The White House has traditionally remained at arms-length from the Justice Department's decisions regarding civil and criminal law enforcement, not because presidents are legally obligated to do so, but because the norm of DOJ's relative independence is so well entrenched.

With the election of Donald J. Trump to a second term in 2024, this settlement was abruptly shattered. Within a year, the President went far beyond the steps taken during his first term to exert an unprecedented level of personal control over the administrative state. Relying on a maximalist unitary executive theory of his Article II authority, the President in short order dismissed or forced out hundreds of thousands of career staff, dismantled agencies, fired independent agency heads, and politicized the Department of Justice, among other steps.

Up to 300,000 members of the federal civil service are estimated to have been terminated in the tumultuous process spearheaded by the

White House Department of Government Efficiency. Numbers tell only part of the story. The reductions in force affected key staff at several public health and safety agencies, including the Food and Drug Administration, Centers for Disease Control, and the Environmental Protection Agency, and compromised vital government functions at the Departments of Energy, State, Homeland Security, and Defense. The administration disbanded or gutted several outside advisory groups that provide agencies critical independent expertise on drug and vaccine approvals and public health and safety standards, among other sensitive regulatory matters. The administration unilaterally dissolved the U.S. Agency for International Development, disabled enforcement at the Consumer Financial Protection Bureau, and cut the Education Department in half. Throughout the process, senior administration officials persistently disparaged federal employees and denigrated their work.

Asserting unprecedented control over independent agencies, the President fired members of the National Labor Relations Board and the Merit Systems Protection Board without cause, and removed a member of the Federal Reserve Board for cause based on unproven allegations. He also dismissed nineteen agency Inspectors General—the internal officials who monitor agency waste fraud and abuse—and the top military lawyers for the Army, Air Force, and Navy, who provide commanders legal advice to ensure that military operations conform to domestic and international law.

The President repeatedly flouted the Impoundment Control Act, seizing control of congressionally appropriated funds, including disaster relief appropriated to the Federal Emergency Management Agency, infrastructure funding for the Transportation Department, and numerous public health grants, and withholding it from states and grantees on a partisan basis.

Also shortly after the President took office, the Justice Department was swiftly converted into a political weapon, with the President personally directing investigations and prosecutions of political foes, in a drastic shift from prior administrations. The Attorney General publicly pledged fealty to the President and, at his behest, dismissed career prosecutors who had worked on past cases involving him, and fired prosecutors who refused to indict his chosen targets. Scores of career prosecutors and FBI officials resigned rather than follow orders they viewed as unlawful or unethical, and thousands more employees left the department, in a mass exodus unparalleled in the nation's history.

It will take time for the full picture of these events to come into view but their cumulative effect in the short term is monumental. The federal government is now more partisan and less professional than at any time in the modern era; it has lost substantial expertise and capacity. In taking the steps described above, the President has consistently pushed statutory and constitutional boundaries, asserted untested legal positions, and violated longstanding norms. While some of his actions may be legal, many are not, at least under current law.

Regardless, a new status quo has been set. In a series of sparsely worded emergency docket orders, the Supreme Court let most of the President's policies stand while litigation challenging them plays out. The Court may ultimately ratify some of the President's actions—a majority of Justices is widely expected to approve his authority to fire independent agency heads, for example—while rejecting others. And many challenges will be resolved by the lower courts. But whatever the legal outcomes, there is little doubt that the federal government has been substantially transformed and the changes may be difficult to reverse.

Profound questions remain about the long-term consequences of this shift, leaving a pressing set of questions for scholars, policymakers, journalists, and others to explore. Perhaps the projected trillions (later downgraded to billions) of dollars in costs savings from the administration's mass firings and personnel reforms will materialize—though judging by the analyses to date, it seems doubtful. More plausible is that the downsizing—which seemed alternately selective and indiscriminate—will result in a deficit of expertise, experience, and judgment, which could manifest in concrete harms felt by the public, such as less safety and more risk to our food, drug, air, and water supplies, our transportation systems, and our counter-terrorism operations, along with weakened consumer protection and fewer constraints on market abuses, civil rights violations, and more.

A failure to enforce ethics rules will lead, inexorably, to an erosion of ethics in government. Without independent internal agency watchdogs, there will likely be more fraud, corruption, and abuse of power in government. Without expert outside advisory bodies helping to inform government regulation, many decisions that we normally expect to be based on sound science or economics will instead be driven primarily or exclusively by partisan politics. More people will question the government's credibility when it disseminates the essential public health, scientific, and economic information on which citizens and private markets depend, and public trust in government, already eroded as a historical matter, may sink further.

A new president could rebuild the Justice Department—restore its tradition of professionalism and non-partisanship and reestablish an arms-length relationship with the White House. Given the extensive damage and sizable loss of talent the agency has suffered, however, that project will be hard; resisting the temptation to simply commandeer DOJ for his or her own political benefit will require a leader with tremendous discipline and self-restraint. It will be difficult for our democracy to survive, though, if the U.S. Department of Justice remains a political tool to punish the enemies and help the friends of whoever occupies the White House.

No one disputes that the federal government needs constructive reform to improve performance, reduce cost, and modernize personnel rules. But the second Trump presidency did not bring us that. Instead, the upheaval of this period has taken us in the wrong direction, back to a time when loyalty was prized over expertise and presidential overreach threatened to topple our rules-based system. The administrative state is kept in check by a balance of power among Congress, the president and the courts—a balance that is currently off-kilter, tilting too far toward the presidency. And public faith in government depends on persistent demonstrations of integrity, fairness, and fidelity to law, which this administration has forsaken. History will decide if we can right the balance, and restore the faith.

<h1 style="text-align:center">19</h1>

FACING OUR FISCAL CHALLENGES AT 250

HOWELL E. JACKSON

As the nation enters the back half of its third century, fiscal challenges are very much in the news. The Trump 2.0 White House has laid claim to expansive fiscal powers, withholding congressional appropriations and levying tariffs without clear legislative basis. At the same time, mounting deficits push the country's public debt to record levels, risking a genuine debt crisis. Such a crisis would have serious distributional consequences as the cost of government spending is passed on to future generations and current inequalities are exacerbated as moneyed interests squeeze out programs for the young and vulnerable.

Throughout our history, fiscal challenges of a similar sort have periodically led to sensible realignments of the structure and oversight of the federal budget, both to rebalance power between the Executive and Congress and to restore fiscal stability in the face of ballooning expenditures. These reforms have occurred roughly every fifty years since the Civil War, and, on that cadence, we are soon due for another round of fiscal tune-ups. Once again it is time to come up with new institutional structures to restore fiscal balance and accommodate the realities of today's budgeting practices within our democratic traditions. The good news is that history says we are up to the task.

At the dawn of the republic, federal budgeting was simple. The Executive—initially Alexander Hamilton and later the Departments—sent budget requests directly to Congress. Congress soon established two committees, Ways and Means in the House, and Finance in the Senate, to coordinate a legislative response. In the First Congress, spending bills took the form of large lump-sum grants at the departmental level but quickly morphed into line-itemization of spending authority. Given the relatively small scale of federal operations through the first half of the nineteenth century, these simple processes were fit for purpose.

With the Civil War, federal spending skyrocketed. By the nation's Centennial, Congress responded by moving spending decisions to House and Senate Appropriations Committees and leaving tax matters to House Ways and Means and Senate Finance. During late-nineteenth-century industrialization, standing committees pushed their way into fiscal matters by sanctioning spending on public works through authorizing legislation, prompting battles with Appropriators and leadership and further fragmenting budget authority.

Order was restored shortly before the nation's 150th birthday with post-World War I reforms in 1921 creating the Bureau of the Budget (later the Office of Management and Budget "OMB") to produce, for the first time since Hamilton, a unified executive budget proposal. To counterbalance expanded executive budget authority, Congress also created the predecessor of the Government Accountability Office (GAO) to give itself professional staff to monitor implementation of spending decisions.

The reforms of the 1920s ushered in what is often called classical budgeting. Members of the Appropriations Committees and executive officials collaborated on annual spending decisions based on a shared view of national priorities, with the president's budget taken seriously as a first draft for appropriations. Congress backed away from detailed line-itemization and aligned appropriations with more general programs, projects, and activities proposed in executive budgets. While negotiations in this era sometimes produced substantial deficits—during the New Deal and especially World War II—they also constrained spending growth in the post-war years, allowing the public-debt-to-GDP ratio to decline from 106 percent in 1946 to 23 percent in 1974.

Classical budgeting began to break down in the 1960s. Congressional majorities sought to implement Great Society initiatives, such as Medicare and Medicaid, through "backdoor" tactics outside the fiscally conservative oversight of Appropriations. The status quo was further strained by President Nixon's impoundments of contracting authority for environmental and other projects, many enacted without Appropriations Committee signoff. Seven years of these "Budget Wars" prompted our last major fiscal reforms, adopted just over half a century ago and slightly more than a half-century after the 1921 refresh.

The Congressional Budget and Impoundment Control Act of 1974 established the basic contours of modern federal budgeting. The Act aimed to strengthen congressional control over spending, creating a bipartisan Congressional Budget Office to provide economic expertise and counterbalance the growing power of OMB. The 1974 reforms also limited presidential impoundments to safeguard legislative spending prerogatives. The Act was understood not just as a way to ensure congressional spending primacy, but also as a mechanism to impose fiscal discipline within Congress by creating new budget committees and mechanisms—annual budget resolutions and, if needed, reconciliation bills—to constrain appropriations, ensure adequate revenues, and police backdoor spending, including entitlements.

These reforms had their moment but have not aged well. Through the end of the twentieth century, the 1974 structure, supplemented by additional legislation directly targeting deficits, eventually (and briefly) brought the budget into balance in the waning years of the Clinton Presidency, as public debt-to-GDP fell to 33 percent in 2002. But with President George W. Bush's tax cuts, fiscal discipline crumbled. The 1974 toolkit—particularly reconciliation—was coopted from a mechanism to impose fiscal discipline into the go-to vehicle to advance tax cuts or spending enhancements whenever the president has cooperative partners in Congress. At the same time, the White House—regardless of party—stopped playing a forceful role in setting long-range targets, with the president's annual budget routinely derided as "dead on arrival" on Capitol Hill. Thus, the two mechanisms adopted to produce fiscal balance over the last hundred years—the Bureau of the Budget/OMB in 1921 and the Budget Committees in 1974—have passed their sell-by dates.

Another weakness of modern budgeting has been the complexification of spending procedures at both ends of Pennsylvania Avenue. On the congressional side, budgetary pressures from post-1974 measures, such as sequestration and pay-as-you-go, motivated Appropriations Committees to structure spending bills with ever-increasing granularity. They subdivide the federal government's 2,000 budget accounts into tens of thousands of subcomponents, laced with an ever-increasing number of itemized restrictions on specific types of spending (like payroll or IT), topped off with thousands of earmarks. While these restrictions no doubt fall within Congress's constitutionally assigned power of the purse, this legislated granularity would be unrecognizable to the Founders—a far cry from the lump-sum departmental appropriations the First Congress granted Hamilton or the then-contemporaneous practices of British Parliaments established following the Glorious Revolution.

Faced with the same pressures and constraints of legislated granularity, the White House—under both Republican and Democratic administrations—has struggled to find wiggle room. Administrations have made creative use of transfer and reprogramming authority to move funds across and within accounts and have sought, where possible, more open-ended authority, as with Overseas Contingency Operations during the wars in Iraq and Afghanistan and the Dodd-Frank Act's funding arrangements for the CFPB, as well as the Biden Administration's failed effort to expand student loan forgiveness. OMB Director Russell Vought has turbo-charged executive spending creativity in the second Trump Administration, but he builds on Executive boundary-pushing that had been underway for decades.

Exactly how current budgetary controversies will play out over the next few years is unknowable. Some in Congress have responded to Trump-era excesses by calling for greater specificity in appropriations and tighter control over Executive implementation, an understandable reaction but one likely to exacerbate legislated rigidity. Alternatively, the courts could acquiesce to Executive claims of constitutional authority to withhold and redirect appropriated funds on a muscular view of Article II in derogation of traditional understandings of Congress's power of the purse.

More optimistically, some compromise could emerge whereby Congress backs away from the granularity of recent years, following the model of other developed economies that rely on more flexible grants tied to policy objectives and policed through post-enactment legislative oversight. We need not, and should not, revert to the department-level funding grants that the First Congress gave Hamilton, but the country should, in my view, be headed somewhat back in that direction. As our early history teaches, the Constitution allows Congress considerable latitude in how it structures spending bills. Political accountability can be achieved in many ways: by Hill staffers writing highly granular bills in a politicized environment or by agency personnel with subject matter expertise allocating lump-sum allotments from Congress or through direct White House control backstopped by congressional oversight. The real challenge is how to balance pragmatic and democratic concerns: Along a continuum of legislated spending specificity, what is most likely to achieve the most efficient application of public resources with an acceptable degree of democratic legitimacy?

The nation's 250th anniversary also presents an opportunity to adopt new institutional structures better suited to restoring fiscal balance for the remainder of our third century, as public-debt levels spike toward 130 percent or more of GDP in the next ten years. One approach now under consideration would be to delegate long-term fiscal planning to a super committee charged with proposing a reform program subject to fast-track approval in Congress. The base-closing commission of a few decades ago offers one model, but experiences with such committees on fiscal matters have proven ineffective in the past.

Alternatively, or in addition, one could imagine processes designed to force presidential candidates to articulate credible fiscal programs as part of our four-year election cycles, giving the winning candidate's program a strong political tailwind upon entering office. While politicians of both parties have been loath to put responsible fiscal policies before the voters, an impressive array of civil-society organizations—from the Committee for a Responsible Federal Budget to the Penn-Wharton Budget Model to the newly established Yale Budget Lab—have proven themselves capable of speaking fiscal truth to power. They could be harnessed to support a non-governmental structure that might, with effort and philanthropic support, force presidential candidates to put forward and defend credible fiscal plans.

The country's fiscal challenges in 2026 are formidable, but history teaches that we can adopt effective and innovative reforms when circumstances demand. The nation's 250th birthday would be an excellent occasion to put our collective shoulders to this critical wheel.

20

"Merciless Indian Savages" or "Distinct, Independent Political Communities"?

Joseph William Singer

Indian Nations occupy two distinct places in American history and law. American Indians are mentioned only once in the Declaration of Independence. They are in a phrase complaining about King George III's alliances with Indian nations to oppose American invasion of Indian country, and they are described, not as nations, but as "merciless Indian Savages." Nor was this a slip of the tongue or a brief emotional outburst. The lawyer for the plaintiffs in the 1823 Supreme Court case of *Johnson v. M'Intosh* similarly referred to Native peoples as "savage tribes," and even Chief Justice John Marshall described them as "fierce savages." On the other hand, both the lawyer for the defendants and the Supreme Court itself referred to them as "tribes or nations" or "Indian nations." And the 1832 case of *Worcester v. Georgia* referred to "Indian nations" as "distinct, independent political communities, having territorial boundaries, within which their authority is exclusive, and having a right to all the lands within those boundaries, which is not only acknowledged, but guarantied by the United States."

The contrast between "savages" and "nations" reflects a deep ambivalence about the relationship between the United States and the Indian nations. Over the course of U.S. history, the "savages" formulation sometimes prevailed, either to justify removal of Indians from lands east of the Mississippi River from the 1830s to the 1860s or as a reason to "civilize" the Indians by outlawing tribal religion, promoting conversion to Christianity, privatizing tribal lands, and kidnapping tribal children to be educated at harsh boarding schools. But, in other eras of U.S. history, the United States treated Indian nations as distinct political communities with inherent sovereignty and the power to enforce their own laws within their own territory. That was the case in colonial times and the early Republic when the U.S. entered treaties with Indian nations, and the New Deal era when the U.S. encouraged Indian nations to adopt written constitutions and to revitalize their governments. It has also been the general national policy ever since 1975 when the United States embraced self-determination for Tribes.

It is possible to graduate from many (but not all) law schools in the United States and never hear the words "tribal sovereignty." Many residents of the United States (including law students) are unaware of the fact that the United States has never conquered the 575 federally-recognized Indian nations who retain their inherent sovereignty and continue to thrive as "distinct, independent political communities." Every president since Richard Nixon, whether Republican or Democratic, has affirmed the "government-to-government" relationship between the United States and the various Indian nations, and every Congress since that time has, with some exceptions, respected tribal sovereignty. Just last year, on December 18, 2025, President Trump signed a congressional bill recognizing the inherent sovereignty of the Lumbee Tribe of North Carolina.

The persistence of tribal sovereignty is not as well-known, understood, or celebrated as it should be. The United States (and post-apartheid South Africa) are unique in the world in their recognition of robust tribal governments. Yet many Americans do not know this or appreciate this. They were taught American history in a manner that swept the Indian nations aside. Maps of the United States rarely include Indian country. If Tribes are mentioned at all in history classes, they are relics of the past rather than thriving nations of today. The truth is that United States law recognizes tribal sovereignty even though Tribes are within the geographic borders of the United States and the states within which they are situated.

Tribal sovereignty should be celebrated, not ignored. The fact that the United States recognizes the Native sovereigns that have been here for thousands of years means that it has chosen to limit its own powers to preserve room for the original inhabitants to exercise their ancient sovereign powers. Powerful nations, if those so choose, can invade, dominate, and absorb weaker nations. The fact that the U.S. has chosen to respect tribal sovereignty, at least in part, is to its credit.

The United States went to war with Iraq the first time because Iraq had invaded and occupied a smaller nation on the grounds that it was an errant province. International law protects sovereign states from invasion by more powerful neighbors. The persistence of tribal sovereignty is a testament to the norm of self-determination which condemns both imperialism and colonialism. The United States itself originated with the belief that it had a right to self-determination. The U.S. has not always honored the Tribes' right to self-determination, but since 1975 (and at other times in U.S. history) it has recognized and respected the inherent sovereignty of 575 Indian nations.

Yet the old notions remain. The Supreme Court, in particular, has trouble seeing why it should defer to tribal sovereignty just because Congress does. In 2016, for example, the Supreme Court divided 4–4 in a case about whether the Tribal Court of the Mississippi Band of Choctaw Indians could hear a case by a tribal member against a nonmember corporation when its employee sexually abused a tribal child. The company leased land from the Tribe, obtained a business license from the Tribe, and agreed to participate in an unpaid internship program for tribal minors. The sexual abuse of the Choctaw child took place on Choctaw land within Choctaw territory. One might think that the Tribe would have the power to protect its own children from harm on tribal lands. The 4–4 vote meant that the Supreme Court did not find the case to be easy.

The Supreme Court had held in 1981, in the case of *Montana v. United States*, that Tribes can regulate non-Indians "who enter consensual relationships with the tribe . . . through commercial dealing, contracts, leases, or other arrangements" and/or who engage in conduct on nonmember land when it "threatens or has some direct effect on the political integrity, the economic security, or the health or welfare of the tribe." One might think that the rape of a tribal child on tribal land within tribal territory threatens the health or welfare of the Tribe, especially when it arises out of three consensual relationships with the Tribe. The "*Montana* exceptions" fit like a glove, but the Fifth Circuit's 2–1 ruling in the *Choctaw* case was affirmed by the Supreme Court by only a 4–4 vote without opinion. Four Justices thought non-Indians should not have to appear in tribal courts to answer a civil claim even when they enter tribal land within the Tribe's territory and rape a tribal child.

Perhaps four of the Justices regret their ruling in *Montana* that authorized tribal court suits by Tribes or their members against nonmembers when they harm tribal interests. Perhaps they imagine that Tribes will be unfair to non-Indians, given the sorry history of mistreatment of Indian nations by the states. Perhaps they sympathize with non-Indians who are ignorant of tribal sovereignty and never contemplated being subject to the regulatory powers of tribal councils and courts. If so, we are seeing the echoes of the attitude toward Native nations displayed in the Declaration of Independence.

Yet in 2020, the Supreme Court held by a vote of 5–4 in the *McGirt* decision that because Congress had never formally disestablished the Muscogee Reservation in Oklahoma that it persists to this day. To the surprise of many, maps had to be changed because much of the state of Oklahoma is now also Indian Country. That means that non-Indians entering tribal lands may well be subject to tribal law.

The split votes in the *Choctaw* and *McGirt* cases tell us that the contest between the "merciless savages" view and the "independent political communities" view continues to haunt American law.

PART VI

ELECTIONS

For many people, the idea of democracy is synonymous with the guarantee of free and fair elections. How those elections actually take place, however, and what precisely makes them "free and fair," is a complicated matter. Nick Stephanopoulos argues that the strength of our decentralized, state-run, localist electoral system is that it is highly resistant to top-down authoritarian interference. The downside is that it is also resistant to much-needed top-down improvements and reforms. Larry Schwartztol worries that the Electoral College poses a double threat to democracy and should be abolished. First, it sometimes produces the democratically counterintuitive result that the presidential candidate who receives the most national votes nevertheless loses the election. Second, its complicated structure invites legal and political instability and even, as we saw on January 6, 2021, violence. These election law experts shine a critical light on both the strengths and fragilities of our basic democratic infrastructure.

21

Our Bulwarks Against Losing—or Improving—Our Democracy

Nicholas O. Stephanopoulos

In his second term as president, Donald Trump has attempted a host of actions that can fairly be labeled authoritarian or anti-democratic. Elections are the foundation of democracy. Yet Trump issued an executive order purporting to make voting more difficult and urged Congress to pass a bill codifying similar voting restrictions. Democracy requires freedom of the press. But Trump's FCC launched investigations of major networks after coverage critical of the President and threatened their broadcast licenses. Democracy depends on the rule of law. However, Trump pardoned everyone involved in the January 6, 2021 attack on the Capitol while his DOJ prosecuted several of his political opponents.

This bill of particulars could be lengthened, but is troubling enough as it is. Here I want to focus, though, not on Trump's authoritarian intent (which is plain enough) but on a key word in the prior paragraph: *attempted*. Trump has *attempted* many anti-democratic actions in his second term. But most of these efforts have failed. For example, courts blocked his anti-voting executive order, and Congress has been unable to enact any new voting burdens into law. Similarly, the major networks are still on the air and continue to release many stories unfavorable to the administration. And while Trump's January 6 pardons are irreversible, almost all of the DOJ's prosecutions of Trump's political adversaries have foundered.

What explains this combination of blatant authoritarian intent and limited authoritarian results? One factor is probably temperamental; Trump's chaotic governing style means that, across all areas (not just those related to democracy), many objectives are announced but relatively few are realized. Another driver may be Trump's low and sinking popularity. Globally, successful subverters of democracy tend to enjoy overwhelming popular support, which enables them to bend institutions to their will. In contrast, an unpopular president invites opposition from legislators, courts, states, and other actors.

But personality and public disapproval are contingent explanations, in that another president might be more organized and more popular. A deeper, more durable reason for Trump's inability to go further down the road to authoritarianism, in my view, is the dispersion of power under the American political system. This dispersion has several familiar dimensions. Legislation must be signed by the president and passed by a bicameral Congress, one of whose chambers usually operates under a supermajority rule. Federal courts possess—and freely exercise—the power of judicial review. Even a unitarist president like Trump lacks full control over the administrative state. States possess a good deal of authority and frequently use it to resist the federal government. And our federalism is complemented by our localism: the delegation of many important tasks to thousands of local governments, which also often frustrate federal initiatives.

My perspective on the Trump presidency (to date) therefore differs from that of scholars like Steven Levitsky, Daniel Ziblatt, Tom Ginsburg, and Aziz Huq. They observe Trump's authoritarian intent, manifested in an array of actions, and conclude that American democracy has significantly declined. Thanks to the gulf between Trump's intent and his more modest impact, I think American democracy has demonstrated its considerable resilience. And I'm not alone in this less alarmist camp. David Landau and Hannah and Samuel Wiseman emphasize the role of federalism. "The dispersal of core functions, including judging, law enforcement, and . . . electoral administration, likely acts as a bulwark that slows moves toward authoritarianism." Kurt Weyland stresses the sheer number of veto gates in American politics. "[I]ts dense web of checks and balances and federalism with its resourceful state and city governments . . . preclude[ ] the president from imposing his will and establishing authoritarian preeminence."

Though I agree with these points, I want to call attention to their dark side, too. The same diffusion of power that prevents most authoritarian designs from succeeding also thwarts many efforts to *improve* our democracy. Bicameralism, the Senate filibuster, judicial review, the administrative state, federalism, and localism—these features of our system favor the status quo over *any* alternative, malignant or benign. To illustrate contemporary American vetocracy (Francis Fukuyama's apt term), consider the project of electoral reform.

In March 2025, Trump issued an executive order that, among other things, sought to require eligible voters to provide documentary proof of citizenship to register to vote and to bar states from counting mail-in ballots received after election day. These would have been substantial changes had they been implemented. But they never went into effect. Various federal judges preliminarily enjoined portions of the order, and a district court in Washington, DC ultimately held that Trump lacked the authority to mandate these shifts in electoral policy. "Put simply," stated the court, "our Constitution does not allow the President to impose unilateral changes to federal election procedures."

After Trump's executive order went nowhere, the House passed the so-called SAVE America Act in February 2026. This bill would have required both proof of citizenship to register to vote and proof of identification to cast a ballot. But this bill has remained a bill. When it reached the Senate floor in March 2026, Democrats predictably filibustered it. Republicans fell well short of the sixty votes needed for cloture.

Four years earlier, the shoe was on the other foot. Joe Biden was president and Democrats had majorities in both chambers of Congress. One of their top priorities (originally numbered H.R. 1 to indicate its importance) was a sprawling electoral reform bill eventually titled the Freedom to Vote: John R. Lewis Act. This behemoth aimed to facilitate voter registration and voting, curb partisan gerrymandering, revive a dormant provision of the Voting Rights Act, deter election subversion, expand campaign finance disclosure, and introduce public financing for congressional elections. But this bill, too, couldn't navigate the treacherous route to congressional approval. It passed the House and then was filibustered in the Senate, where forty-eight Democrats—two shy of the necessary fifty—backed eliminating the filibuster for electoral legislation. Had the bill been enacted, right-wing critics would have pounced with a barrage of lawsuits. The conservative Supreme Court would likely have been sympathetic to many of these claims.

We find ourselves in a limbo, then, where fragmented power stops moves toward both authoritarianism and a sounder democracy. One response to this stasis—the attitude of Landau, Weyland, and the Wisemans—is to welcome it. The difficulty of altering the status quo protects us from malicious actors who want to undermine our democracy. We should be grateful for these obstacles, on this account, even if they also inhibit democratic progress.

There's wisdom in this stance, but it's arguably too risk-averse given all the problems of modern American democracy: low turnout, rampant gerrymandering, pervasive misalignment between public policy and public opinion. Another, less passive option is to concentrate on state and local, rather than federal, change. Most of the hurdles to federal action—the Senate filibuster, aggressive judicial review, recalcitrant sub-federal governments—are lower or absent at the state and local level. So believers in a more participatory, more representative, democracy could push states and localities to adopt their preferred policies. These campaigns aren't certain to bear fruit either, but their odds are much higher than attempts to shift federal law.

State and local activism, however, has its own drawbacks. It can be harnessed for authoritarian as easily as for democratic purposes. At best, it leads to patchwork, not uniform, improvement. And seemingly appealing reforms (like curbs on congressional gerrymandering) can backfire if they're implemented by some states but not others. In the longer term, proponents of a better democracy thus can't ignore the federal government despite all the impediments to federal action.

With respect to such action, I have a pair of concluding thoughts. One is simply that democratic advocates must strike when the iron is hot. Moments when sweeping positive change is possible—like 2021–2022, when Congress debated, but failed to enact, largescale electoral reform—are exceedingly rare. It's a tragedy if these opportunities are wasted.

The other point is that "generic" reforms—pro-democratic measures desirable under any circumstances—must be complemented by steps crafted specifically to combat the threat of authoritarianism. Thanks to the fragmentation of power in the American system, this threat is sometimes overstated. But the Trump presidency shows that it's nevertheless more acute than most observers previously thought. This isn't the place to develop a comprehensive anti-authoritarian agenda. Suffice to say, though, that the next version of H.R. 1 should address not just elections but also declarations of emergency, law enforcement deployments, civil service protections, DOJ independence, and court reform. These may be secondary bulwarks against democratic decline, but recent years have established that they, too, require reinforcement.

22

Rebuilding the Architecture of Presidential Elections

Larry Schwartztol

From the beginning of our democracy, the constitutional machinery for electing presidents has been combustible. Mostly it chugs along, adapting over time to evolving norms of presidential politics. But since the earliest days of the Republic, it has occasionally failed, sometimes spectacularly. At the center of many of these failures sits the Electoral College. Reformers have long sought (and repeatedly failed) to abolish the Electoral College. One central criticism of the Electoral College is that it sometimes results in the candidate with the most national votes losing, an outcome in tension with the democratic principle of one-person-one-vote. Yet there is another, equally pressing concern that today has become especially acute: the Electoral College is a source of profound instability in our political system. In a time of disorienting political, social, technological, and economic change, abolishing the Electoral College would fortify the structural stability of American democracy.

The original Constitution's basic architecture for selecting presidents mostly remains in place. Each state receives a number of electors equal to its congressional delegation and enjoys broad power to determine the manner in which electors are appointed. (Since the mid-nineteenth century, all states have established popular elections as the way to choose their electors; but they are not required by the Constitution to do so, and in the earliest years of the Republic, many legislatures simply appointed electors directly.) Electors then meet in their respective state capitals to vote. After the electoral votes are counted in Congress, the winner (assuming he gets a majority) becomes president. If no candidate receives a majority of electoral votes, the House of Representatives (voting by state, rather than individual member) chooses the president from among the three top electoral-vote recipients.

This structure has always fit uneasily with modern understandings of presidential legitimacy. The Electoral College winner usually prevails in the national popular vote, but not always—and at the end of the day, the popular vote has no legal force. That democratic deficit is profound even when the president is elected without incident through the Electoral College's principal process. But it becomes even more problematic in light of the possibility that a presidential contest could be thrown to the House of Representatives. Though this has not happened since 1824, it remains a loaded constitutional gun. An electoral-vote tie or even a modest third-party showing could deny both major candidates a majority and send the choice to the House, which would not be bound by the will of the electorate. This "wrong winner" problem—a structure in which a person may be elected despite losing the popular vote—has provoked longstanding criticism, which gained renewed salience following the election of presidents who lost the popular vote in 2000 and 2016.

In addition to this democratic deficit, the Electoral College has always been a source of legal and political instability. This is because it is convoluted, dispersed among many institutional actors, and filled with gaps that matter when something goes wrong. This first became vividly apparent in 1800. The Framers did not anticipate organized parties, and in 1800 Thomas Jefferson wound up in an electoral vote tie with his running mate, Aaron Burr. (Under the original Constitution, each elector cast two votes; the winner becomes president, and the runner-up became vice president.) The election went to the House, where lame-duck Federalists prolonged a deadlock that required thirty-six ballots to resolve and prompted serious talk of violence and disunion. The breakdown was so spectacular that it spurred a constitutional amendment. The Twelfth Amendment, ratified in 1804, provided that electors would vote separately for president and vice president (thus enabling party tickets) and that if the House deadlocked in a contingent election the vice president would assume the office on inauguration day.

The Electoral College has continued to periodically bring the country to the brink. Following the election of 1876, Congress received competing slates of electors from four states. With no constitutional process for adjudicating those disputes, the election remained unresolved until two days before inauguration day, with very real talk of political violence or military intervention in the event of dueling claims to take the oath. The 2000 election did not come quite so close to the cliff's edge: the Supreme Court decided *Bush v. Gore*, after which Al Gore conceded, a little over a month before the inauguration. But the only reason the election came down to the determination of five justices in the first place is that, under the Electoral College, Bush's tiny, contested 537-vote margin in Florida superseded Gore's substantial national popular vote victory.

And the *Bush v. Gore* decision was shaped by the complexities and ambiguities in the Electoral College's legal structure. The Court's determination that Florida's process must end immediately, with no further effort at a fair recount, turned in part on a statutory deadline that could determine which electoral votes Congress would count in the event of a dispute. And the Court's ruling (as well as Gore's concession) took place against the backdrop of active steps by the Florida legislature to declare that the state's election had "failed" and that it was therefore directly appointing Bush's electors. Had the dispute continued to the joint session of Congress, the country likely would have had to navigate a crisis in legally uncharted waters.

Twenty years later, the 2020 election vividly highlighted the Electoral College's destabilizing potential. The January 6 attack on the Capitol reflected many causes, including a concerted campaign of disinformation and the active engagement of extremist organizations. But the ultimate target for the attack was the joint session of Congress at which the electoral votes were to be counted. On one hand, the Constitution set out an extremely limited job for Congress that day: tallying the electoral votes. But its ambiguities and silences created an opening for the lawyers who urged a last stand against the election's rightful outcome. For those lawyers, the absence of constitutional guidance on how to resolve disputes about which electoral votes to count meant that even frivolous disputes— objections based on untested or disproven facts, without regard for the prior determinations of courts, governors, or other institutional actors— could be presented as essentially political questions for the assembled members of Congress to resolve. Legal memos directed to Vice President Pence urged him to either unilaterally declare Trump the winner or force a contingent election in the House. (These arguments lacked legal merit for many reasons, including their disregard for the clear requirements of federal statutes governing the counting process. But they sought to leverage constitutional ambiguity and complexity to justify that legally free-wheeling approach.) While these lawyers may not have argued directly for a violent assault, they reinforced the idea that Vice President Pence and the assembled Congress members would get to decide the election, not just count votes. And that legal provocation provided the predicate for the mob seeking to coerce a decision in favor of Trump.

Given these serious shortcomings, it is unsurprising that reformers have long sought to amend this constitutional structure. Since 1825, there have been over 700 amendments proposed in Congress that would abolish or modify the Electoral College system. Indeed, a proposed amendment to move to a national popular vote passed in the House in 1969, but fell short of the supermajority needed to pass the Senate. (In response to the January 6 crisis, Congress passed a statute clarifying the process of counting votes and mitigating some of the most serious risks. These reforms were valuable, but no statutory reform could cure the deficiencies in the basic constitutional structure.)

While amending the Constitution is always a herculean political task, many observers consider the obstacles to replacing the Electoral College to be especially daunting in the current environment. The multiple supermajority requirements necessary to pass an amendment mean that a determined minority can pose an insurmountable obstacle. In theory, reforming the Electoral College need not divide Americans among partisan lines. As a practical matter, however, there are two elections in living memory in which a Republican has won an electoral vote majority despite losing the popular vote. This recent history likely locks in a partisan valence to this issue, at least for the moment, and makes national supermajorities elusive.

Are we stuck in a constitutional rut, saddled with a bug-ridden system that we lack the capacity to overhaul? Maybe not. Historically, America has had long periods of amendment droughts followed by bursts of constitutional change. Indeed, following Reconstruction, the country went forty-three years without passing an amendment. Then, between 1913 and 1971, it adopted eleven. Without attempting to catalogue the necessary or sufficient conditions for such change, the amendments passed in the twentieth century generally reflected periods of intense social change, political realignments, and concrete problems arising from existing constitutional structures.

While it is hard to know if we are in such a constitutional moment, we are clearly in a period of transformational change in the institution of the presidency. The accretion of power within the executive branch, facilitated by the Supreme Court's expansive view of presidential power, has been underway for decades. But in his second administration, President Trump has accelerated these trends and pushed the limits of the presidency in novel and radical ways. Among other things, he has deployed the might of the federal government to punish critics and perceived enemies; militarized immigration enforcement in American cities; and pursued unilateral military adventurism. President Trump has also made unprecedented attempts to exert executive branch control over federal elections. These are the sorts of dramatic shifts that have inspired constitutional change in the past.

All of these threats and instabilities militate in favor of abolishing the Electoral College, with its constitutional ambiguities and countermajoritarian leanings. For better or worse, presidential elections have become the center of gravity for national political debate and participation; they are the organizing structure for national discussions about how to solve big problems. They deserve a more stable constitutional structure built for the twenty-first century.

PART VII

CRIME, PUNISHMENT, AND STATE POWER

A criminal system is like a fingerprint of a democracy—it tells you a lot about its true identity. And the revelations are troubling. Alexandra Natapoff argues that the American criminal system has historically treated rule of law as a kind of luxury item: often unavailable to ordinary and vulnerable people while benefitting a small, privileged class. Today, however, many elite, formerly high-functioning criminal institutions are faltering under political pressure. As a result, she muses, even the privileged are learning what it feels like to live without the full protections of rule of law. That institutional faltering, in turn, is producing new and dramatic dynamics. Adriaan Lanni documents the surprising resistance of grand juries to high-profile prosecutions brought by the Trump administration. She argues for a reinvigoration of this foundational form of popular control over the criminal process, expressing hope that grand jury skepticism will extend into ordinary criminal cases. Andrew Crespo points out that Congress has the authority to restrict or even rescind the federal prosecution power altogether. He argues that recent federal abuses of prosecutorial authority militate for its elimination, leaving the prosecutorial function in state and local hands where it has traditionally resided. Due in part to that tradition of localism, Carol Steiker predicts that, notwithstanding the global trend toward the abolition of capital punishment, the death penalty will remain an entrenched if shrinking part of the U.S. criminal system. Finally, although immigration is technically a matter of civil and not criminal law, Sabi Ardalan and Phil Torrey demonstrate how the skyrocketing use of immigration detention is dehumanizing and punitive in ways that are neither necessary nor justified, and thus distorting that all-important democratic fingerprint.

23

American Criminal Law: From Inequality to Impunity

Alexandra Natapoff

An unmarked car screeches up to the curb and the doors pop open. Heavily armed officers spill out into the street, guns pointed, and the terrified crowd scatters. Officers chase down the slowest runners, tackling them to the ground and throwing them into the back of the car before they speed away down the dark street.

In 2026, this story became shockingly familiar, describing ICE agents dragging people unlawfully off the streets. But this particular tale of governance failure is not about ICE. It is from 2015 in West Baltimore, where a gang of police officers known as the Gun Trace Task Force ran rampant for nearly a decade. These officers terrorized residents with so-called "door pops," robbed homes, made false arrests, and generally struck fear into Baltimore's poorest neighborhoods. When residents and defendants reported the conduct, they were disbelieved and ignored.

American rule of law has long failed the vulnerable, even as it offers enormous benefits to the privileged. Our criminal system routinely tolerates official lawlessness, state violence, and other egregious governance failures in disadvantaged communities and against ordinary people in ways that would never be tolerated in wealthier communities or by more powerful people. Millions of Americans suffer from systemic breakdowns in the basic operations of the criminal process: illegal stop-and-frisk programs, racially motivated arrest practices, unconstitutional bail proceedings, profiteering from fines and fees, abysmal failures to provide constitutionally-required defense counsel, harsh sentences for minor conduct, and violent, even lethal jail conditions. From Rodney King to George Floyd, and for millions of poor and working people whose names we will never know, the criminal system is a place that exacerbates their disadvantages and where rule of law is a luxury item they can't afford.

Rule of law, however, is not rocket science. Even as the criminal process repeatedly fails at the enormous bottom of the penal pyramid, it clearly knows how to lavish due process and care on a small, elite, high functioning top. Wealthy defendants with excellent lawyers typically get the full benefit of their constitutional rights, protected by official norms of legal precision and restraint. Until recently, at the U.S. Department of Justice and the FBI, in well-resourced federal courts and in high-profile financial cases, we have seen over and over how rule of law can work well when we want it to: based on facts, according to law, with a measure of care, respect, and attention to the equities. No institution is perfect, of course, and there is plenty of injustice in elite legal spaces. But at the top of the penal pyramid, for a fortunate minority, rule of law has worked about as well as could be expected in a constitutional democracy run by actual human beings.

That is, until now. Today, we are witnessing governance failures and the unraveling of basic criminal legal principles in elite spaces. In 2026, a presidential pardon can be openly sought through million-dollar campaign donations. The U.S. Department of Justice's enforcement priorities, as well as those of the FBI, are being redirected away from traditional criminal law enforcement and toward political reward and retribution. Meanwhile, lawyers and law firms adverse to the administration have been threatened with discipline and even prosecution just for doing their jobs, as have judges and politicians who engage in the standard checks and balances contemplated by the separation of powers. As a result of these distortions, criminal justice institutions that used to represent the gold standard are turning into a cautionary tale about law's fragility in the face of unchecked, unprincipled power. We know that criminal law often fails those with too little power. But it also falters in the face of those with too much.

Although this recent demise is extreme, its basic ingredients are not new. The powerful and wealthy, for example, have always enjoyed zones of impunity. Wall Street bankers have long gotten away with defrauding millions of consumers. Police have long gotten away with killing unarmed Black people. Powerful sex offenders routinely escaped accountability.

Rule of law is not self-executing, and its all-too-human agents have always accommodated power and influence to some extent. But today's unapologetic embrace of elite and politicized impunity exceeds even those egregious failures.

The monetary piece isn't entirely novel either. The American criminal system has a well-known alter ego as a revenue generator, extracting fines and fees from poor and working people in millions of low-level cases. By contrast, today's highly profitable leniency market—from campaign donations to millions in financial and other benefits for both the pardoner and the pardoned—feeds off of serious cases and the wealthiest offenders.

The predicates for the current wave of violent immigration enforcement are also old, rooted in our collective tolerance of routine violence against people labeled "criminal." Today's vilification of criminal immigrants wouldn't work so well if we hadn't spent the last forty years dehumanizing people who commit crimes while stripping them of protections against the state. In the normal course of things, U.S. law casually accepts that police may forcibly arrest and incarcerate people merely because they violate a traffic ordinance or cannot pay a fine. Civilian police forces have been given military equipment to use against their own city residents. Violence and rape remain common in our prisons and jails. ICE's excesses are not *sui generis* but rather descendants of the kinds of official violence that have been routinely deployed by the criminal system for years. Indeed, Baltimore's abusive Gun Trace Task Force was ostensibly created in 2007 to go after "the worst of the worst," the very same justification used today to support ICE's unprecedented expansion.

Even the market for lenience is not new. Criminal guilt has been a legally tradable commodity since at least the 1970s. Ninety-five percent of all convictions in this country are the result of a plea deal in which defendants trade away their constitutional rights in exchange for lesser punishment. Defendants who cooperate can often escape liability altogether, a kind of poor man's pardon where defendants pay the government with information, access to friends and family, and even by risking their own lives. Criminal justice has always been negotiable. But today's market has devolved into an open bazaar for the well-connected.

Put differently, the federal government and the privately powerful are cashing in on the enormous amount of authority and elbow room that we have given law enforcement to make legally and ethically problematic decisions. We collectively tolerated those compromises, or just ignored them, when their costs were imposed mainly on the vulnerable. But now, the murky waters from the basement of the criminal system have risen up into the main house and are visibly flooding the living room. The flood is startling; many living room inhabitants never imagined that such things could happen in such well-resourced, protected spaces. To be sure, some of the current excesses are obviously illegal or unconstitutional. But at least some represent technically legal exercises of existing criminal authority—unfettered law enforcement selection discretion, negotiations over guilt, making money off of criminal cases—that have been on the books for ages. The kinds of official violence, unequal treatment, craven instrumentalism, and gross unfairness that we have long excused in ordinary courts and jails and in disadvantaged communities around the country have mutated into new legal disorders. These maladies are now infecting the highest echelons of the criminal system, in places that once served as exemplars of lawful restraint.

These are foundational democratic challenges. A criminal system is a kind of governance fingerprint: it reflects our communal tolerance not only of crime, violence, and victimization, but also of social inequality, unchecked power, and official lawlessness. In 1776, the criminal system was relatively tiny and bore almost no resemblance to the one that we have today. And yet even then, the Founders recognized the existential need to constrain the carceral power of the state. Much of the Constitution's Bill of Rights exists precisely because the Founders feared the threat of executive branch criminal enforcement overreach. Two hundred and fifty years later, our high tolerance for executive discretion, state violence, and unprincipled enforcement in our least powerful communities has made its way up into the highest levels of governance. Rule of law in the criminal system has always been elusive for the powerless. Now the rest of us are learning what that feels like.

24

RESTORING THE POWER OF THE PEOPLE IN THE CRIMINAL PROCESS

ADRIAAN LANNI

In the first year of President Trump's second term, a surprising site of resistance emerged: The people, primarily in the form of the grand jury, rejected several politically-charged federal prosecutions. These high-profile cases highlight how rare and difficult it is in most cases for the grand jury to influence prosecutions. My hope is that these celebrated decisions will encourage grand juries and trial juries to consider rejecting criminal charges in ordinary cases as well—and will likewise encourage legislatures to empower grand juries to reclaim a larger role in regulating criminal prosecution.

The right of the people to check overzealous prosecutions is enshrined in the constitutional rights to a federal grand jury and to a trial by jury in felony cases. These protections were inspired by some famous examples, such as the 1735 case of John Peter Zenger, a newspaper printer prosecuted for seditious libel based on statements in the paper critical of the colonial governor. Two separate grand juries refused to indict Zenger, but the prosecutor proceeded without a grand jury by filing an information to the court. Although the judge instructed the trial jury to decide only whether Zenger had published the issues in question, the jury, perhaps responding to defense counsel's closing that the question before the court was "the cause of liberty," acquitted Zenger.

In the first year of Trump's second term, as the federal prosecution power has been wielded against protesters and political opponents of the President, grand juries have reinvigorated this Founding-era tradition. In one instance, well-publicized because of its absurdity, a man threw a sandwich at a federal agent as part of a protest against the federal deployment in the District of Columbia. A grand jury refused to issue an indictment. After prosecutors downgraded the charge to a misdemeanor assault to avoid the grand jury requirement, the trial jury acquitted him. The grand jury and trial jury offer a particularly potent form of resistance to government overreach because, unlike judges, law firms, corporations, and universities, it is difficult for the president or other executive branch officials to retaliate against, or even criticize, a series of popular bodies like the grand jury or trial jury.

The recent "no bills" by federal grand juries in politically-charged cases have generated widespread attention precisely because no bills are so rare. The evolution of the criminal justice system since the Founding has made it very difficult for the people to serve as a meaningful check on prosecutions. Despite the original conception of the grand jury as independent from the other branches of government, in practice the prosecutor has enormous influence over the modern grand jury, controlling all the evidence that is presented, with no opportunity to hear from the defense. In the recent politically-charged cases, the grand jury knew enough about the context of these prosecutions to exercise independent judgment, but this is not the case for most grand juries in ordinary cases.

Other developments in criminal justice have added additional barriers to meaningful popular oversight. Due to the steep rise in plea bargaining in the late twentieth century, fewer than 5 percent of cases ever reach a trial jury. The proliferation of broad and overlapping criminal laws, high mandatory sentences, and recidivist statutes exposes many defendants to severe sentences, a situation that encourages plea bargains and also risks outcomes that are out of step with popular notions of fairness. For example, one study published by James Gwin in the *Harvard Law and Policy Review* suggests that the U.S. Sentencing Guidelines may be significantly harsher than community sentiment. Following a conviction in twenty federal trials, individual jurors informed of the defendant's prior record were asked for a sentencing recommendation. The study found that the low-end Guidelines range for each case was almost five times higher than the median jurors' recommendation, and 92 percent of the jurors recommended a sentence that was below the Guidelines' recommended minimum for the offense.

Modern grand jurors and trial jurors in ordinary felony cases are more likely to object to the severity of the potential sentence or the prosecutor's choice of charges than to the prosecution itself. But grand and trial jurors cannot act on this instinct because they are typically not informed of the range of penalties facing the defendant or alternative charges that might have been brought.

Is there a way to reinvigorate the people's oversight of the criminal process, not only in high-profile politically-charged prosecutions, but in ordinary cases as well? Scholars have proposed various reforms to empower the grand jury. Reform proposals include forbidding prosecutors from resubmitting cases to a second grand jury after an initial rejection, giving defendants a right to testify, and informing grand jurors of the penalties associated with the charges and of their power to reject charges even in cases supported by probable cause.

More controversially, some scholars, including myself, have proposed appointing an attorney independent of the prosecutor's office to advise the grand jury, not only on probable cause, but also on the range of potential charges available. Under this approach, the grand jury procedure would be transformed from a review of the prosecutor's proposed charges to a more interactive process permitting grand jurors to consult their own attorney and to participate in an informed way in formulating the charges. Empowering the grand jury to formulate charges would move the grand jury closer to its origins, when grand juries had the power to bring charges of their choosing based on their own knowledge and investigation of the facts.

The death of the jury trial is much harder to reverse. Eliminating the harsh sentencing provisions that have encouraged plea bargains might be a first step. A reformed grand jury might deter prosecutors from the most extreme instances of overcharging, somewhat reducing the pressure to plead guilty. But ultimately, jury trials are likely to remain rare, which means that it is more important than ever to ensure that the grand jury exercises some popular control over the all-important initiation of the criminal process.

As a check on a populist president, it is remarkable that grand juries and trial juries have succeeded where so many elite actors (including the judiciary and Congress) have so far struggled. Ordinary people may find it difficult to influence policy, but given half a chance they know injustice when they see it. If we can trust laypeople to protect relatively powerful and well-resourced defendants from authoritarianism, we should also trust them to protect the powerless from a system that has lost touch with common sense.

25

THE LAST FEDERAL PROSECUTORS

ANDREW MANUEL CRESPO

Should the federal government have the power to prosecute people for crimes?

Not long ago that question would have seemed radical to pose. But 250 years into our national experiment and, critically, a year into Donald Trump's second presidency, none can ignore the massive banner now hanging ominously from the façade of the Department of Justice's headquarters in Washington, DC. Unfurled in February 2026, the towering bolt of fabric depicts Trump's scowling visage, carrying a message all too clear. Any pretense that the President's personal politics will be kept out of federal prosecutions—a once bedrock tenet of our constitutional democracy—is gone. In this new America, opposition is punished, loyalty is pardoned, and the rule of law, with its insistence on impersonal prosecutions, is in tatters.

Against this authoritarian backdrop, it is only natural to ask whether the power being abused ought to exist.

Confronted over the banner, the Department made the point explicit. "We are proud at this Department of Justice," a spokesperson said, "to make America safe again at President Trump's direction." The sign might as well read "under new ownership."

Not that we needed a banner to make the point. Upending centuries of constitutional norms, President Trump spent the first year of his second term personally directing federal prosecutors—including some of his own former attorneys, now installed as senior Department leaders—to persecute his political opponents. Former FBI Director James Comey, New York Attorney General Letitia James, Senator Adam Schiff. All tried at various points to hold Trump to account. All were prosecuted or investigated once he took office, as Attorney General Pam Bondi snapped to execute his commands. "They impeached me twice," Trump wrote her in an online missive inadvertently made public. "They're all guilty as hell. . . . We can't delay any longer. . . . JUSTICE MUST BE SERVED, NOW!!!"

Comey was indicted five days later, James two weeks after that.

Meanwhile, two governors of the Federal Reserve face federal criminal investigations as Trump tries to browbeat them into lowering interest rates. In the case against one, Fed Chairman Jerome Powell, a federal judge bracingly wrote that "the Government has offered no evidence whatsoever that Powell committed any crime other than displeasing the President," and held that the investigation's "dominant (if not sole) purpose is to harass and pressure Powell" into yielding to Trump's will.

Federal legislators and state officials are similarly targeted. Prosecutors attempted to indict multiple members of Congress for urging military officers to obey the Constitution and disregard unlawful orders. Trump decried their message as "SEDITIOUS BEHAVIOR, punishable by DEATH!" and called for their prosecutions. Then, on January 20, 2026—one year to the day after Trump's second inauguration—federal prosecutors served criminal subpoenas on Minnesota Governor Tim Walz, the former Democratic vice-presidential nominee, and other Democratic officeholders who dared speak out when Trump sent a deadly deployment of ICE agents into Minneapolis. Weeks earlier, his prosecutors opened a transparently diversionary criminal investigation into the widow of a woman whom those agents shot dead in the street.

All this, in just one year.

Trump has meanwhile turned leniency into a bounty for those showing fealty. Then-Acting Deputy Attorney General Emil Bove—Trump's former personal attorney—moved to dismiss a pending criminal case against New York City Mayor Eric Adams while openly asserting that the President wanted a compliant mayor in office. And let's not forget that Trump began his second term by pardoning hundreds of people convicted of ransacking the Capitol and assaulting police officers on January 6, 2021, all in an effort, urged on by Trump himself, to prevent the inauguration of Trump's electoral opponent, Joseph Biden.

When power is so nakedly personalized, the critical question can't be avoided. Should the president have the power to prosecute? In a world dominated by an ever-ascendant unitary executive theory of constitutional authority, that question quickly morphs into another: Should the federal prosecution power exist at all?

This is not a fanciful hypothetical. Congress clearly has the authority to restrict or rescind the federal prosecution power. Notably, were it to do so, it would be restoring a balance familiar at the nation's founding. As legal historian Jed Shugerman recounts, the robust federal prosecution power familiar today is a relatively recent invention. The first attorneys general were part-time solo practitioners offering occasional legal advice with no staff and no department. Federal district attorneys, scattered across the country and largely unsupervised, answered principally to the Treasury Department, whose primary concern was collecting federal revenue. They were paid a fee per conviction. Congress did not create the Department of Justice until 1870 and did not establish salaries for federal prosecutors until 1896.

For much of our history, this marginal, disorganized form of federal prosecution was a narrowly circumscribed function of the national government. The sweeping prosecutorial power Trump now wields is thus not some constitutional inheritance. It is a modern construction that Congress can reconsider.

Restricting that power would comport well with our national tradition of localism and the democratic accountability it promotes. Heather Gerken, the country's leading theorist of progressive federalism, argues that devolving power to local communities better serves democracy by protecting "racial minorities and dissenters"—two groups squarely in Trump's crosshairs. These citizens hold more "power at the local level than they do at the national," Gerken explains, which makes them more "efficacious political actors" with genuine "muscle to protect themselves."

The late Bill Stuntz pressed a related argument specifically about prosecution. The "decline of local democratic control over criminal justice" can produce pernicious outcomes, he argued, as policymakers far removed from the communities they govern come to treat prosecutions as "political symbols or legal abstractions" rather than decisions that "define neighborhood life" for real people.

Still, I suspect some may have an instinct toward reform over abolition. We should work to restore the post-Watergate consensus favoring prosecutorial independence, they might say, rather than void the power altogether. But Trump's actions lay bare an inconvenient truth. That old system was built almost entirely on norms. And once broken, those norms are painfully hard to restore. We now face a prosecutorial order in which political imprisonments, and indeed political executions ("by DEATH!," he says), are a genuine possibility. Hoped-for renormalization simply cannot meet the moment. Only concrete legal change can ensure that prosecutorial abuse is checked by meaningful electoral oversight, as consistently occurs in the states where attorneys general and district attorneys face the disciplining power of the ballot box. The federal government alone gives its chief executive—the president—the power to prosecute, and we now know just how dangerous that power can be.

Even so, some may ask: Don't we need federal prosecutions to address truly national crimes? What of national security threats, or widescale financial fraud? Here it bears remembering, we will still have states. California is the world's fifth largest economy. The New York City police department operates a global intelligence bureau with officers stationed around the world. These are sophisticated sovereigns whose prosecutors have long handled complex cases rivaling those in federal court. And crucially, abolishing federal criminal prosecution need not mean abolishing federal investigations: The FBI, the SEC, and the CIA could still develop evidence and refer it to state prosecutors, continuing a long tradition of cooperative federalism. Likewise, the Department of Justice could still perform its noncriminal functions and pursue civil litigation—on voting rights, police abuses, financial misconduct—and seek structural injunctions far better positioned to effect systemic change than isolated prosecutions of "a few bad apples."

Of course localism isn't perfect. Some progressives, recalling the civil rights battles of the last century, may yet wonder: Who will seek justice for victims of racial terror in places where local prosecutors refuse to act? To be sure, a handful of federal prosecutors in the Department's storied Civil Rights Division have at times pursued prosecutions that some liberals cheered. But nostalgia for the days when Robert Kennedy and Thurgood Marshall ran the Department ought not blind us to the ends to which its awesome powers are being bent today. Likewise, while racial injustices assuredly persist, we are past the days of rampant state sanctioned lynchings. There are few places in America today where prosecutable murders would be passed over by a locally elected district attorney *and* the state attorney general but yet prosecuted by the Department of Justice. Even in the Obama administration, Eric Garner's family never did see the prosecution they sought.

Most fundamentally, I suspect the instinct that we need federal prosecutorial power may stem from a more basic intuition that criminal law is a natural and important instrument of governance—a needful tool against serious social wrongs. As Ben Levin and Kate Levine observe, even many who generally favor decarceration still turn to the criminal law "to solve social problems." Here, "federal" may simply be an intensifier—a way of saying we need extra powerful criminal law ("a federal case") to address extra important wrongs.

Against this instinct, it is worth considering whether the authoritarian moment we are now living through may hold a lesson—if we let it teach us—about the limits of what Jonathan Simon calls "governing through crime." As Angela Davis warned from her cell in the Marin County Jail over half a century ago, "Fascism is a process." And in that process, the same law-enforcement apparatus that built up the largest prison system in the history of the world might one day be turned, Davis warned, against "even moderate Democrats."

That one day may be today. But if there is a silver lining in this terrifying time, it is that many federal prosecutors are drawing a line in the sand. When Trump sought to extort Eric Adams, Acting U.S. Attorney Danielle Sassoon and other senior leaders in her office resigned in protest. When ICE homicides in Minneapolis were met with criminal investigations of a surviving family member, a dozen senior prosecutors quit.

These principled prosecutors are hardly alone. While the Trump administration fired over 200 Department of Justice lawyers this past year, thousands more have resigned, hollowing out the Department's once hallowed halls.

From their front-row seats, these prosecutors saw how quickly federal criminal law can become a tool of authoritarian oppression. To their credit, they walked away from that fearsome power. Perhaps they should be the last to wield it.

26

THE FUTURE OF CAPITAL PUNISHMENT

CAROL S. STEIKER

The nation's 250th anniversary is an invitation to consider the arc of our governance choices in the context of global developments. When I speak on the topic of capital punishment, one of the most frequent questions I encounter is whether there is a realistic possibility of national and worldwide abolition of the death penalty in the foreseeable future. This query is not surprising in light of the dramatic pace of change over the past half-century. For millennia, the death penalty was a historical constant with only a few outlier abolitionist jurisdictions both inside and outside the U.S. until the latter half of the twentieth century. Then, with startling speed, the practice went into dramatic decline. In the 1970s, only a small minority of nations had fully abolished capital punishment. Today, more than half of the roughly 200 countries in the world have fully abolished by law, and more than two-thirds have done so in either law or practice.

So the question naturally arises whether the death penalty is a practice akin to chattel slavery that will soon be universally morally condemned and relegated to the dustbin of history, or whether it is more like state-sanctioned religious persecution, which has substantially diminished and is widely criticized, but still remains firmly entrenched in various forms in many places around the globe. Scholars of the death penalty disagree about its future trajectory, invoking different aspects of the recent past to support contrary views.

As an opponent of capital punishment, I wish I could join those who see worldwide abolition on the horizon. But the best evidence seems to suggest that the death penalty will remain an entrenched practice for the foreseeable future, though perhaps an increasingly isolated one, much in the same way (and for some of the same reasons, such as autocratic or theocratic rule) as state-sanctioned religious persecution.

Those who forecast a global rejection of capital punishment rely on the strong trend line of the past half-century. Jurisdictions embracing abolition have included not only almost all of Europe and South America but also many countries in Africa, a former stronghold of capital punishment. In addition to the large number of countries that have completely abolished the practice, many retentionist countries have substantially reduced their use of the death penalty. Although official numbers are not available, China is widely recognized as the world's leader in executions by a large margin. Yet experts also agree that China has very substantially reduced its reliance on the death penalty in the past 15–20 years. Within the U.S., Texas has long been the nation's leader in executions, and it too has substantially reduced its execution rate, with the annual execution count in recent years holding at less than a quarter of the count in 2000.

In the moral realm as well, the death penalty has seen its status shift with increasing speed from an accepted tool of criminal justice to a violation of fundamental rights. Many human rights organizations around the world have taken the position that capital punishment violates the right to life and the protection against "cruel, inhuman, or degrading" punishment enshrined in the Universal Declaration of Human Rights. While the practice is not universally outlawed by international treaties, the trend there, too, has been toward increasingly stringent limitations on its use and even total abolition. For example, the European Convention on Human Rights prohibits the death penalty in all circumstances, including war.

In the court of public opinion as well, the death penalty is losing ground. Religious leaders, especially in many Christian denominations, increasingly take categorical stands against capital punishment, even submitting amicus briefs in court proceedings urging judicial restriction or abolition of the practice. Public opinion polling in the U.S. has revealed that support for the death penalty has hit historic lows in recent years after several decades of decline. Part of this decline is driven by demographics, with younger people, including those who identify as Republicans, opposing capital punishment in much greater numbers than older generations—a trend that supports a prediction of further decline in the practice.

Despite the tremendous momentum of these truly remarkable changes over the past half century, there are substantial reasons to doubt that worldwide abolition is on the horizon. Although two-thirds of the countries in the world have abolished the death penalty in law or practice, retentionist countries include highly populous nations, resulting in more than half of the world's population living in jurisdictions where capital punishment remains in force.

Retentionist countries differ from abolitionist regimes in ways suggesting they will strongly resist abolition in the foreseeable future. The single most common trait among abolitionist countries is democratic governance. Autocratic leaders have powerful motivations to employ the death penalty that include demonstrating their power, punishing their political enemies, quelling unrest, and maintaining social order. In addition to authoritarian rule, another common feature among retentionist states is a majority Muslim population and a legal system that incorporates elements of Sharia law. Although not all Muslims believe that capital punishment is required by their faith, many Muslim political leaders insist that it is mandated by the Qur'an and the Sunnah for certain offenses. In the retentionist world outside of China, global executions hit their highest figure in a decade in 2025, driven largely by a strong uptick in the Muslim world, especially in Saudi Arabia and Iran.

Though some retentionist regimes have seen declines in executions and increasing restrictions on the use of the death penalty, this shrinking footprint may not augur impending abolition. The narrowing of the death penalty to the most serious crimes and procedural reforms that improve its fairness in application may well fortify the practice against criticism and attempts at abolition. A narrower, fairer death penalty may prove to be a more stable and enduring one.

Moreover, several developed democracies, including the U.S. and Japan, retain and use the death penalty, undercutting the argument that democracy requires its abolition and giving retentionist states a handy comeback to depictions of them as uncivilized autocracies. The U.S., in particular, because of its global power, provides a shield for other nations that wish to retain the death penalty. Given its federal structure, the U.S. itself is unlikely to achieve nationwide abolition through legislative repeal of the death penalty in all fifty state legislatures and Congress.

The only realistic hope for the complete abolition of the American death penalty lies in the U.S. Supreme Court declaring it an unconstitutional practice. The prospects for such a ruling looked promising a decade ago, but the current conservative supermajority on the Supreme Court makes it highly unlikely for at least a generation.

But the future of contested practices is difficult to predict. To return to the example of chattel slavery, many people—slavery abolitionists among them—believed that abolition in the U.S. was an impossible pipedream in the decades leading up to the Civil War. Or consider marriage equality for same-sex couples. In the 1980s, when the Supreme Court upheld the criminalization of consensual gay sex, the prospects for national recognition of such a right seemed dim. Sometimes big changes happen faster than anyone might foresee.

Even if, as I predict, worldwide abolition of capital punishment does not occur in the near term, in the sense of the next generation or two, its trajectory of decline seems to portend its eventual abolition in the long term. If the practice continues to become more isolated and contested, and a global consensus about its fundamental immorality ultimately coheres—even if these things happen slowly and bumpily—the death penalty will eventually die. Christians who were put to death in the Roman Colosseum 2,000 years ago could not possibly have imagined Rome's current practice of lighting the Colosseum to celebrate when new jurisdictions abolish the death penalty. The transformation of the meaning of that historic site over the long sweep of history is a reminder of the inevitability of massive change over time and the hopeful possibility that such change will entail the abandonment of cruel and brutal practices.

27

DECARCERATING IMMIGRATION

SABRINEH ARDALAN AND PHILIP L. TORREY

An Iranian Christian asylum seeker with severe back pain detained for over a year. A Guatemalan man with cognitive impairments imprisoned for nearly a year and a half whose health declined so precipitously he asked to be deported, rather than stay detained and continue with his case on appeal. A woman held in solitary confinement for months because of a mental health condition that caused her to believe that she had superpowers. Several women placed in isolation after speaking out about medical abuse they endured while detained in a privately-run prison.

These are just a few examples of the harms that immigrants detained by U.S. immigration officials in prisons and county jails across the country have experienced. While the number of individuals detained has drastically increased under the current presidential administration, these abuses are not unique to this moment. They span multiple facilities, across multiple presidential administrations and Congressional terms. They are inconsistent with due process, with human rights, and with basic principles of civilized, humane governance. To advance justice and demonstrate our commitment to equality under law, this carceral system of immigration detention must be re-envisioned.

The problem has gotten worse in recent years. Immigration detention numbers reached an all-time high in 2026, with hundreds of thousands incarcerated and billions of tax dollars spent on immigration detention. Less than ten years ago, the average number of immigrants detained each day was fewer than 20,000. In early 2026, it surpassed 70,000. Indeed, the United States has one of the most expansive (and expensive) immigration detention systems in the world, with dire consequences for the health and safety of immigrants. Between January 2025 and March 2026, forty-one immigrants in ICE detention died, which is a rate of about one death every six days.

This inhumane system is not only morally offensive, but also inconsistent with its own legal foundations. The Supreme Court has emphasized that immigration detention is not intended to be punitive. Rather, its primary purpose is ostensibly to ensure that immigrants attend their immigration court hearings and comply with court orders. There are other ways of achieving that goal without incarcerating immigrants for months and even years at a time, without using solitary confinement as punishment, and without denying access to adequate medical or mental health care.

Indeed, the current system of immigration detention did not even exist until the mid- to late-1990s when the criminalization of immigrants became a centerpiece of federal legislation. As congressional demands for detention grew, the private prison industry expanded to meet those demands. Today, an overwhelming majority of immigrants are detained in privately run, for-profit prisons, which make millions of dollars each year from government contracts. With $45 billion of funding allocated by Congress last year, Immigration and Customs Enforcement ("ICE") is attempting to expand these prisons even further to include commercial warehouses retrofitted to detain immigrants, among other measures to increase bed capacity. At the local level, the federal government pays counties to reserve beds in jails for immigration detention, which in turn incentivizes the government to fill the beds with immigrants.

Contrary to official assertions, the vast majority of those detained have no criminal convictions. Narratives about the dangerousness of immigrants stoke fears in communities that then lend support to the detention of immigrants, even though those narratives are demonstrably false. In fact, a new report stated that recent changes in ICE apprehension policies have resulted in a roughly 2,450 percent increase in the number of individuals detained with no criminal record.

There is nothing inevitable about these draconian incarceration policies. Numerous obvious steps can be taken, both federally and locally, to end reliance on an inherently punitive form of incarceration that endangers the mental and physical health of immigrants. An important first step would include releasing vulnerable populations and eliminating solitary confinement. In the criminal context, states have already taken steps to end the use of solitary confinement; the same can be done in immigration detention. States can also place limits on, and even end, agreements with ICE to detain immigrants within their jurisdictions. Congress and the executive should follow suit.

Greater accountability, transparency, and oversight are also needed at the very least to ensure meaningful screening for medical and mental health conditions and other vulnerabilities. Incarceration is a last resort: we should prioritize releasing vulnerable immigrants from detention and preventing their incarceration in the first place.

To the extent that immigration detention aims to ensure that immigrants appear at their immigration court proceedings, assigning counsel to immigrants is a cost-effective mechanism for reaching the same result. Studies have repeatedly shown that most immigrants who have legal representation reliably appear in court for their hearings. Yet, the right to counsel is generally at the immigrant's own expense, which means few detained immigrants have legal representation. Lawyers are cheaper than jail. Investing in meaningful access to counsel would respond to concerns about immigrants attending court or reporting to immigration officials while avoiding some of the system's worst abuses.

In a nation of immigrants, the most important change might be to remind ourselves of our oldest commitments. Changing the narrative about immigrants and creating greater connections across communities can help break down barriers and build understanding. As parents, workers, caregivers, employers, and children, immigrants are crucial, contributing members of our society. Our country has an obligation to safeguard their rights, not place their lives at risk.

PART VIII

THE ENVIRONMENT

Environmental law is the primary governance mechanism through which we address some of the most pressing policy issues of the day, including our food, health, air and water pollution, agriculture, and climate change. But the world is changing fast and environmental law is struggling to keep up. Richard Lazarus fears that climate change is proving too much for our political infrastructure. While all three branches of government successfully cooperated in the 1970s and 1980s to create strong environmental laws, today's executive branch, Congress and the Supreme Court have each failed to address climate change, even exhibiting hostility toward much-needed regulation. In a similar vein, Emily Broad Leib worries about the across-the-board failure to craft a strong national food policy. In its absence, the American food system contributes significantly to pollution and global warming while tolerating widespread hunger and food insecurity. Kristen Stilt takes a step back and attributes such failures of vision to a historical lack of ecological consciousness. As she puts it, our contemporary legal framework was never built to protect nature, but rather "to manage the orderly exploitation of the environment." Together, these scholars sketch a rich roadmap for future generations of environmental lawyers, policymakers, and concerned Americans.

28

MEETING THE CHALLENGE OF ADDRESSING CLIMATE CHANGE

RICHARD J. LAZARUS

It is a frightening moment in the history of modern environmental law in the United States. Environmental lawmaking has never been easy. Yet in many respects, its story of the past fifty years is one of enormous success—air, water, and hazardous waste pollution have decreased dramatically along important dimensions while the economy has grown exponentially.

Making climate change law, however, tells a vastly different story. Both the current administration and the Supreme Court are actively undermining longstanding principles of both administrative law and separation of powers in ways that prevent long overdue constructive climate lawmaking. The United States and the entire world currently face the potentially catastrophic problem of climate change—with the kicker that the longer it takes to bring down greenhouse gas emissions the exponentially harder it becomes to do so before their worst impacts occur. Tragically, however, climate lawmaking has proven to be environmental lawmaking's worst nightmare in the U.S.—the vast temporal and spatial dimensions of the costs and benefits of restricting greenhouse emissions have defied the short-term focus of most people and therefore also those of elected officials who both seek their votes and are responsive to major donors to their campaigns from the fossil fuel industry. Congress has all but shut down on the subject.

That is why during the past three decades, no president or Congress has yet been able to enact laws to address the climate issue in a meaningful and comprehensive way. And the second Trump administration is insanely doing just the opposite—creating yet another nightmare in facing up to the climate challenge. The Trump administration's express policy on climate change is to "drive a dagger straight into the heart of the climate change religion." And to that stunning end, President Trump's appointed head of the Environmental Protection Agency has repealed what the administration characterizes as the "holy grail" of federal government authority to regulate greenhouse gas emissions that cause climate change—EPA's 2009 determination that greenhouse gas emissions in the United States cause or contribute to climate change that endangers public health and welfare.

The administration's repeated references to religion are downright bizarre. Yet they are not at all incidental to the extent that they expose the ideological zealotry motivating the administration's effort to destroy any ability of the U.S. to address what scientists and essentially the rest of the world all agree is one of the greatest threats to humankind. This ideological extremism includes: repealing the 2009 endangerment determination in order to ensure the executive branch lacks any legal authority to restrict greenhouse gas emissions at all, blocking development of wind and solar sources of renewable energy, launching preemptive lawsuits to deny the states the authority to fill the gap left by the lack of federal regulation, and ordering existing coal fired power plants that are no longer economically viable to burn coal (one of the nation's largest sources of greenhouse gas emissions).

The ideological extremity of the Trump administration on climate change in particular and environmental protection more generally, however, did not come out of nowhere. It can be fairly traced to the evolution and then devolution of modern environmental law in the United States over the past fifty years. And that devolution is itself grounded in the extraordinary shifts in the relative power exercised by the three branches of federal government and their willingness to exercise that power in shaping the nation's environmental laws.

At various times and in contrasting combinations during the 1970s and 1980s, a powerful Congress, judiciary, and executive branch worked together to establish a highly resilient and effective foundation of environmental laws. Within the past twenty-five years, however, there have been seismic whipsawing shifts within the White House on the policy wisdom of strict environmental laws, especially in response to the overwhelming difficulty of the climate issue. Fifty years ago, the rise of environmental law could not be denied, notwithstanding repeated unsuccessful efforts to weaken its requirements. In its sixth decade, by contrast, its once settled foundations are increasingly threatened.

The Supreme Court has in turn fueled that threat rather than served as an effective backstop to dampen it. The Court has reacted to the challenge of climate change by further undermining the federal government's ability to address the problem effectively. And not just for making climate law. But for lawmaking within both the executive and legislative branches in general.

Here, moreover, there is no small irony. In the 1970s and 1980s, the entire federal judiciary, including the Supreme Court, responded to the nation's overriding commitment to more environmental protection with supportive rulings. Congress passed dozens of new laws, and the courts embraced the challenge to ensure their implementation. The courts endorsed "hard look" judicial review of agency factfinding to ensure that federal agencies strictly complied with the lofty goals and ambitions of this new generation of laws. Judicial decisions increased citizen suit access to ensure stricter enforcement of the new statutory requirements. The courts regularly rejected federal regulatory takings claims. They dismissed outright Commerce Clause and nondelegation doctrine challenges to congressional authority.

Famously, the Supreme Court in its 1984 opinion in *Chevron v. EPA* announced a new framework for judicial review of agency interpretation of statutes administered by the agency pursuant to congressional delegation of lawmaking authority. The Court not only rejected the proposition that an agency rule must be supported by clear congressional authorization but required courts to defer to reasonable agency interpretation of statutory language it administered so long as its reading *was not contrary* to the clear mandate of the statute. While *Chevron* itself initially provided agencies with discretionary authority to allow environmental rules to be more cost effective, the ruling ultimately provided agencies with the authority needed to toughen environmental controls in the absence of new legislation caused by the congressional shutdown. Not only environmental law but federal administrative law, constitutional law, and other cross-cutting areas of law themselves all transformed to create a foundation to support a modern administrative state capable of address-ing pressing national issues on a timely basis.

In response to the climate issue and to the congressional lawmaking paralysis it has created, however, the current Court is in the process of dismantling that foundation: not just to the detriment of environmental law, but for federal lawmaking and the role of administrative agencies in general. In short, for a majority of the Justices concerned with safe-guarding separation of powers, the executive branch's efforts to address climate change in ambitious ways notwithstanding the absence of new legislation was the paradigmatic example of what had become wrong with executive branch lawmaking more generally.

It is no mere happenstance that the Court's very first "shadow docket" ruling was climate-related. A five-Justice majority in February 2016 took the then-unprecedented action of staying Obama's EPA Clean Power Plan—which regulated for the first time greenhouse gas emissions from existing coal fired power plants—while the case was still pending before the D.C. Circuit and after that court had denied such a stay. The Court has since dramatically expanded this highly questionable practice in doz-ens of Court rulings, in which the Justices issue orders of major import in the absence of full briefing, argument, or meaningful deliberation. These orders have seriously undermined the Court's integrity and perpetuated the image that the Justices are impulsively ideological rather than consid-ered and deliberative.

Nor is it a coincidence that the Court, six years later in *West Virginia v. EPA*, first invoked the aggressive "major questions doctrine" to upend the EPA's subsequent effort during the Biden administration to regulate those same sources of greenhouse gases. The Court's new doctrine, which effec-tively flipped *Chevron* on its head, provided that federal agencies like EPA could promulgate significant, potentially transformative rules, like those regulating greenhouse gas emissions across the nation, only if the agency could establish "clear congressional authorization." *West Virginia* was a far cry from *Chevron*, which had ruled that courts should uphold reasonable agency interpretations only if *contradicted* by clear congressional intent. Not surprisingly, two years later, the Court formally overruled *Chevron* in *Loper Bright Enterprises v. Raimondo*. The Court has accordingly under-mined not just EPA's ability to address pressing problems like climate change, but in the face of a deadlocked Congress, the federal executive branch's overall ability to address pressing problems of any kind.

The Court's hostility toward agency regulation contrasts sharply with its tolerance for deregulatory dismantling. The Court has not yet suggested any interest in putting similar limits on the current administration's efforts to destroy the federal government's long-term ability to restrict greenhouse gas emissions or promote alternative renewable sources of energy now or in the future—by dismissing career agency experts without any legal process and by ceasing all climate scientific research, notwithstanding its support from existing congressional appropriations. Forebodingly, several Justices instead seem ready to make it even harder still to address the climate issue in a constructive way. Justices Thomas, Alito, and Gorsuch have written or joined concurring opinions that, relying on long ago rejected notions of Commerce Clause and nondelegation doctrine limits on congressional power, suggest that even congressional enactments that seek to clearly authorize federal climate regulation would be unconstitutional.

The Justices need to be part of the solution rather than, as they are now, a significant part of the problem. Climate change lawmaking efforts, whether by federal agencies under existing law or ultimately (finally) in the future by Congress more expressly conferring broad and capacious lawmaking authority on agencies, are not properly viewed as threats to fundamental separation of powers principles that therefore must be rejected. The need for climate change law to avert potential catastrophe instead underscores the brilliance of the Constitution, which allows the executive and legislative branches the necessary leeway to address the nation's needs in dynamic, ambitious, and innovative ways. Absent that necessary mind-shift on the Court, there is good reason to fear for our future.

29

FOUNDING IDEALS AND THE FUTURE OF AMERICAN FOOD POLICY

EMILY M. BROAD LEIB

Thomas Jefferson famously said, "Those who labor in the earth are the chosen people of God, if ever he had a chosen people, whose breasts he has made his peculiar deposit for substantial and genuine virtue." Jefferson mythologized agriculture and farmers, believing that "agriculture is the most healthful, most useful and most noble employment of man." And though the words "food" and "farm" do not appear in the Declaration of Independence, themes of food and agriculture abound, such as concerns over blockage of trade, taxing of food products like sugar and tea, and the unwanted quartering—including housing and feeding—of British soldiers.

Jefferson would not recognize today's food and agriculture system. Far from the most "healthful" industry, global food production is responsible for a third of greenhouse gas emissions. Food waste (about a third of the global food supply) is responsible for 8–10 percent of global emissions. In 2018 in the United States, 1.5 million deaths—over half of all deaths—were caused by conditions that could have been prevented with improved diet, such as type 2 diabetes, heart disease, stroke, and various cancers. Food insecurity spikes in the wake of the COVID-19 pandemic, recent supply chain disruptions, and inflation highlight persistent failures and inequities in the food system.

Despite the food system's centrality to our national health, economy, and environment, we have failed to craft a strong, comprehensive, modern food policy. We continue to sanction, even to subsidize pollution. We allow food production to contribute to climate degradation. We permit food insecurity to persist: 14 million American children still go to bed hungry every night. These failures are failures not of resources or technology but of vision. We have no coordinated or strategic federal plan for food in the way that we do for national security, energy, or other comparable sectors.

Food is regulated by more than fifteen federal agencies—many of which have conflicting authorities and missions. In recent years, numerous experts have called on the U.S. government to create structures that coordinate and prioritize a coherent vision for the food system. Yet unlike peer countries—such as Australia, Canada, and the United Kingdom—the U.S. has failed to develop a national food strategy or appoint a national food leader with authority to set and achieve long-term, whole-of-government priorities.

This is problematic because the food system is multifaceted, and many elements interact with one another, sometimes in counterproductive ways. For example, the U.S. farm bill provides direct payments and subsidized crop insurance that primarily support, not healthy foods, but commodity crops such as soybeans, corn, and cotton. By contrast, the Dietary Guidelines for Americans have long recommended that at least half the diet be made up of fruits and vegetables, which are known as "specialty crops" and left out of most farm bill programs. Similarly, U.S. laws set standards for state and local drinking water under the Safe Drinking Water Act, yet runoff from agricultural production that contaminates drinking water is exempt from the Clean Water Act's permitting requirements.

The political swings of the past decade have compounded the problem. Lack of vision, leadership, and strategy have allowed fluctuations in agricultural funding supports, food security programs, and environmental regulations without thought for long-term food system outcomes.

There is, however, one unique area of food policy that has exhibited growing agreement across the political spectrum: addressing diet-related disease. Robert F. Kennedy, Jr.'s "Make America Healthy Again" movement has galvanized support across parties for taking diet seriously as a driver of health. While many aspects of RFK Jr.'s platform are not bipartisan—and face critiques for failing to follow scientific evidence—the elements related to food and diet demonstrate broad appeal. RFK Jr. oversaw the publication of an interagency MAHA report and strategy that outline how the U.S. food system causes chronic disease and lay out plans to address it, including better regulating food additives; developing a national definition of "ultra-processed food;" improving meals in schools and hospitals; and increasing transparency in food labeling. HHS and FDA have taken steps to implement many of these proposals. States have responded positively: In 2025, dozens of states introduced bills aligned with MAHA goals, such as banning or requiring warning labels on foods with certain additives or banning certain additives or ultra-processed food in schools. Many states that enacted such policies in 2025 were red states, such as Texas, Louisiana, and West Virginia.

Unlike many of the Trump administration's policies, diet-related disease policies show alignment and even consistency with previous efforts from the other side of the aisle. In 2022, the Biden Administration released a National Strategy for Hunger, Nutrition, and Health, aiming to end hunger and reduce diet-related diseases by 2030. The Biden administration also initiated an effort to improve post-market review of food additives and proposed regulations for front-of-package labeling. State bills proposing to ban additives in food or in schools in 2025 were modeled on legislation California enacted in 2023 and 2024; in 2025 California also banned "ultraprocessed foods of concern" in schools. And many MAHA priorities echo Michelle Obama's "Let's Move" campaign, which endeavored to improve school meals, support better food labeling, and increase food access.

While vital for public health, this policy bright spot is an outlier. Most of American food policy remains an unhealthy, conflicted, counterproductive mess. The Biden Strategy on Hunger, Nutrition, and Health—while admirable in its efforts to address hunger and diet-related disease—failed to include priorities related to climate change. Among 196 commitments, climate was mentioned only once, in a pledge to research the connection between climate and food security. The MAHA movement has not found success with the elements of its strategy related to food production and environment, including better regulating pesticides and fertilizers, and addressing soil contamination. American food policy still tolerates food insecurity on a scale unseen in peer nations. The Biden administration tried to address the problem by increasing access to SNAP among other approaches, but both the first and current Trump administrations have overseen vastly reduced access to the program, despite the acknowledged connection between food insecurity and the diet-related disease that is a MAHA priority.

We should ensure that today's well-founded commitments to tackle diet-related disease persist into future administrations and find success. But even that narrow commitment will fall short if it remains in isolation. Rather, we must convert that commitment into interest in the entire food system, and into a strategy that sets long-term priorities and provides vision and leadership. This means addressing how food production affects soil, water, and climate. It means enshrining our responsibility to ensure food security. The U.S. is one of the very few nations that still has not formally recognized a right to food, even though we are better positioned than many nations to make it a reality. We should stop being an outlier.

Thomas Jefferson was right. Food is central to the environment, to the economy, to health, and to equality. On the 250th anniversary of our nation, it is long past time to get beyond partisan gamesmanship and short-sighted policies and recognize the "healthful, useful and noble" value of a robust, comprehensive, and aspirational national food policy.

30

THE LAW AGAINST THE LAND

KRISTEN A. STILT

The United States Constitution is a document of profound silences. In its architecture of governance—its balance of powers, enumeration of rights, and framework for commerce and defense—there is no mention of the land itself. There is no recognition of how the new country acquired the land upon which the provisions of the Constitution would operate, nor of the existing belief systems about the natural world that the Constitution would supersede on that land. Animals, plants, waters, and ecosystems exist entirely outside the Constitution's textual bounds.

This is not an oversight, but the philosophical bedrock upon which our now-perilous relationship with the nonhuman world was built. Fundamentally, the Constitution is a document about power more than perpetuity, and this silence on the nonhuman world is its most enduring and dangerous legacy.

The authors of *The Federalist Papers*, for example, consumed with existential threats of faction, tyranny, and economic instability, viewed the American landscape not as a finite community or interdependent web of life, but as a vast, untamed field for political experiment. It was an inventory of resources to be exploited, a wilderness to be conquered, and a commodity to be distributed in the service of building a new republic. Nature, including all nonhuman life, was the assumed and infinite backdrop for human drama, without any interests or intrinsic value.

This ethos was codified in policies such as the Land Ordinance of 1785, which created a mechanism for the efficient privatization and sale of the wilderness, and it endured until the Homestead Act of 1862. As the historian Roderick Frazier Nash writes in *Wilderness and the American Mind*, the prevailing American sentiment was that wilderness was something to be feared, conquered, and improved. The Constitution facilitated this very project: the conversion of a continent's ecological capital into a nation's economic and political power.

This Constitutional DNA is now the heart of modern American environmental law. Our contemporary legal framework is not designed to protect nature from humanity, but to mediate disputes among humans over the allocation of natural resources. It is a system built to manage the orderly exploitation of the environment, with conservation measures appearing largely as afterthoughts—emergency brakes on a machine geared for consumption.

Given the Constitution's ecological silence and its anthropocentric legacy, the path forward lies not in its text, but in its most fundamental assumptions. The document is driven by the implicit recognition of national self-preservation. Today, the single greatest threat to that endurance is state-sponsored ecological collapse. Indeed, arguably much of the global geopolitical tumult we are experiencing is in great part emerging from conditions of climate change.

A recent groundbreaking lawsuit, while unsuccessful, brought this argument out of academic and scientific theory and into the federal judiciary. In *Juliana v. United States*, a group of young plaintiffs argued that the federal government's actions promoting a fossil fuel-based economy violated their constitutional rights to life and property and that the government failed to protect essential public trust resources. They made a common sense and profound claim: Existing rights are meaningless without a climate system capable of sustaining life.

In 2020, the Ninth Circuit Court of Appeals dismissed the case on the grounds of standing and noted that the judiciary was not the proper branch of government to create a remedy for climate change. However, the majority opinion conceded the terrifying reality of the plaintiffs' claims, writing that a "substantial evidentiary record documents that the federal government has long promoted fossil fuel use despite knowing that it can cause catastrophic climate change, and that failure to change existing policy may hasten an environmental apocalypse." The court acknowledged the existential crisis and claimed impotence in the face of it.

It was Judge Josephine Staton's dissent that forged a new constitutional argument. Her rebuke argues that the Constitution cannot be interpreted to permit national suicide. "It is as if an asteroid were barreling toward Earth," she wrote, "and the government decided to shut down our only defense." She clearly and profoundly advanced the common-sense view that "the Constitution does not condone the Nation's willful destruction."

Her dissent articulates the core of a constitutional interpretation crucial for our current times: The government's duty to preserve the country is implicit in the document's very existence. The Founders' desire for the nation to last for "posterity" cannot be squared with government actions that guarantee that posterity will inherit a ruined world.

Any survivable path forward requires a fundamental shift in our governing ethos—a recognition that the perpetuity of the nation is ecologically contingent. Such a shift would move beyond just passing stronger environmental laws: those would still operate within the old paradigm of mitigating human-caused harm. Instead, it would require bringing the more-than-human world into our legal and ethical frameworks. This is not a call for nature as a fourth branch of government, but for a significant change in how the existing branches interpret their mandates.

The Declaration of Independence asserted our rights to pursue "life, liberty, and . . . happiness." The Constitution's Preamble promised to "secure the Blessings of Liberty to ourselves and our Posterity." Both these promises are null and void on an uninhabitable planet. The constitutional duty to "provide for the common defense" must be expanded to include defending the nation against the existential threats of climate change and ecological collapse.

This argument for de-centering humanity in our legal framework is not an altruistic plea for the planet. It is a pragmatic argument for human survival. The profound irony is that our species' steadfast refusal to grant legal or ethical consideration to the nonhuman world *on its own terms* now directly threatens the stability of the human world. The constitutional framework, designed to ensure the stability of the nation, has been interpreted in a way that facilitates its ruin. To save ourselves, we must re-read our own founding document and rediscover the implicit duty it contains: a government's sacred obligation not to destroy the country it is sworn to protect. The most anthropocentric goal of all—our own survival—now paradoxically depends on abandoning the very idea of human supremacy.

PART IX

THE FUTURE OF ECONOMIC GOVERNANCE

Perhaps nowhere does this collection exhibit its intellectual divergences more dramatically than in this section on money, labor, corporate power, capitalism, and concentrated wealth. From the corporate law perspective, Mariana Pargendler describes the recent decline of the legal checks and balances that once constrained American corporations and supported the growth of capital markets. She concludes that "U.S. law is now moving toward developing-world cronyism, where controlling shareholders face few constraints and shape laws in their favor." Mark Roe describes the corporate legal landscape from the perspective of America's robust history of populist anti-finance, anti-corporate politics. He flags the puzzling populist tolerance for the new breed of tech billionaire, musing that economics can never fully explain corporate structure or behavior without accounting for popular politics. In a structural vein, Yochai Benkler characterizes the United States as "a liberal oligarchic republic" designed primarily around the protection of wealth. Describing the Republican and Democratic parties as "the Tweedledum and Tweedledee of neoliberalism," Benkler concludes that current American politics are largely explicable as "the misdirected rebellion of the working classes against the destruction of their life prospects in the service of oligarchy." Benjamin Sachs zeroes in on the rise and fall of labor unions and other membership organizations as the key to understanding American economic governance and democracy. Like Benkler, he emphasizes America's concentrated wealth and unparalleled levels of social, political, and economic inequality, arguing that new laws are needed to build and enable membership organizations that can meaningfully redistribute power.

Christine Desan reminds us that there are many ways to design money itself, some of them more or less egalitarian, all of them requiring public support and subsidy. She mourns how "the privatized practice of money creation has swallowed the public sourcing of value," and urges us to rethink how we permit private interests to design and control the flow of the money on which we all rely. Finally, Jared Ellias deplores the short-sighted legal and policy choices that have turned the specialized bank-ruptcy system—designed to manage financial crises—into a backstop for managing social problems. As he puts it, bankruptcy court is ill-suited to decide "how best to prevent youth sexual assault, mitigate wildfire risk in arid regions, or regulate the safe use of prescription opioids." In fascinating ways, these six scholars adopt entirely different, perhaps even incompatible conceptual frameworks for addressing surprisingly similar questions.

31

Corporate Governance and Private Power

Mariana Pargendler

Two and a half centuries after the Declaration of Independence, U.S. law faces a paradox the Founders could scarcely have imagined: The nation built to resist concentrated power has created private institutions whose reach can rival the state itself. Corporate law is thus a constitutional problem in miniature, allocating power and structuring accountability. The checks and balances that have been a hallmark of the system's capital markets success, and of social ordering more generally, today are under enormous strain. U.S. law is now moving toward developing-world cronyism, where controlling shareholders face few constraints and shape laws in their favor. Paradoxically, these same powerful institutions, capable of shaping their own legal environment, have largely accommodated rather than resisted new concentrations of executive power, suggesting that private and public power may be mutually reinforcing rather than countervailing.

The modern business corporation—so ubiquitous it seems natural—is, in historical terms, a recent invention. In 1776, business corporations were rare, chartered sparingly for special purposes. The Constitution does not mention them. That same year, Adam Smith's *The Wealth of Nations* warned that when managers administer "other people's money," "negligence and profusion" would inevitably follow. Smith identified two enduring risks in the early corporations of that time: they might fail through mismanagement; and they might embody monopolies harming consumers. Now, add environmental degradation challenging planetary limits and the sheer concentration of private power challenging democratic control.

The past 250 years defied Adam Smith's skepticism. Corporations became the dominant engine of economic life. State law endows corporations with their basic attributes—including legal personality, limited liability, entity shielding, and regulatory partitioning—enabling large-scale enterprise and constraining the regulatory powers of the state itself. Law does not merely regulate corporations; it constitutes them. And law remains indispensable to managing the agency costs and the social costs of corporate activity.

By 2026, American corporations stand at the center of our era's defining challenges: artificial intelligence, climate transition, social media's influence on minds and democracy, and geopolitical competition with China. Yet the U.S. corporate landscape is shifting dramatically. Public markets have grown more concentrated, both in terms of the market value commanded by the largest firms and in the prevalence of controlling shareholders among them. Private markets have exploded while remaining opaque. Dual-class structures increasingly cement founder control. The dispersed shareholders of mid-century textbooks have given way to the "Big Three" institutional investors, introducing a different form of concentration in firms that lack controlling shareholders. U.S. capital markets increasingly host foreign firms and investors.

American corporate law can be understood through two seemingly opposed but ultimately complementary narratives. The *market-centric view* emphasizes private ordering and regulatory competition. Corporate law is viewed as a product, which states effectively "sell" in exchange for franchise fees. Delaware has long dominated by offering flexibility and predictability, as well as substantial discretion for corporate boards in the name of shareholder interests. The "genius of American corporate law," in this view, lies precisely in responsiveness to shareholders' and managers' interests without democratic accountability.

The corporate accountability view tells a different story. Far from *laissez-faire*, the United States developed the world's most elaborate regulatory and enforcement apparatus for public companies. The SEC, created during the New Deal, became a model exported globally. U.S. markets demand unusual transparency, and a sophisticated plaintiffs' bar makes litigation frequent and consequential.

Delaware's equity tradition further complicates the purely permissive story. Corporate action is "twice tested": not only for technical compliance but for conformity with equity. U.S. courts developed veil-piercing, fiduciary duties for controlling shareholders, and derivative suits earlier and more extensively than peer jurisdictions. As Mark Roe has famously argued, state competition operates in the shadow of federal power: the threat of federalization disciplines states toward minority shareholder protection and other concerns.

This accountability infrastructure arose from diverse pressures. In Roe's account, a tradition of American populism has historically curbed the power of financial institutions. Nonprofit activism shaped corporate behavior and laws toward social and environmental goals. What I have called a "corporate governance obsession" promised checks and balances within firms to address problems from corruption to systemic risk. These narratives are best understood as complements, reflecting an uneasy compromise between enabling markets and constraining the abuse of private power.

That already-imperfect compromise now faces further strain. Delaware's 2024 and 2025 amendments represent a troubling retreat from American corporate law's accountability tradition. Responding to judicial constraint of controlling shareholder power and equitable policing of conflicted transactions (including an extraordinary pay package for the world's richest man), the Delaware legislature moved toward bright-line rules making a wide array of potentially problematic transactions unreviewable, leaving fewer constraints on controlling shareholders, and creating more obstacles to shareholder litigation. These reforms were not merely technocratic endeavors. They followed attacks on judges, credible reincorporation threats to Texas and Nevada, and intense lobbying by increasingly powerful controlling shareholders and the private equity industry—reflecting the subversion of the existing legal order by powerful interests.

This shift marks a major departure from longstanding U.S. corporate governance principles. U.S. law is rolling back corporate accountability mechanisms and regulations across the board. As I have argued elsewhere, in other nations controlling shareholders appeal to nationalism to justify their control and role in society. Here, a similar trend is dismantling legal constraints that once aimed to confine controllers' power. At the federal level, proposals to route securities disputes into arbitration would neutralize much of the private enforcement machinery. Efforts to weaken shareholder proposals on social and environmental matters further reduce accountability. Together with the Delaware retreat, these developments suggest a broader unwinding of the regulatory and judicial infrastructure built over decades which constitutes a key pillar of the U.S. system.

This unwinding has a political context. The international rise of authoritarian regimes has often transformed corporate governance both through the direct exercise of state power and through the cooptation of private enterprise. In the U.S., corporations appear increasingly entangled with government as well. Ironically, to fight China, the U.S. is abandoning its arm's-length tradition and moving closer to China in key respects. Recent breaks include new strategic state shareholdings and even the adoption of a "golden share" in connection with a foreign acquisition. Whereas earlier experiments with U.S. state ownership came in times of crisis, such as when the federal government took shares in major financial institutions and car companies following the 2008 financial meltdown, current state incursions are occurring without an acute crisis. The government is pressing corporate leaders to favor government policies through a combination of political carrots and sticks. Corporate leaders' abrupt shifts in public posture suggest dependence when political risk becomes existential. Concerns about cronyism, selective intervention, and politicized enterprise are mounting.

The 250th anniversary of American law arrives as U.S. corporate and capital markets law, often celebrated as the envy of the world, faces these daunting new challenges. Legal scholars have overwhelmingly favored a narrow, "modular" view of corporate law focused on investor protection alone, with other social concerns outsourced to other areas of law. This view is untenable: it has long had its share of critics and is incomplete in its own terms. Even standard corporate rules aimed at protecting shareholders from managers have broader social consequences. Expropriation by controlling shareholders is economically regressive and further concentrates wealth and power. Derivative suits for failure of oversight serve to strengthen the bite of sanctions imposed by other areas of law. Transparency aimed at investors produces broader positive externalities in terms of social control. Social concerns are not fully separable, and distortions created by corporate law—the field governing residual discretion—are not easily addressed elsewhere. The narrowing of the field's scope by the law-and-economics tradition has reduced our ability to resist the ongoing backlash.

The task ahead is to preserve corporations' vitality and capacity for innovation for the social good in the face of these societal challenges. Much remains to be done in perfecting democratic controls and legitimacy of corporations, which have long been unsatisfying. Law, including corporate law, has an important role to play. The first step is resisting the erosion of basic principles that have distinguished U.S. corporate governance and inspired jurisdictions worldwide.

32

America's Anti-Corporate, Anti-Finance Populism: Yesterday and Today

Mark J. Roe

There has long been a popular sense that corporations were too strong, Wall Street too powerful, and financial firms too rich. For a considerable length of American history, American populism aimed to weaken Wall Street, and largely succeeded. Americans' historical distrust of finance made it much weaker than it was in other nations; industry spanned the continent in the late nineteenth century, while that popular distrust largely confined banks—the key financial institution of the time—to a state-by-state presence. Weakened, localized finance meant that financial players could not, unlike in other nations, play a large role in the large American corporation and the financial channels that powered it.

The impact of populist politics started in the nation's early days. We started with a nation-spanning bank that, according to its architects like Alexander Hamilton, could and would power national commerce and American manufacturing. But the nation-spanning bank met its demise at the hands of Andrew Jackson and American populism. Andrew Jackson's populist veto message, denying rechartering to the Second Bank of the United States set the foundation: right from the near-start (1832), we had no nationwide financial institution that could directly knit together regions, the country, and nationwide business. And we had no central regulator that could stabilize the inherently unstable fractional reserve, deposit-based banking system, which was then central to the flow of funds in the country—no pension funds, no mutual funds, no private equity. Then, during the Civil War, Lincoln's government created national banks, which were "national" only in name. They were local in operation, barred from operating beyond a single location. The consequence: As American industry went national at the end of the nineteenth century, the core financial channel stayed local. No other major nation had as rudimentary a banking system as the United States.

Twentieth century American developments stuck to this path: insurance companies saw and began exploiting national opportunities that the banks couldn't. A scandal, an investigation, and strong public attention (the chief investigator, a New York lawyer, anticipated it would be the "most tremendous job in the United States") led to laws barring the biggest insurers from owning stock. The investigation propelled New York lawyer—Charles Evans Hughes—nearly to the presidency. In the New Deal, finance was again rechanneled but not through nation-spanning banks. Local operation was reaffirmed.

I analyzed these historical phenomena in *Strong Managers, Weak Owners* as not just discrete one-after-another anti-finance actions, but as foundational to the structure of the large, continent-spanning American public corporation. Financial institutions couldn't play a major role in large firms, so we needed better stock markets and better bond markets to finance American growth.

And for the most part, we got them. As a consequence, the ownership of the large American firm was diffuse—we had no powerful banks or insurers, as was common elsewhere in the world. Boards, not financiers, became central to running the firm, more so than they would have been if American finance could have played a bigger role. Some modern corporate techniques, such as the 1980s hostile takeover (by which outsiders offered to buy up a public company's stock with the aim of running the company better) were corporate transactional reactions to the largely unchecked decisional power of the American CEO and the American board. Their power was unchecked in part because financial owners played less of a role than they would otherwise have played, due to American populism.

Looking abroad, we saw something else: financial systems and corporate networks with more regulation and more banker voice and ownership in large firms. The powerful German banks and the Japanese main banking system were illustrative. Some of these results abroad came, I posited in *Political Determinants of Corporate Finance*, from a regulatory and popular setup that differed from that in the United States. More people abroad were less concerned with bank, industrial, and financial power, as long as it was regulated and well-controlled by the central government. And the tools that pulled the diffusely-owned American firm back from drifting away from disciplined action—the hostile takeover and high, stock-based compensation, for example—were scorned abroad. That inhibited foreign firms from distributing their ownership diffusely.

And today?

Today, new players have emerged. They are the billionaire owner-founders of the most successful twenty-first century tech corporations. These billionaire owners are strong inside the American corporation, and they have not induced the same popular blowback that earlier hit financial moguls and financial institutions. This absence of blowback is a significant change, affecting corporate governance, economic power, and law.

The financial firms still can be targets of popular distrust, as John Coates shows in *The Problem of Twelve*. But the modern distrust differs from the old populism. In the past decade, several of the largest financial firms—BlackRock, Vanguard, and State Street—pursued a corporate social responsibility (CSR) agenda that doesn't map onto an American consensus. They found themselves attacked in American politics. In anti-CSR and states unenthusiastic about DEI diversity policies, these new large financial institutions were criticized and sued for advancing what political opponents said was a political agenda that was not attuned to getting the best investments returns for pensioners. This is a different kind of anti-finance populism than that which dominated for much of America's past.

And something else is going on today. The newly powerful corporate players are not banks (at all) or even assets managers (like BlackRock). They're owners and founders of the large twenty-first century corporation. Think: Elon Musk (of course), Jeff Bezos, Jensen Huang, Mark Zuckerberg, and other founder-leaders, often in tech. They get major media attention. While admiration is not the universal tone for that attention, there's no sustained popular or political move to bring them to heel and reduce their power and status. In fact, it's the opposite. States hunger to have these players present, and the tech players can and do influence lawmakers to produce the business laws that they want. There's no sustained opposition. Think: Occupy Wall Street was peripheral even at its strongest moments. And then it faded.

Why haven't these new corporate titans encountered populist opposition as strong as that which Wall Street and the banks faced historically? Perhaps it's because, whatever they do that's objectionable to popular opinion, they get a benefit of the doubt because they're creating new features for American lives that people appreciate. After all, where would we be without Google searches today? And it's free. Or, how about Amazon? They might extract value from small business and employees, but for consumers the merchandise arrives on one's doorstop tomorrow. Perhaps that's the reason—consumer friendliness.

But that hasn't always been the case. John D. Rockefeller didn't get that political free pass when he built and dominated American oil at the end of the nineteenth century. He was not treated positively in the media and the polity despite the fact that he made refined oil accessible to more Americans. Instead, he got negative media attention and a Supreme-Court-ordered dissolution of his powerful oil monopoly in the Standard Oil Company of New Jersey.

Other possibilities could be in play. One, today's new business titans are still young and active; not an older retired generation living off wealth produced long ago. The new media shows their smiles and their activity; twenty-first century media—the internet, et cetera—make them seem more like real people than the Robber Barons probably seemed to ordinary Americans.

Two, they're rich and they're sought after for political support. The new technologies of the twenty-first century allow more tech start-ups to grow rapidly, so that the firm reaches scale and major political influence even before the founder passes the business to a new generation or to professional managers. The fact that there are more such dominant entrepreneurs today (often in tech) means they're harder for politicians to challenge. They have not been targeted as relentlessly as finance once was in America.

Three, American populism has other targets today. Much of the population dislikes elites (in finance, still, but also in the national media, and in universities). And many react negatively to DEI and CSR. If their populist vigor aims at universities today more than before, then maybe today's populist players lack the bandwidth to go after the otherwise quite visible, quite powerful, new entrepreneurial class. A good many Americans may well think that the elite universities—and their kids' lack of access to them—block their children's progress more visibly than the new elites.

All told, there's something for corporate analysts and observers, as well as policymakers, scholars, and journalists, to ponder. What the large corporation looks like, and which ownership structures survive or suffer a demise, can be, and has been, largely determined by political currents and preferences. Today's populist ethos vis-à-vis the large corporation and finance differs greatly from the populist ethos that long dominated in America. In figuring out why the large corporation looks the way it does, economics counts. But sometimes it counts only if it fits the political ethos of the time.

33

SOCIAL DEMOCRACY AGAINST LIBERAL OLIGARCHY

YOCHAI BENKLER

The liberal oligarchic republic is the form of government that pulls all capitalist societies into its gravitational well. Governments that fiscally depend on selling debt into financial markets and taxing market transactions are impelled to place the defense of wealth (oligarchy) as a central pillar of their governing program. How much this imperative defines the entire system of government, fully submitting to the oligarchic pull, and how much counterforces drive toward democracy—governance *for* the majority of a nation's people—has been a terrain of struggle in all capitalist societies. It has shaped the entire trajectory of American history.

From birth, the United States was a liberal oligarchic republic like the Dutch Republic before it, more liberal (legitimated in terms of individual freedom structured as rights) than Venice or Genoa, and more republican (legitimated in terms of representativeness) than Britain. From birth, its governance structure reflected an unholy alliance between Southern planters whose wealth depended on property in enslaved workers of African descent and Northern merchants, investors, and professionals, against the democratic pull of white smallholders and a handful of abolitionists. Alongside persistent denial of full juridical personhood to women and Americans of African descent, property and taxpaying qualifications were a site of struggle for the franchise throughout the antebellum period even among those "all men" recognized as equal bearers of "certain unalienable Rights."

Nineteenth century radical reformers knew that formal equality of liberal rights or the franchise was not the most foundational requirement for democracy. "Talk not of free agency to him whose only freedom is to choose his own method to die," said Galusha Grow, later the first

Republican Speaker of the House, in 1852. "Let the public domain," he argued in support of free land grants, "be set apart as the patrimony of labor, by preventing its being absorbed by capital." "The struggle between labor and capital is unequal at best. . . . And in that struggle, is it for this Government to stretch forth its arm to aid the strong against the weak? Shall it continue, by its legislation, to elevate and enrich idleness on the wail and the woe of industry?"

Grow and the National Reformers, who passed the Homestead Act of 1862, were the most successful among the radical reformers who sought transformation of the material conditions of life and production as a precondition to, and sole guarantor of, democracy in America. Thaddeus Stevens's model of land reform during Reconstruction sought, and failed, to ground emancipation in real material independence for the formerly enslaved families, because he understood that formal liberal equality, including in the vote, was no guarantee of real freedom. A generation later, the People's Party's Ocala Program demanded public banks and granaries to socialize working credit for farmers, as a bulwark against the power of bankers; regulation or nationalization of railroads to liberate them from the power of carriers; and a monetary policy that served the people's interests, rather than those of the financial rentiers.

Oligarchy was victorious in the Gilded Age. Its power reached its first peak. The People's Party and workers' mobilization were defeated by the combination of an unrepresentative electoral system, often corrupt, and a judiciary single-mindedly dedicated to the defense of property and wealth. For over a generation, the federal judiciary leveraged the constitution to defeat democratic reform in the states, while using the labor injunction to deploy coercive violence to suppress worker mobilization.

The collapse of laissez faire liberalism birthed the New Deal, and Roosevelt's declaration of Freedom From Want as one of the four freedoms provided a temporary victory. It won a pared-back version of more ambitious programs for transforming production in the name of real freedom. For a generation it offered white working men and their families a degree of security. In the 1960s, the Great Society promised to expand that freedom to Black Americans and women.

The March for Jobs and Freedom and *A Freedom Budget for All Americans* combined racial justice with labor advocacy and calls for broad class coalitions, led by A. Philip Randolph and Bayard Rustin alongside Martin Luther King. In the 1970s, Coretta Scott King's leadership in support of the Humphrey-Hawkins Full Employment Act tried to do the same, even as labor was weakening. But Jesse Jackson's Rainbow Coalition was the last time that racial justice politics on the left emphasized economic improvement and class coalition politics on par with identity-based anti-domination. Since the 1990s, the Democratic Party and vaguely "left" politics increasingly focused on the politics of anti-domination unmoored from economic power and class. That change was both a tactical retreat in the face of capital's victories in the 1980s, and a consequence of the transformation of the Democratic coalition in relation to labor.

After 1970, capital rebelled. By the 1980s, oligarchy was victorious. Privatization, deregulation, globalization, and financialization provided capital with escape routes from the New Deal settlement, enabling the escape of the 1 percent and imposing stagnation and declining life prospects on the bottom 80 percent. The GOP became a coalition of capitalists and financial rentiers allied with the alienated white working classes, both skilled and unskilled. Right-spin identity politics focused on religion, white identity, and traditional male dominance held that coalition together, harnessing backlash against the civil rights revolution, the women's movement, and secularization of the public sphere. For forty years capitalists and rentiers told their working-class allies that they could make it in a free market if only they worked hard enough—an outright lie—but what really mattered was that their identity was to be valued—a misdirection.

The Democratic Party, in turn, became the coalition of the professional and managerial class (PMC), embracing their own variant of neoliberalism, expressed as meritocracy that rewards the hard working, talented, and well-educated with well-earned superstar salaries—also a lie—and using a left-spin identity politics to harness working class women and the racialized working class and underclass to the party of the PMC, but doing nothing to alleviate their economic immiseration. Certainly, anti-domination victories improved the condition of PMC Black Americans and women fundamentally. But the condition of the urban racialized underclass, subject to intensified state violence and repressive welfare administration, or of the working classes, however racialized or gendered, is no better and, for many, worse.

Since the 1990s the two parties became the Tweedledum and Tweedledee of neoliberalism.

Trump's victories, the destroyed trust in elite institutions, and the anomie that has gripped America as it approached its 250th anniversary have been the misdirected rebellion of the working classes against the destruction of their life prospects in the service of oligarchy. As Walter Benjamin wrote in 1936, "Fascism attempts to organize the newly created proletarian masses without affecting the property structure which the masses strive to eliminate. . . . The masses have a right to change property relations; Fascism seeks to give them an expression while preserving property. The logical result of Fascism is the introduction of aesthetics into political life."

Only a politics directly focused on taming the oligarchic impulse of American polity can begin to redirect us away from the aesthetic and alienated toward a democratic pathway. Such a politics must harness the power of the state as a counterpower to capital, and direct its institutional program toward dampening the market imperatives that undermine most Americans' ability to live self-directed, dignified lives. It requires a real Freedom From Want agenda, one that seeks to partially decommodify access to basic needs, broadly defined. It requires meaningful socialization of labor, knowledge, infrastructure, and credit markets, to liberate the many from the socially destructive effects of a system built on the liberal myth of free contracting under formal equality, but functioning in practice as a system of intensified exploitation veiled behind that myth.

The United States arrives at its 250th anniversary as the most unequal among the world's wealthy societies. It ranks well below most wealthy countries, and all Nordic social democracies, on global indexes of democracy, health, and education, as well as those measuring its alleged greatest strengths: intergenerational mobility and economic freedom. This sorry state is a direct result of the nearly absolute victory of oligarchy over democracy in the past half century. Only a politics and program of social democratic transformation can wrest real freedom from the jaws of capital in America.

34

Law for Organizing: Combating the Crisis of Inequality

Benjamin Sachs

In the years preceding the second Trump Administration, and as we approached the 250th anniversary of the Declaration of Independence, it had become clear that the United States was facing dual crises of inequality. One was a crisis of economic inequality. The other a crisis of political inequality. And these crises reinforced one another: As wealth became more concentrated in fewer and fewer hands, the now *ultra*-wealthy became more able to translate their economic power into political influence, which then could be used to push for policies that enabled greater wealth accumulation, and on and on. Political science captured this dynamic in various ways. In 2011, Jeffrey Winters wrote an influential book about oligarchies in which he established that the United States was functioning as one. As he put it: "Regardless of the other ways in which political power might be equal—such as one-person-one-vote or an equal right to speak or participate—yawning differences in material power create enormous inequalities in political influence and account for key political outcomes won by oligarchs."

As stark as the political science findings of the last decade were, they are not stark enough to capture the reality of the second Trump Administration. Wealth concentration is accelerating at a dizzying pace. Today, the five wealthiest people in the United States have a combined net worth of 1.8 trillion dollars, which amounts to about 1 percent of the total net worth of all U.S. households. At the beginning of 2026, Jeff Bezos, who owns Amazon, was worth more than $250 billion. It would take an Amazon warehouse worker five million years of full-time work to earn that much money. The situation is equally dire in the political realm. The *New York Times* recently reported that, in 2024, 300 billionaires and their families accounted for nearly 20 percent of all the contributions in federal elections. Indeed, it now seems that the ultra-wealthy—individuals and corporations—are able to simply buy government policy. For example, when he took office for the second time President Trump pledged to fight tech monopolies and decried crypto currency as a scam, but following millions of dollars in contributions from Meta, Nvidia, OpenAI, and the crypto industry, the administration has taken decidedly different policy tacks. Thus, the President has issued an executive order to block state regulation of AI, approved the sale of Nvidia's AI chips to China, signed other executive orders loosening oversight of cryptocurrency, and disbanded a DOJ cryptocurrency enforcement team. Individual billionaires have also acquired unrivaled policy influence. To take one example, Marc Rowan, who is the chief executive of a private equity firm, played a major role in designing the administration's assault on higher education. Winters was right—America looks more and more like an oligarchy.

Addressing the economic and political inequality behind this slide into oligarchy must be a central project of our law as we start the next 250 years of American government. The project will require a comprehensive slate of interventions, but key among them must be legal reforms designed to facilitate organizing by the poor and working class. As Kate Andrias and I have argued, laws that facilitate the building of membership organizations, like labor unions, can enable poor and working class people to build the economic and political power necessary to combat inequality and resist oligarchy.

In fact, much of the increase in economic and political inequality that has plagued the United States over the last decades is attributable to the decline in the presence and power of such organizations. When they were active and strong, labor unions in the U.S. were able to force a redistribution of wealth from capital to labor and ensure that labor received an increasing share of the proceeds of economic output. With union density plummeting from a high of 35 percent to a paltry 6 percent today, more and more of the rewards of economic activity are going to capital, with a predictable and profound impact on economic inequality. The same is true for politics. Unions offered, for a time, a strong collective political voice for workers, enabling them to successfully push for redistributive economic policies. Without unions, the poor and working class have lost much of their voice in politics.

Law is a central part of this story. When Congress enacted the Wagner Act in 1935, it helped generate a massive increase in union organizing: In the six years that followed the Act's passage, more than six million workers joined unions. Of course, law is also central to the story of union decline: Since 1935, courts (and Congress with the Taft-Hartley Act) substantially weakened American labor law and thereby empowered employers to fight unions, which they have done with great success. But both of these dynamics point to the same conclusion: When it comes to the feasibility of poor and working class organizing, law matters.

Labor unions, it is important to stress, are but one example of the type of organization that could contribute to solving the crises of inequality. Membership organizations of multiple types could play such a role. Thus, for example, tenants' unions have voiced collective demands to landlords, and to city and state governments, at various times and places in U.S. history and, if they were able to grow, could take on this role at a much greater scale. There have also been important organizing efforts among debtors and students that could presage a way to provide collective voice and power in these sectors.

Based on the successes and failures of the Wagner Act, and drawing on a wide literature on social movements, Professor Andrias and I suggested the elements that a law consciously designed to enable such organizing should have. We concluded that such a law should grant organizing rights explicitly so that it can serve as a "frame" for organizing—akin to the role labor law played when organizers told their coworkers in the 1930s that "the President wants you to join a union." The law should also offer a simple and easily accessible mechanism for financing organizations, like the system that allows workers to have union dues deducted from their paychecks and sent directly to their union. Such a law should provide space for organizing, whether physical or digital, and ensure that those spaces are free from surveillance. The law, critically, must protect participants from retaliation. It must facilitate ways for organizations, especially nascent ones, to make real, practical change in participants' lives, most commonly by mandating bargaining between the organization and the relevant set of counter parties. And, finally, such a law should protect peaceful forms of protest and disruption, including the right to strike.

By adopting organizing-enabling laws for these multiple contexts—labor, housing, education, debt, and others—the law could spur organizing among workers, tenants, students, and borrowers and thus facilitate the construction of powerful membership organizations. These organizations would be positioned to make both economic and political demands. Workers can demand higher wages from their employers and higher minimum wage legislation from federal and state government; tenants can push for lower rents and better rent control laws; students can insist that universities and state governments slow the growth of tuition costs; borrowers can bargain for lower interest rates and for legislation requiring debt forgiveness. In all cases, the organizations would give their poor and working-class members the ability to countervail the power of wealth and oligarchy.

Critical questions remain. One is the obvious practical question of political prospects, and, indeed, organizing laws stand little chance of enactment by Congress in the foreseeable future. But the prospects for enacting such legislation may well be better in certain states and cities where the effects could be just as powerful as federal legislation, even if more geographically circumscribed.

Another question is how to ensure that the membership organizations the law facilitates are in fact committed to redistribution of wealth and political power. To some extent, the answer is straightforward: If the organizations are governed democratically, then they will reflect the interests of their members, which means that a tenants' union, or a labor union, or a debtors' union will advance positions that drive in the direction of economic equality. But this also means that it is critical for a law of organizing to require that the organizations it facilitates are governed internally by democratic procedures.

In sum, membership organizations of poor and working-class Americans can be a central part of the effort to combat inequality. By developing countervailing power, such organizations can demand a more equitable distribution of wealth and a more equal distribution of political voice. If we want to build that kind of country, enabling the growth of such organizations must be a central project of our law.

35

THE REVOLUTIONARY CHALLENGE OF EQUALITY: TOWARD A REDESIGN OF AMERICAN MONEY

CHRISTINE DESAN

Two hundred and fifty years ago, Americans identified equality as a foundational goal. In the decades that followed, they (we) engineered money according to a design that undermined that end. The system today creates and delivers dollars that draw on public commitment to hold value but prioritize private profit as they issue. The system is both productive and discriminatory. It fuels a powerful market and shapes that market disproportionately to aid the advantaged. It has coalesced incrementally, improvisationally, and at times accidentally, but has huge cumulative impact. We will reach our revolutionary end only when we remake our money.

According to James Madison, "establishing political equality among all" would further "the great object" of smoothing factional strife. While their differences relentlessly drove people apart, wise practice could bring people together. The trick was to avoid increasing unmerited accumulation of riches and "by the silent operation of laws . . . reduce extreme wealth towards a state of mediocrity, and raise extreme indigence towards a state of comfort (Madison, *On Parties*, 1792)."

At the time of this writing, Elon Musk had a net wealth of $809,000,000,000. By contrast according to Forbes Advisor, 25 percent of all Americans have less than $1,000 in savings. Fifty percent of them, in each generation except the boomers, have less than $5,000 in savings. Musk can give millions to a political campaign without feeling the impact; most Americans would sacrifice essential funds to give $100. Political equality is an empty promise in the face of that difference.

If we want to understand how money ends up, we need to look at how it starts. Inequality in our society has many drivers—but one of them is the way we make the money that captures value and carries it between us every day. The American dollar rests on government engineering and collective support. That public sourcing is constantly operating—but it is just as pervasively denied. The hijack has turned money inside out, sanctifying its private allotment rather than its common creation.

The story begins with a mystery. Money is meant to capture value, but value is a concept that no economist has ever managed to define. We can agree about measuring distance or weight, but comparing the worth of an apple, an education, a piece of land, or our health? How do you create a unit that identifies and entails value?

Again and again, moneys arise out of ingredients basic to communities: They sustain themselves on periodic contributions from their members and learn to organize those resources. The magic occurs when a community receives a contribution in advance and gives its member a token in return, creating a credit that can be used later when the contribution would have been due. The unit holds material value that everyone recognizes because others also owe the community. If the community agrees to honor the token as a credit taken from anyone's hand, the token can travel. Presto—we have created a money that circulates and holds a value everyone recognizes, all in the form of a credit issued by the community. It is a public creation, collectively sourced.

The strategy is empowering. Now a polity can create tokens to spend, mobilizing just the resources it needs while collecting contributions later in a neatly packaged form. At the same time, individuals can use the new medium to compare, store, and transfer value. Exchange expands, curated and enforced by the very community that makes the medium. As private demand for money joins public demand, communities experiment with ways of expanding the liquid value.

Each design choice matters. Consider different ways of delivering money into circulation. For centuries, European monarchs demanded taxes in metal coin, monopolizing the mints that made it. Coin carried its own collateral—the silver or gold that made it up—and mints could sell people bringing in bullion more coin for private use. The medium supported royal authority but drove medieval privation and prompted voyages of extractive exploration. Compare money made during the Civil War by the Union government. It paid its soldiers and suppliers in promises printed in green ink on paper. "Greenbacks" circulated into the civilian population until taken back in taxes, a medium transparently dependent on the fiscal authority of Congress. As the Supreme Court held, that body had abundant authority to tie "the poor man's cattle, and horses, and corn" to the "rich man's bonds and notes." Each relied on "the national credit" and bore its ebbs and flows in value. *Knox v. Lee*, 75 U.S. 533, 561 (1870).

Now the plot twist. A design variation went viral in the early modern world. All the moneys sampled above issued directly from and brought power to public authorities, be it a British king or the U.S. Congress. But money's creation and diffusion could be privatized. Governments could partner with investors to issue money for profit.

The innovation of privatized money drew on powerful ideological currents. Fighting against oppressive royal control, English liberals identified individual interests as the productive heart of human agency. "Can any man tell better than yourselves, where your shoe pincheth you, and what is most expedient for you to do?" asked the author of *Vox Plebis, or The People's Outcry Against Oppression* (1646). Claims for political equality of individuals, their rights to private property and contract followed. The discourse was emancipatory when aimed against the abuses of the Crown and toward the cause of representative government. It also carried the capacity, unbound by exhilarated proponents, to obscure the community that anchored those individuals.

The trend toward privatized money-making by banks followed. Improvised first by the British and adopted early by the Americans, the logic endorsed individual agency as interest-driven. Here is how it works. A government borrows from a group of investors in their promises-to-pay, call them "bank notes." The government then treats those promises, those bank notes, as money. Spent and taxed in by the national authority, bank notes then function effectively as the sovereign medium. See 12 U.S.C. §411; 31 USC § 5103.

The innovation had enormous political and distributive consequences. Even as the government enabled the medium with public support, it now paid creditors to make the monetary base, giving them tremendous power. The arrangement advertised private expertise in matters monetary and endorsed individual agency as rational and efficient, thus an appropriate repository of that power. Further, it institutionalized an orientation toward profit as the compass that sent a public medium into circulation.

A similar strategy created and multiplied money for individual borrowers. American states, left by the Constitution without authority to make the federal dollar, chartered banks to multiply it in private credit instead. The strategy remade corporations, once considered public in purpose, into distinctly commercial vehicles and those commercial vehicles into institutions essential for irrigating exchange. They spread currency across countrysides far from political centers, making markets along the lines that bankers drew. The practice invited economists to strip the economy of its collective matrix and medium; it appeared to be driven by individuated determinations. "Speculation by competent men," gushed Justice Holmes about trade in commodities futures, "is the self-adjustment of society to the probable." *Board of Trade v. Christie Grain & Stock Co.*, 198 U.S. 236, 247 (1905).

When Congress established the Federal Reserve in 1913, it institutionalized a government agency out of network of commercial banks at the heart of the U.S. economy. Today those banks make the vast majority of the money supply. The Federal Reserve wields a trillion-dollar budget to support them, elaborating the financial infrastructure that embraces shadow banking and its analogues. Practice itself appears to confirm that interest-driven action comprises the market because we have engineered it to that mold. A public medium starts its distributive journey exactly as those institutions lend.

The privatized practice of money creation has swallowed the public sourcing of value. As that foundation disappears from view, it takes with it the possibilities that would flow from understanding money as a concerted initiative to create value collectively recognized. We are left with a system that erects a market for profit on the underlying contributions of a community while depleting it. This is the infrastructure that has generated the chasm between American billionaires and the ordinary American family with less than $1,000 in the bank. If we want to close that gap, we need to reimagine how we can design our money to reward the public participation in its creation.

36

AMERICA'S COURTS OF LAST RESORT: THE BANKRUPTCY SYSTEM

JARED ELLIAS

The U.S. Constitution, ratified in 1788, always contemplated a federal bankruptcy system. It would take Congress more than one hundred years to implement the first permanent bankruptcy law (in 1898) and nearly two hundred years to implement the first bankruptcy law that corporations found highly useful (in 1978). Since then, the U.S. bankruptcy system has become a key part of the infrastructure of the global economy, with American bankruptcy judges overseeing the restructuring of giant American and non-U.S. firms alike.

But there is another highly influential, and often controversial aspect of the famous U.S. bankruptcy system: the way in which it increasingly functions as a court of last resort, a forum where social problems land when elected officials cannot, or will not, provide a comprehensive response. Over the past decades, Chapter 11 has absorbed crises as varied as mass pollution, destructive wildfires, and institutional failures that enabled widespread sexual abuse of children. In each instance, the breadth of harm would seem to warrant comprehensive legislative action. Yet too often, the primary governmental response emerges instead through piecemeal Chapter 11 proceedings overseen by individual bankruptcy judges. Bankruptcy law became federal law, in part, because the Framers of the Constitution understood that state legislatures would have incentives to create rules that favored their own borrowers over creditors in other states. As I will explain, bankruptcy is now being asked to solve a different type of political dysfunction for which it was not designed: the unwillingness of politicians to lead on pressing societal issues.

Bankruptcy is ill-suited to be the primary institutional forum for resolving mass harms. Bankruptcy judges have jurisdiction over the debtor and its property and possess deep expertise in bankruptcy law. However, they lack a general mandate to redesign regulatory regimes, conduct public investigations, or marshal public resources when private assets are inadequate. Assigning hard distributive choices to an unelected judge can diffuse responsibility and allow elected officials to evade accountability while turning to more politically tractable priorities. But the federal bankruptcy system is no substitute for Congress or state legislatures. Bankruptcy courts do not possess independent substantive expertise in the deeply technical questions these cases raise, such as how best to prevent youth sexual assault, mitigate wildfire risk in arid regions, or regulate the safe use of prescription opioids.

To develop this claim, I offer three brief recent examples—Boy Scouts of America, Purdue Pharma, and the Pacific Gas & Electric Corporation—in which large-scale social failures were transformed into Chapter 11 cases, with the tools and bargaining environment of Chapter 11 shaping the ultimate solution. As George Triantis and I have argued elsewhere, political branches can capture bankruptcy's coordinating benefits by working alongside the bankruptcy process while deploying their own expertise and fiscal capacity, but this is a clear second-best solution to difficult societal problems compared to comprehensive legislation and regulatory enforcement.

First, beginning in 1890, parents across the country entrusted their children to youth groups organized by, or affiliated with, Boy Scouts of America ("BSA"). Some participants later alleged that they had been sexually abused in connection with BSA programming. A surge of litigation led BSA to file for Chapter 11 protection in 2020. At the time of the filing, BSA leadership estimated that more than 7,800 former leaders had abused over 12,000 children over a seventy-two-year period, yet more than 80,000 individuals ultimately filed sexual abuse claims in the bankruptcy case.

Judge Silverstein had to guide the case toward a resolution that balanced two imperatives: compensating survivors and preserving the viability of a major American institution—which, as of December 2019, served approximately two million American children—through reorganization. Yet she did not possess the tools available to a legislature or executive agency, such as convening public hearings or designing prospective legal reforms to address the systemic failures that tens of thousands of individuals alleged they had endured.

In a second example, the opioid maker Purdue Pharma filed for Chapter 11 in 2019, beset by litigation from survivors of opioid abuse, their families, and governmental entities. Judge Robert Drain presided over a process that was, by many accounts, effective, but that raised important questions of legitimacy and fairness. For example, many questioned whether the process provided survivors with their "day in court" despite significant efforts from Judge Drain and the attorneys involved to provide victims with a voice. Had Congress created a federal process, it could have both marshaled the assets of wrongdoers and considered what was needed to make victims whole, while addressing the safe use of painkillers. Most settlement proceeds were directed not to victims but to state and local governments for addiction treatment and abatement programs. A centralized legislative process might have produced more transparent and politically accountable decisions about those allocations. The bankruptcy court could coordinate claims and approve a comprehensive settlement, but it could not confer democratic legitimacy on those policy choices or access resources beyond the assets of Purdue Pharma's bankruptcy estate.

Finally, Pacific Gas & Electric Company ("PG&E"), Northern California's largest investor-owned public utility, filed for bankruptcy in 2019 after the company's equipment contributed to catastrophic wildfires that caused extensive loss of life and property. A chief culprit was climate change and the resulting unprecedented dry landscape, which increased the risks associated with PG&E's power transmission business. The state legislature subsequently enacted legislation that shaped the Chapter 11 plan, but the outcome, unsatisfactory to many observers, was ultimately governed by bankruptcy law. Judge Montali was constrained to the tools available under the bankruptcy code, and when the company stretched to satisfy wildfire claims, he confirmed a plan that compensated fire survivors through a risky structure that ultimately left them with payments that were not large enough to make them whole. Only years later did PG&E, under new leadership, undertake some of the more the ambitious and costly wildfire-mitigation efforts that many observers regarded as necessary at the time of the restructuring.

While these examples may appear distinct, they share a common structure. Each involved harms that affected tens of thousands of Americans and, through their families, hundreds of thousands more. Each also raised broader policy questions about how American society would continue to deal with serious challenges, such as the ongoing risks created by youth educational programs, power transmission in California as the climate changed, and safe use of painkillers. In every instance, the harm was handled by bankruptcy judges deploying the tools of Chapter 11 rather than elected officials drawing fully on agency expertise and the fiscal capacity to tax or borrow in order to supplement private assets and more fully compensate victims.

It need not be this way. For example, after the September 11 attacks, Congress created a comprehensive, publicly funded compensation program and also implemented reforms in airport security. In the cases described here, by contrast, the judges overseeing the restructurings were largely confined to the assets of a single debtor. Although Chapter 11 can incorporate certain governance reforms into a confirmed plan, it does not empower courts to regulate similarly situated firms outside bankruptcy.

To be sure, the bankruptcy system is an important and competent forum for resolving complex financial distress. But these cases reflect a deeper failure of the American constitutional order and vision. It is doubtful that the Framers of the Constitution contemplated that the bankruptcy system would be used to make up for these types of weaknesses in the political branches.

Systemic societal harms warrant comprehensive and democratically accountable responses, not merely the ad hoc resolution of claims within a single debtor's reorganization. The rule of law would be strengthened if elected officials assumed a more central role in confronting mass failures, supplementing and guiding the bankruptcy process rather than treating it as a substitute for democratic policymaking.

PART X

NEW TECHNOLOGIES AND THE FUTURE OF KNOWLEDGE AND DEMOCRACY

Law and governance are inextricably shaped by the technologies on which we rely to build our lives and communities. When those technologies change, our democracy changes too. Lawrence Lessig argues that the unregulated race for AI development reveals the failure of our entire constitutional framework. Congress is our primary institution for rational national policymaking and it has become dysfunctional. Neither the Supreme Court nor the executive branch have the capacity or incentives to fill the breach and protect us from the threat of an all-powerful AI created and controlled by private interests. Lessig concludes: "Our constitution has failed. It is time we begin the process of crafting its replacement." Jonathan Zittrain takes a step back and describes how numerous new technologies—including the internet and encryption as well as AI—shift the power balance between individuals and government and destabilize longstanding legal protections. Zittrain asserts that we need to collectively rethink the basic contours of government and insist that technology serve our democracy, rather than leaving such profound decisions to private ordering and chance. Ruth Okediji reminds us that the creation and protection of intellectual property is itself an exercise in economic development, nation-building and cultural expression. She identifies the disjuncture between federal IP law on the one hand, and more pluralistic Native American tribal and global intellectual property regimes on the other, and she argues that "the constitutional organization of knowledge itself" depends on appreciating this "layered sovereignty" regime. Glenn Cohen brings all this uncertainty close to home by describing revolutionary reproductive technologies—including aggressive gene editing and the creation of sperm or eggs from skin cells—that are changing the very meaning of who can reproduce, with whom, and how. He worries that the Supreme Court has been entirely silent, offering no guidance on these fundamental questions implicating dignity, access, and equality, and he warns that this "constitutional vacuum is not healthy for a political system."

37

The Failure of Our Constitutional Design and the Threat of AI

Lawrence Lessig

At the core of our Framers' constitutional design was a policymaker named "Congress." Given pride of place in the Constitution, Article I, and dominating debate at the Federal Convention, Congress was meant to be a diverse (in our Framers' limited view of diversity) and representative body of Americans, "dependent," as Madison promised, at least in the House, "on the people alone," whereby "the people," as he explained in *Federalist 57*, he meant "not the rich more than the poor."

The core truth about now is that Congress is a failed institution. The causes are many. Early in our history, partisan politics transformed the body from a deliberative one into a competitive one. That competition was debilitating at certain periods—see, for example, the Civil War. But there have been important periods when parties have not been debilitating. After World War II, for example, when one party nominally dominated Congress, partisan politics were robust but not debilitating. Because there were effectively four parties in Congress (conservative Republicans, conservative Democrats, liberal Republicans, liberal Democrats), and none claimed a majority, a norm of compromise and collaboration developed as the only method by which legislation could be passed. But when Barry Goldwater signaled the transformation that Ronald Reagan would effect, a transformation from non-ideological parties to ideological ones, that began the slow slide in Congress from a functioning body to a body that can no longer function.

This transformation has only been exacerbated by a media ecosystem that rewards extremism and clownishness over compromise and competence. The business model of parties in Congress today is not to work with the other to accomplish something. The business model is to build a big enough majority to annihilate the other. And what fuels the expansion of a majority is the hatred among its supporters that might be driven toward the other.

Even more debilitating is the corrupting dependence that Congress has developed upon private money to fund public campaigns. Members of Congress and candidates for Congress spend anywhere between 30 percent and 70 percent of their time raising money. That money they raise comes not from the average American, but from a tiny fraction of the 1 percent. This dynamic has only been exacerbated by the rise of super PACs. In the 2024 election, 75 percent of the $5 billion in super PAC money spent to affect congressional races was spent in just twenty-four districts. We do not have what Madison promised; we have its opposite precisely. Not a Congress "dependent on the people alone," whereby the people is meant "not the rich more than the poor"; instead, we have a Congress dependent first upon the rich. This translates into the rich's perpetual ability to veto the capacity of Congress to address the problems that are most pressing for most Americans, not to mention the poor.

This general failure of Congress has, over the last eighty years, inspired other institutions to step into the breach. For much of that period, it was the Supreme Court that determined to correct the democratic failings of Congress. The first example was apportionment. That intervention then led the Court to consider a range of democracy-enhancing measures. Yet the current Court has reversed this trend, intervening not in ways that enhance democratic equality but that exacerbate democratic inequality. The Court has refused, for example, to block partisan gerrymandering and, most prominently, has effectively barred legislatures and the people from addressing the corrupting influence of money.

More recently, we've seen the federal executive step into the breach. In a trend that began with Clinton and that has now culminated in the extraordinary claims to power by Donald Trump, presidents have felt entitled by the necessity of the moment to grab more and more policy-making authority under Article II, given the perpetual systemic failure of Article I. Authoritarianism regularly follows from populist disgust with the institutions of representative democracy. In this way (as well as others), America is not exceptional.

This institutional failure would be bad enough in any context. In ordinary times, no nation can long live without the capacity for rational policy makers to respond to changed circumstances and arising threats in a sensible way. But given the threats that are now emerging with the rise of artificial intelligence, America desperately needs a capacity to govern sensibly. Though AI promises enormous benefits to society—indeed, utopian benefits to society—no invisible hand will guide the technology companies in the direction of a general benefit to humanity, rather than a partial benefit to technology owners. And even more concerning is the anxiety articulated by those closest to the technology that the technology is too powerful for humans to control.

Yet the race among AI companies to develop god-like AI continues nonetheless. In the interindustry competition among major AI laboratories, each is running as fast as it can to achieve artificial general intelligence (AGI). And when anyone raises the suggestion that perhaps that race should be paused until safety measures are at least understood, and the possibility of annihilating humanity removed, that suggestion is ridiculed by pointing to the international competition between the United States and China. If we don't get there first, we will be devastated by the other, or so the argument goes. And so, a general race toward humanity's cliff continues, with everyone recognizing that no one has built the brakes necessary to stop us before we go over, but with everyone hoping someone will before we do in fact go over.

It is easy enough to identify the enormous policy challenges that we as a nation face: climate change, economic inequality, access to health care, economic security, a safe and clean environment, and, maybe most pressingly, avoiding the catastrophic threats that AI technology presents. But unless we can shift our attention from the particular threats to the source of our inability to address those threats sensibly—namely, the failed institution that is Congress—we will never succeed in addressing any of those challenges. We need to acknowledge that the machine our Framers built to address our common threats has failed: The political theory that premised the design has long been proven false; the evolving norms of partisan polarization, tied to an evolving practice of a corrupt system for funding elections, has taken a badly designed system and rendered it fundamentally dysfunctional.

Thus, at this 250th anniversary of a Declaration of certain "truths" held to be "self-evident," we need the courage to "hold" one more truth as self-evident: Our constitution has failed. It is time we begin the process of crafting its replacement.

38

GAINING POWER, LOSING CONTROL: RETHINKING THE CONSTITUTION'S VALUES AMIDST NEW TECHNOLOGIES

JONATHAN ZITTRAIN

When I was around ten, I had a discussion with my mother, a lawyer, that must have had something to do with rights. She theatrically invoked an aphorism that seemed profound to me at the time: "Your right to swing your fist ends where my nose begins." It captures the notion that most of the individual liberties enshrined in the Constitution and its Bill of Rights are realized only through reconciling our freedoms with those of others, or with the legitimate and compelling interests of the state.

But the world can change, sometimes prompting a re-evaluation of how such lines have been drawn. The tech and internet boom that began in the late 1990s and is in full flower today requires us to re-evaluate how we have been striking these balances. From copyright to encryption, panoptic surveillance to AI, technology is redistributing power and knowledge in fundamental ways.

The key issue is that technology is moving more and more from the realm of chance to the realm of the knowable and doable. Sometimes it means individuals can elude governmental power where that power had not been previously contested or resented. Other times it means governments are emboldened in deeply troubling ways that cannot be trusted to be reined in through the traditional recognition and exercise of legal rights.

Copyright, for example, has long been in tension with First Amendment rights. Copyright's substantial restrictions on our behavior—which could entail monetary damages for, say, making a friend an old-fashioned mix tape or publicly belting out a song without permission—have been held immune from First Amendment scrutiny only because the copyright statute offers some countervailing release valves, such as the ability of mix tape makers or karaoke singers to cite fair use as a defense. Technological change, however, disrupts the balance between free expression and property rights. In the late 1990s, digital rights management, "DRM," promised a world where our own DVD players or e-book readers could enforce novel limits on how we use their contents without any need for legal protection—simply preventing us from making those mix tapes through software and hardware restrictions.

Fair use doesn't help there, since it's merely a legal defense to an infringement claim, not an affirmative guarantee that we can engage in the legally protected activities. It thus offers no help if the tech can be contrived by content owners and device manufacturers to provide a barrier.

The use of private tech to change balances of affordances previously struck by public authorities cut the other way, too, undermining property rights. DRM notwithstanding, publishers pointed out that networking everyone to everyone else was giving rise to peer-to-peer file sharing, producing a world where copyright's legitimate restrictions could be flouted at a scale far larger than clumsily made mix tapes. Thus, both sides of the copyright wars feared tech disturbing their long-settled habits and entitlements.

While copyright holders had some luck getting Congress to tighten up copyright law, it wasn't a decisive victory. There was no going back to the way things had been before the internet came along.

The copyright wars instead ended with a new status quo. A smaller music industry offering music as a convenient, above-board, temporary subscription rather than a forever purchase. Shared playlists took the place of mix tapes, with implications not only for copyright but for privacy. The consumption of content is now exquisitely monitored and tracked in ways that librarians lending out books and records would never contemplate doing for (or to) their patrons.

Another example is the new tension between encryption and lawful surveillance. The availability of cheap, effective encryption raised the prospect that the public at large could store their notes and documents in their smartphones, and if they weren't around to share their passwords, law enforcement officers couldn't access them, even if they'd gotten a warrant. This was called the "going dark" problem, and a number of prosecutors and investigators lamented the way in which the Fourth

Amendment's warrant requirement could be mooted. They called for new governmental mandates to prevent smartphone makers from allowing their customers to put such documents beyond the reach of lawful process.

As with copyright, the prior balance credibly seesawed the other way, too. Many people share keys to their files with smartphone makers so that they can recover their data if they forget their own passwords, and they place their documents in cloud storage that isn't typically protected the way smartphones can be. People associated with a targeted device can be lawfully compelled to cough up their passwords or fingerprints.

Moreover, smartphones are now only a tiny slice of our digital footprints. At the time the Court originally took up questions of government electronic eavesdropping in the 1960s, eavesdropping required people to be troubling themselves to use old school telephones, or for police to be physically proximate to their suspects, continuously listening. Today, there's a kaleidoscopic panoply of ways in which we already record ourselves, whether or not communicating with others, all subject to eavesdropping at a distance: smart TVs, health monitors, digital assistants, online vehicles. Going incandescent is thus as much a worry as going dark, as the sheer volume and depth of what a warrant might yield about someone is unrecognizable compared to the prior century.

Indeed, storage of everyone's information within a handful of private Fort Knoxes—Gmail accounts, cloud storage lockers, a handful of mobile network providers, and the like—has given rise to general searches like "Tell me everyone who was within 100 feet of this location last Saturday morning," or "Here's a file that's contraband. Which of your customers' accounts have it?" We have yet to work out the significance of this development for our privacy. Maybe a shallow search of everyone's data, with any hits serving as the basis for a more intrusive search, is a more privacy-respecting way to solve a crime than jumping straight to intrusive searches of suspects initially identified through less accurate means. But there's been no sustained reflection by Congress or the judiciary to answer that question to account for a drastically changed world.

Today we're in the grip of AI's revolution, and the First, Fourth, and Fifth Amendments are about to become subject to larger private gambles over previously publicly-struck balances.

Many people already run their life's puzzles large and small through chatbot advisors. These advisors are configured to be kind, patient, encouraging, and increasingly accurate on factual matters both simple and byzantine. As these bots make the small hop from text on our devices to voices in our ears, and take into account our prior questions and conversations with them, they eliminate the logistical and financial frictions of consulting lawyers, doctors, therapists, or other human specialists who have historically assisted with weighty decisions. But while those human advisors owe us duties of loyalty and confidentiality, recognized and enforced through law and guild, there's no such special protection for chatbot consultations. What might previously have been largely protected by law from later public surveillance (including spousal privilege), or unreachable as a practical matter because human-to-human conversations are more evanescent, is now accessible and searchable with the lightest of process.

Yet this imbalance, too, could cut the other way with significant consequences for the professions and public safety. Nipping at the heels of the corporate server-based AI chat models—only one subpoena away from the government—are open-weight models that can run locally on a laptop or smartphone. In an echo of that early twenty-first century free-for-all of peer-to-peer music sharing, a few technically-adept engineers could remove any safety tuning a model maker had deigned to add to a publicly-released model, share the new model with anyone who cares to take it, and people can get bomb recipes or have their AI companions patiently and kindly encourage and abet their fevered follies. The loyalty and confidentiality that learned professionals owe their clients, patients, and penitents are by law and custom tempered by instances in which those professionals must report harmful activity, such as the prospect that someone has engaged in child abuse or is carrying a dangerous and communicable disease.

All of these dramatic changes have profound implications for our collective governance decisions. 1776's Revolution was informed by the trauma of public power: a prior government not responsive to or fully respectful of individual rights. The new American Republic was to be empowered and capable in ways that let it get to the work of governing, while limited by the Constitution and the soon-following Bill of Rights.

But the power of that government, as well as of the individuals it governed was, by today's standards, astonishingly limited. The world two centuries ago was marked by the limits of the natural world, full of chance and caprice. Today's technology converts chance into near certainty for those who control it, with extraordinary accompanying power that defies regulation by traditional means. Power and knowledge that enormous should not be left to private ordering, or meta-chance. An impotent government in the face of wildly augmented individuals is a recipe for anarchy. Individuals tracked and herded by all-seeing authorities is a recipe for tyranny. Old ways of thinking will not be enough to stave off these threats.

The shape of this new governance physics is uncertain and dynamic. The way forward is not simply to refactor piecemeal the scope of individual constitutional rights established 250 years ago, though that's not a bad exercise. Rather, it's to come together once again as a polity to see if we can agree on where the boundaries should lie between individual and governmental power, and to bring technological affordances in line with that. It may even turn out that there are some technological advances that should be abjured on all sides, because no one individual or set of institutions can be expected to reasonably make use of them. Either way, these are decisions that we need to confront together.

39

INTELLECTUAL PROPERTY AND LAYERED SOVEREIGNTY

RUTH L. OKEDIJI

The Copyright and Patent Clause of the Constitution supports a nation-building project that centralizes control over knowledge and shapes American ideas about authorship, innovation, and cultural value. At the same time, sovereign Native American tribes possess authority over their own knowledge and cultural expression that predates the Constitution and that persists absent clear congressional displacement. The result is an under-theorized and unstable overlap between federal intellectual property (IP) law and tribal systems of knowledge governance.

Article I, Section 8, Clause 8 grants Congress power "To promote the progress of science and useful arts, by securing for limited times to authors and inventors the exclusive right to their respective writings and discoveries." From the Founding, Congress has wielded this authority to promote domestic industry, structure national markets, and exercise control over knowledge production. The Patent Act of 1790, though formally open to foreign inventors, served American industrial development and technological self-sufficiency. Trademark law similarly structured national markets, with territorial use in U.S. commerce becoming a defining limitation on protection.

Copyright law reinforced this national orientation through requirements such as registration and deposit, which eventually contributed to the Library of Congress' role as a repository of national knowledge. The federal emphasis on print culture and standardized dissemination helped produce a public sphere organized around literacy, uniform texts, and shared norms of public discourse. This print-centered regime was central to the formation of a national identity in the early American republic.

This national project sits in tension with the United States' layered sovereignty. Tribal nations are distinct political communities with inherent sovereignty over internal affairs, including the governance of knowledge and innovation. As "domestic dependent nations," they retain sovereign authority unless it has been clearly divested by Congress. That sovereignty includes the regulation of knowledge systems that originate within tribal communities and cultural traditions.

The doctrinal stakes of this tension appear most clearly in two unresolved problems.

First, a recognition problem: When, if ever, must federal or state courts give legal effect to tribal IP regimes? Federal patent and copyright law presumptively applies nationwide, including in Indian Country, yet Congress has provided little guidance on whether tribal law governing traditional knowledge, cultural expression, or innovation should be recognized—particularly where it diverges from federal eligibility rules or ownership concepts.

Second, an enforcement problem: Against whom may tribal IP law operate? While tribal authority over members and internal affairs is well established, its extension to non-members—especially non-tribal entities commercializing knowledge goods originating on tribal lands—remains contested.

These domestic tensions are compounded by emerging international frameworks. As Indigenous knowledge becomes more salient in global markets, disputes over traditional knowledge and genetic resources increasingly implicate tribal, federal, and international law. One result is that knowledge may be recognized and protected under tribal or international norms while remaining unprotected under federal law.

In response, many tribes have enacted their own IP regimes governing traditional knowledge, cultural expressions, and innovation. These efforts create a parallel legal system grounded in tribal sovereignty that define ownership, control, and permissible use according to Indigenous legal orders.

At the international level, these concerns are reflected in instruments such as the 2024 WIPO Treaty on IP, Genetic Resources and Associated Traditional Knowledge. Indigenous groups, including many Native American tribes, have been among the most active proponents of such agreements. But ratification by the U.S. seems a distant possibility and even if that happens, this treaty does not represent the full knowledge governance regime Indigenous peoples seek.

The result is a structurally unstable IP landscape in which courts lack a coherent framework for allocating authority across overlapping sovereigns. This instability is most visible in disputes involving appropriation of tribal knowledge by non-tribal actors, or conflicts between tribal regulatory systems and federally protected IP rights. Courts confronting these disputes must address recurring questions about which law governs and how competing regimes interact. The main guiding principle in sorting out these disputes should be a presumption of co-existence that rests on three doctrinal foundations.

First, federal IP statutes should not be understood to displace tribal law absent a clear statement from Congress or an irreconcilable conflict. The comprehensiveness of federal IP regulation alone is not evidence of field preemption.

Second, under established canons of federal Indian law, ambiguities in federal statutes affecting tribal sovereignty must be resolved in favor of retaining tribal authority. Where Congress has not clearly indicated displacement, courts should presume that tribes retain regulatory authority over knowledge, cultural expression, and innovation within their jurisdiction.

Third, courts should treat the overlapping IP regimes as a choice-of-law problem. They should evaluate the relative regulatory interests of each sovereign, considering factors such as the origin of the knowledge, the identity of the parties, the locus of conduct, and the degree of interference with federal objectives. This analysis may support concurrent application of federal and tribal regimes rather than mutual exclusion.

Consider a dispute in which a non-tribal biotechnology firm commercializes a plant-derived compound based on knowledge originating within a tribal community that does not satisfy federal patent eligibility standards. Under an exclusivity model, the absence of federal protection would foreclose legal remedy. Under a coexistence model, however, a court would ask whether Congress has clearly displaced tribal regulation; in the absence of such displacement, tribal law remains operative, and ambiguities are resolved in favor of tribal sovereignty. The court would then apply a structured choice-of-law analysis, which may support recognition of tribal rights at least where conduct is closely connected to tribal lands or knowledge systems.

This approach does not displace federal IP law. It instead situates it within a plural constitutional order in which multiple sovereigns generate overlapping but partially autonomous regimes of knowledge governance.

One can see the tensions inherent in this regime as productive rather than destabilizing. Properly understood, federal IP law already operates within a constitutional structure that accommodates multiple sovereigns. What has been missing is not authority, but a framework for mediation. A presumption of coexistence provides such a framework, allowing courts to give effect to both federal and tribal IP regimes within a single constitutional order.

At stake is not merely the allocation of regulatory authority, but the constitutional organization of knowledge itself. That structure does not simply tolerate overlapping sovereignties—it depends upon their coexistence.

40

REPRODUCTIVE TECHNOLOGIES AND THE FEDERAL CONSTITUTIONAL VACUUM

I. GLENN COHEN

We are on the cusp of some revolutionary new reproductive technologies, and yet the Supreme Court has been silent on how to think about what the federal Constitution might have to say about the *last* wave of technologies dating back *to the early 1980s*. Questions about the propriety of destroying embryos, whether women can lawfully agree to sell their reproductive labor as surrogates, gene editing, radically new forms of family formation, as well as questions of dignity, access, and equality, cut to the quick of what kind of country we are. To the extent we view the federal Constitution as the ultimate repository of those values, the current silence on what the Constitution means feels deafening.

So, why the silence? Is it good or bad? What would a bold constitutionalizing project look like for this space?

Consider In Vitro Gametogenesis (IVG), in which one can take skin or other somatic cells, derive induced pluripotent stem cells, and direct them to become sperm or eggs that could be used for reproduction, as one of the cutting-edge reproductive technologies we may soon see. Indeed, the technology can likely enable cross-sex gametes—sperm from women and eggs from men—enabling both partners of same-sex couples to be equal genetic contributors to reproducing, or potentially for a single individual to contribute sperm and egg to the same child. IVG has been successfully used in animal models, albeit with significant rates of failure and embryo destruction. Even if we are at some point ready for use in human beings in the U.S. that would not be lawful under current law, in part due to an appropriations rider that prohibits the FDA from considering an application to use it.

Or, consider Mitochondrial Replacement Techniques (MRT), currently authorized for limited use in the UK but, by dint of the same appropriations rider, prohibited in the U.S. In lay terms, it involves combining one woman's nuclear DNA with another's mitochondrial DNA and insemination with male sperm, with a goal of avoiding transmitting mitochondrial diseases while retaining genetic relations.

What does the federal Constitution say about the permissible use of these reproductive technologies? Can Congress just block the FDA from reviewing them altogether, thus blocking a necessary step for their entering clinical use? What does the Constitution mean as to more "traditional" (if you will pardon the seeming contradiction in terms) reproductive technologies such as "In Vitro Fertilization" (IVF), artificial insemination, or surrogacy?

Your guess is as good as mine. IVF appears in only three U.S. Supreme Court decisions in history, despite the fact that an estimated 96,000 children were born using the technology in 2023, accounting for 2.3 percent of all U.S. births. None of the opinions really develop the constitutional law. A concurrence in *Webster v. Reproductive Health Care* notes that IVF is not at issue; a dissent in *Dobbs v. Jackson Women's Health* flags that future constitutional issues may arise; and in *Astrue v. Capato ex rel. B.N.C.*, (you have probably never heard of it!) a unanimous Court holds that under rational basis review a state may exclude from Social Security survivor benefits children posthumously born through IVF when the state's intestacy law would block them from inheriting. This small presence in the Court's opinions is in stark contrast to the numerous reproductive technology issues that have been decided by the state courts, dealing with issues such as parentage of children born through surrogacy, embryo disposition disputes, discrimination claims against providers of these services, torts for reproductive wrongdoing, et cetera.

What gives?

One simple answer would be that these state court decisions largely turn on state law and thus evade U.S. Supreme Court review. It is true that the cases primarily turn on state law, but the litigation sometimes features claims of violations of federal constitutional law, even if they are not central to the opinions rendered. And some *lower* federal courts, not many, have spoken to federal constitutional law issues in this space; for example, in 2002's *J.R. v. Utah*, a federal district court found that aspects of Utah's restrictions on the enforcement of surrogacy agreements were unconstitutional.

The few courts and scholars (including this one) that have weighed in on what existing federal constitutional Supreme Court cases might say have tended to anchor the analysis on the Supreme Court's now upended abortion jurisprudence, and three cases from 1942 (*Skinner v. Oklahoma*), 1965 (*Griswold v. Connecticut*), and 1972 (*Eisenstadt v. Baird*), respectively. However, there has been almost no relevant discussion by the Supreme Court in more than fifty years. The first IVF birth in the U.S. happened in 1981, almost a decade *after* the last of these cases, making them poor guides. This trio of cases is about contraception and sterilization, not *producing* offspring.

So what explains the lack of constitutional law in this space? One can only speculate. On the left, before the Court overturned *Roe v Wade*, some reproductive rights advocates might have been wary that pushing for federal constitutional protections for reproductive technology use might have produced unfavorable constitutional law on abortion. Today, they may be worried that resounding losses in reproductive technology rights claims will embolden states to restrict them more.

On the flipside, what explains the fact that other than parentage determinations, where controversies seem inevitable, states have not attempted many restrictions on reproductive technology use? Politics may also furnish an answer. It could be that the fertility care sector has been effective at lobbying. Or, it could be that many who were in favor of or tolerant of abortion restrictions, having achieved their goal, might be wary of the political blowback to restricting reproductive technologies. For example, in 2024, the Alabama Supreme Court ruled that improperly destroyed embryos counted as children for the state's wrongful death of a minor statute. Then-candidate Trump and many in his party tried to distance themselves immediately from the ruling and its potential negative effects on reproductive technology availability—a stinging example of what might happen when one kicks this particular hornet's nest. Indeed, the state's own legislature quickly intervened with an attempted statutory fix.

The broader question is whether this federal constitutional vacuum is good or bad. I have my doubts that this vacuum is healthy for a political system. While much of family law has always been a matter of state law, the introduction of new drugs, devices, and biologics has traditionally been the responsibility of federal authorities to review.

"Ok, big shot, so what should federal constitutional lawmaking in this space look like?" There is a lot of space for development. Three very distinct constitutional programs come to mind, broadly speaking, centered on tradition, equality, and liberation. To be clear, as to each, I am here considering only the negative liberty (freedom from government restriction), not the positive liberty equivalent (such as governmental support).

The <u>Traditionalist</u> view would start with the forms of reproductive family making that have long been part of U.S. history and treat the Constitution as a Procrustean device. Artificial insemination has a surprisingly long history in the United States. The first reported case was Dr. William Pancoast at the Jefferson Medical College in Philadelphia in 1884, shortly after the Fourteenth Amendment was added to the Constitution in 1868. The strictest traditional view might limit constitutional protection to *this* technology and leave states significant authority over the rest, perhaps policed on the margins by Equal Protection law. A more relaxed Traditionalist might also seek to protect different technologies that have a similar goal—allowing women to become pregnant through technological participation of a single additional male partner (their husband or other), but exclude third-party participation.

The <u>Equality</u> view focuses not on the technology but on the interest being served, enabling individuals who cannot do so to reproduce. The narrow version would focus on medical infertility—gonadal damage, the inability to produce sperm and egg, women who had to undergo hysterectomies, etc. It might protect those who, by dint of bad moral luck, lost a medical capability that healthy individuals have. It might be connected to a particular concept of disease as departures from the species' typical desired functioning. On such a view infertile men and women would fall under a federal constitutional aegis, but gay, lesbian, and single individuals (sometimes called "socially infertile" or "dysfertile") would not be so protected and instead forced to duke it out for their usage as part of the political process. While disability has never merited heightened review by the U.S. Supreme Court in Equal Protection analysis, this view might argue that here disability antidiscrimination (protecting those with *medical* infertility) is buttressed by the association with the right to reproduce and family formation. Of course, equality is a somewhat malleable concept, and one could imagine a version of the argument that is more embracing of gays and lesbians, with the kinds of odes to their relationship building we see in opinions like *Obergefell v. Hodges*.

The Liberationist view renders the interest in reproductive technology use not merely as "mimicking" coital reproduction, but perhaps "extending" it. Extending even otherwise healthy women's ability to genetically reproduce much later in life, bringing them parity with men's ability to do so, is viewed as a fit goal for constitutionalism. For lesbian and gay would-be parents, it might embrace new technologies like IVG that would allow *both* partners to be genetic parents. What is worth protecting on this view is not merely same-sex family formation through parental recognition, but *genetic* family formation.

Indeed, we can get even more radically Liberationist. Consider also uterus transplants—currently successfully performed in the U.S. on some assigned female at birth, but at least not yet (perhaps the science will ultimately mean not ever) on those assigned male at birth. A more radical constitutionalizing project would suggest that achieving gender equality means constitutional protections for trans women or even cisgender men might themselves be given the opportunity and challenges of experiencing *pregnancy*, and not merely a *genetic* connection.

Which of these or other (the list is not meant to be exhaustive) conceptions is the right one to guide our polity? In space, no one can hear you scream. And in a constitutional vacuum, the vociferous debate about these issues has heretofore remained quiet.

PART XI

THE INTERNATIONAL LEGAL ORDER

Since the Founding, the United States has always been centrally defined by its relationship to and influential place in the international order. But nearly everything else has changed since 1776. Kristen Eichensehr reminds us that the Framers "drafted the Constitution for a weak and vulnerable new country," and could not have anticipated that the United States would become a global hegemon and architect of the international order. She worries that the unchecked power of the executive branch—also unanticipated by the Framers—is now undoing the enormous benefits of that order. Gerald Neuman also emphasizes America's substantial need for and reliance on international cooperation. He fears that the current administration's "massive repudiation of international cooperation" is a self-inflicted injury that will "inevitably weaken the United States and enhance the power of rival forces." Susan Farbstein highlights the irony that the U.S. was central to the construction of the modern international legal system and its respect for human rights, a project that the U.S. is currently actively undermining. Alex Whiting offers a similar analysis of international criminal law. The United States played a critical role in the establishment of Nuremberg and subsequent war crimes tribunals, even as it refused to join the International Criminal Court. He worries that the current administration's attack on international institutions and its aggressive use of force puts the entire project of international criminal justice at risk. Bill Alford puts these anxieties in historical context, noting that the U.S. has always had an ambivalent relationship to the international order. Even so, he describes the current administration's attack on that order as unprecedented, and he explains why China today is particularly well-situated to fill the leadership void that the United States has left in its wake.

41

FOREIGN RELATIONS AND THE FAILURES OF FORESIGHT

KRISTEN E. EICHENSEHR

Perspectives on government and its problems inevitably rest, at least in part, on one's lived experience. The Framers of the Constitution drew on their own experiences to address concerns about both domestic governmental overreach and international vulnerability. But two failures of foresight at the Founding have led to a present with distinctly different concerns from those against which the Founders tried to guard. The unchecked expansion of executive power domestically has led to presidential actions that risk destabilizing an international order that the Framers would have envied.

The first failure of foresight was domestic. The Declaration of Independence broke with a monarchy that sought an "absolute Tyranny" over its American colonies. Fearful of centralization, the Articles of Confederation established a national government that lacked an executive branch, leading to problems of coordination, defense, and efficacy as compared to other countries. The Constitution tacked in the other direction, creating an executive branch and imbuing it with significant authority, including the Commander-in-Chief power. But the Framers viewed Congress as the more dangerous branch. In *Federalist 48*, Madison described the "executive magistracy" as "carefully limited, both in the extent and the duration of its power," and warned that "the people ought to indulge all their jealousy and exhaust all their precautions" to counter the "enterprising ambition" of the legislature. In *Federalist 51*, Madison further warned that "[i]n republican government, the legislative authority necessarily predominates," and described the presidential veto power as a way to "fortif[y]" a weak executive.

The executive's powers were stronger than the Framers realized, and Congress's incentives to counteract them were much weaker. In *Federalist 51*, Madison envisioned that each branch's ambition would "counteract ambition" by the other. But the near-constant need to run for reelection and the rise of the party system have undercut legislators' willingness to stand up for Congress's institutional prerogatives in foreign affairs. As Justice Jackson warned in *Youngstown Sheet & Tube Co. v. Sawyer*, "Party loyalties and interests, sometimes more binding than law, extend [the president's] effective control into branches of government other than his own and he often may win, as a political leader, what he cannot command under the Constitution."

The second failure of foresight was international. The Framers drafted the Constitution for a weak and vulnerable new country. John Jay worried in *Federalist 4* about foreign nations making war too readily, warning that "nations in general will make war whenever they have a prospect of getting anything by it," and that "absolute monarchs will often make war when their nations are to get nothing by it, but for purposes and objects merely personal." Jay framed the constitutional union as fundamentally defensive, arguing in *Federalist 5* that "weakness and divisions at home would invite dangers from abroad; and that nothing would tend more to secure us from them than union, strength, and good government within ourselves."

The Framers could not foresee the world of the twentieth century in which the United States became a hegemon and the architect of an international legal order that sought to restrain states' resort to force. That legal order has been a boon: The United States has benefited tremendously from the relative stability and order that this system has engendered.

But the Framers' first failure of foresight about the power of the executive is now undoing the benefits of the second. Congress's structural and political weaknesses have left the executive with nearly unchecked power to use force abroad, undermining both the constitutional separation of powers and the international order that the United States previously championed.

The blame for the present reality rests in part with Congress. The ambition that James Madison counted on in *Federalist 51* to counteract others' ambition has turned, for many legislators, into personal ambition for reelection, not ambition to guard Congress's institutional prerogatives against executive encroachment.

In a moment of constitutional rebalancing in the 1970s, Congress did attempt to rein in the executive's national security and foreign policy excesses through a series of statutes designed to allow Congress to maintain an ongoing check on the president via legislative vetoes. Crucial statutes of this era include the War Powers Resolution (WPR), the International Emergency Economic Powers Act, and the National Emergencies Act. But the other two branches thwarted Congress's efforts.

A large share of blame rests with the executive. In recent decades, presidents of both parties have made ever-broader claims of constitutional authority to use force abroad without Congress's authorization and have stretched congressional authorizations for the use of force related to 9/11 and Iraq up to and beyond their breaking points. The executive branch has also skirted Congress's attempts to restrain the president's uses of force through the WPR, using creative lawyering to avoid admitting that the Resolution's restrictions apply and resorting to presidential vetoes to stymie congressional efforts to direct the termination of or prevent the start of hostilities through joint resolutions.

The Supreme Court bears responsibility as well. Its invalidation of legislative vetoes in *INS v. Chadha* in 1983 had the effect of locking in congressional delegations to the president while eliminating the procedural checks Congress had intended to retain over war powers and emergency authorities. The Framers' choice to "fortif[y]" the president with a veto power has proven fateful: To directly restrain the president's use of force and emergency powers, Congress now has to muster a supermajority in both houses to overcome a presidential veto.

It is ironic that the Framers' fear of Congress led to the fateful design choice that has empowered the president to use force in ways that undermine an international order that has afforded the United States a degree of security that would have astounded the Framers. Congress played a crucial role in the construction of that order, including through Senate consent to the ratification of foundational agreements like the U.N. Charter and the North Atlantic Treaty and subsequent congressional support for U.S. participation in international institutions.

Congress could also stop its destruction. Legislators, scholars, and other commentators have made numerous proposals for ways that Congress could reassert itself on use of force matters with benefits for both the domestic *and* international legal orders. But for such proposals to succeed requires legislators—a supermajority of them—to assert Congress's institutional prerogatives.

Looking ahead, the United States must continue to struggle through a problem the Framers did foresee. Madison explained in *Federalist 51* that "[i]n framing a government . . . , the great difficulty lies in this: you must first enable the government to control the governed; and in the next place oblige it to control itself." How—or whether—the government can control itself both domestically and internationally remains very much a work in progress.

42

THE UNITED STATES WILL NEED INTERNATIONAL LAW

GERALD L. NEUMAN

The Declaration of Independence began our national existence with a "decent respect for the opinions of mankind." Two hundred and fifty years later, the United States government is engaged in a massive repudiation of international cooperation and organizations and is devastating its credibility. This self-inflicted injury will inevitably weaken the United States and enhance the power of rival forces. As the Republic will once more learn, it needs international law.

Extrapolating from existing trends in how power is exercised within and across countries shows the challenges democracy will likely face. Consider three schematic scenarios for the United States and the world. In one scenario, the authoritarian networks that currently undermine pluralistic democracies have largely triumphed and the United States has become one authoritarian country among many, with China the dominant power that writes the rules of the road as the United States once did. In the second scenario, a small set of transnational megacorporations in industries such as information technology, communications, alternative finance, and resource extraction have hollowed out the governance of the countries that formerly hosted them, leaving an appearance of self-government in matters that do not impede their operations. In the third, more optimistic scenario, the United States has recovered its democratic pluralism, is rebuilding its institutions, and within the context of a very different balance of power is attempting to win back former allies with whom it had too greatly breached faith.

In the third scenario, international law would be an important tool for polities working together to preserve their democratic character and resisting attempts by authoritarian rivals to reconfigure global power structures in their own favor. International law may also afford mechanisms for restraining corporate absorption of governmental functions and for avoiding descent into the second scenario. I will not speculate here about what the needs of an authoritarian United States would be.

The Framers of the 1787 Constitution understood the value of international law. Their vision need not bind us in the greatly changed circumstances of the twenty-first century, yet it advises us nonetheless. The Constitution was designed to facilitate the participation of a federal republic in a larger system of international cooperation and competition. Some constitutional provisions referred explicitly to international law and its institutions, such as treaties, ambassadors, consuls, alliances, war, and offenses against the law of nations. The Supremacy Clause made treaties the law of the land and obligated the states to comply with them. In fact, stopping violation by individual states of treaty commitments was one of the principal motives for the adoption of the Constitution.

The ability to make credible commitments and keep them is not an infringement of national sovereignty—it is a vehicle for the exercise of national sovereignty in an interdependent world. That was already true with the slow-moving technologies of the eighteenth century, and the current realities of instantaneous communication and rapid movement of people and things only make it more so.

International law also provides known baselines from which international cooperation and competition can occur. Like national private law, it sets expectations of behavior against which deviations can be measured and disputes can be articulated. It enables governments and private actors to estimate risks while investing resources or efforts to achieve shared benefits. Even norms that are purely conventional and have no strong justification on their own can promote orderly interaction and increase predictability. They can provide frameworks for serving the common interests of democracies or for coalitions leaguing together to defend existing international law against authoritarian revision.

Unfortunately, in the current period of official disdain for legal constraint, the United States has worked to undermine one of the most fundamental achievements of the post-war world order, the international prohibition of the acquisition of territory by force. That is an encouragement to conquest that China and Russia will not soon forget. It also gives cover to smaller powers with ongoing territorial disputes or with historical objections to their current borders. The consequences of global temperature rise may also increase the incentives for states to seize their neighbors' land, rivers, and seas. The United States might face such threats not only against its protégés, but perhaps more directly, for example against some of its own maritime resources.

For the weakened United States to engage diplomatically with the world it will also need to return to another principle of respect expressed in the Declaration of Independence: that all of humankind are created equal. Or, in the wording of the Universal Declaration of Human Rights, "All human beings are born free and equal in dignity and rights." Two aspects of that central norm of human rights law deserve to be emphasized here. First, echoing the anticolonial goal of the 1776 U.S. Declaration, the 1948 Universal Declaration confirms equality as between people belonging to independent countries and people belonging to "non-self-governing" territories. Countries that once were colonies have suffered extreme disrespect from U.S. officials in recent times. Second, human equality is not merely a duty owed to governments: it requires respect for individuals, regardless of their race, their sex, or their religion.

Relatedly, the United States will need to return to its modern practice of treating religions equally, in foreign policy and domestically. While that does not mean ignoring religiously motivated violations of human rights, it does mean responding even-handedly rather than championing particular religions as such. Both for accurate perception and for designing strategies, it must be remembered that in global terms all religions are minority religions. Protection cannot be successfully claimed in other countries for one religion unless it is also extended to other religions.

The Declaration of Independence announced that the United States were taking their "separate and equal station" among the peoples of the world. With insight and good fortune the United States has maintained a leading role globally for decades but by now it has overplayed its hand. As prior generations understood, and as should already be clear, the United States needs international law.

43

AMERICAN POWER AND THE FUTURE OF HUMAN RIGHTS

SUSAN H. FARBSTEIN

The international human rights project is, in many ways, an American story. The Declaration of Independence addressed a domestic audience as well as "a candid world," insisting that legitimate governance must be grounded in the protection of fundamental rights. The new republic sought to uphold, not upend, the law of nations.

But the project is also a story of American ambivalence, hypocrisy, and now abandonment. As we observe the 250th anniversary of the Declaration of Independence, the United States is not merely failing to lead the international legal system but is actively undermining it. The question is whether this moment will mark the destruction of the postwar international legal order or become a painful but catalyzing transition toward something more equitable and effective.

THE POSTWAR ARCHITECTURE

From the ruins of the Second World War, the United States helped construct the modern international legal system. American lawyers played central roles in the Nuremberg and Tokyo trials, ensuring that individuals could be held criminally responsible for war crimes and crimes against humanity. The United Nations Charter, drafted in San Francisco with significant American input, fused the prohibition on wars of aggression with a commitment to promote universal respect for fundamental rights. Eleanor Roosevelt chaired the drafting committee of the Universal Declaration of Human Rights, which remains the foundational text of the global human rights system.

Over time, treaty bodies, special rapporteurs, and regional and international courts built a meaningful framework for monitoring and enforcement. American engagement has often been partial and selective, and the system has never worked perfectly. Still, it represents a genuine achievement: a shared understanding, codified in treaties and reinforced by institutions with real investigative and adjudicatory powers, that respecting and protecting human rights is a matter of international concern.

Over the past quarter century, the United States' posture has shifted in consequential ways. The 2003 invasion of Iraq is widely understood as a violation of the UN Charter's prohibition on the use of force. Torture, enforced disappearances, and targeted killings carried out as part of the "war on terror" constituted grave breaches of international humanitarian and human rights law. Yet throughout this period, American officials felt compelled to offer legal rationales for their conduct, whether strained interpretations of self-defense, redefinitions of torture, or novel readings of treaty obligations.

These justifications were often deeply flawed, but they reflected an implicit recognition that international law mattered for human dignity and global security, and that being seen as law-abiding conferred legitimacy upon states. The United States may have bent the rules, but it remained invested in the system it helped create. It still accepted international law as the framework through which its actions should be judged.

FROM EVASION TO REPUDIATION

Now, the United States is tearing up the rule book. It has moved from sometimes evading international norms to openly repudiating them.

On the third anniversary of Russia's full-scale invasion of Ukraine, the United States voted against a General Assembly resolution condemning Russian aggression and reaffirming the UN Charter's core principles. Rather than abstain, it aligned itself with a small group of states including Russia, North Korea, Sudan, and Hungary, that routinely reject foundational tenets of international law. Recent executive actions have withdrawn the United States from numerous international organizations and treaties deemed contrary to U.S. interests, and imposed sanctions on the

International Criminal Court. In short order, the President announced that he sought to reclaim the Panama Canal, acquire Greenland, and make Canada the fifty-first state. A cascade of unlawful acts—from boat strikes in the Caribbean, to the invasion of Venezuela and kidnapping of President Nicolás Maduro, to extrajudicial killings of American citizens on the streets of Minneapolis, to an illegal war of aggression in Iran—make clear that the current administration is no longer trying to work within the international legal framework. The United States seeks to dismantle it.

For many around the world, these events may simply affirm what lived experience has already taught: International law is applied and enforced unevenly. Communities that have endured U.S. military interventions, U.S. support for abusive governments, or impunity for U.S. violations may view these latest developments less as a departure than a confirmation of long-standing realities. This critique is important, but it should not diminish the magnitude of what is being lost now.

Compliance with international law, like any legal framework, has always been imperfect. States have sometimes violated their legal obligations and the UN's structural inequalities have shielded powerful actors from meaningful consequences. But noncompliance is not the same as rejection. To repudiate the institutions themselves—to characterize international legal commitments as optional or antagonistic to national interests—is to erode the architecture that has structured global governance and protected human rights for eighty years.

Earlier U.S. failures could be understood as deviations from professed ideals. Human rights practitioners could still advocate and litigate to insist that the United States live up to international standards. The current posture dismisses such demands. The United States now treats international law not as a binding framework subject to interpretation but as an obstacle to be discarded in pursuit of American interests.

This shift has profound consequences. When the United States disavows the prohibition on aggression or the universality of human rights, it weakens those norms everywhere. It emboldens other bad actors eager to follow suit. It accelerates the fragmentation of the international order. In recasting international law as a mere constraint on sovereignty and dismissing international institutions as "anti-American" or "globalist," the United States is abandoning the very idea that shared rules should govern the exercise of power.

RUPTURE AND POSSIBILITY

One possible future is especially bleak. International institutions wither, leaving survivors of human rights violations with fewer forums to seek justice or redress. Transnational challenges like climate change and mass displacement are addressed through ad hoc deals between powerful actors, with little transparency, accountability, or concern for the most vulnerable.

But another possible future is more hopeful. The shock of U.S. retrenchment could accelerate efforts already underway to diversify leadership in the international legal system, elevate voices from the Global South, and reduce dependence on any single state as guarantor of the rules-based order. Regional human rights systems could gain influence. Coalitions of states could invest in accountability mechanisms insulated from great-power vetoes. Domestic courts could play a larger role in enforcing international norms through transnational litigation.

History offers no guarantees here, but it does offer precedents: moments when rupture led to reimagining. Decolonization reshaped the United Nations. The end of the Cold War enabled the creation of new criminal tribunals. Global civil society invented forms of human rights advocacy that would have been hard to envision when the Universal Declaration was drafted. The current disruption may likewise open space to build a more robust and equitable international legal system—less tethered to postwar power structures, more driven by those impacted by human rights abuse, and more committed to socio-economic rights and atrocity prevention.

The question, on this 250th anniversary of the Declaration of Independence, is whether the United States will continue to engage with and improve the international legal order it helped build, or instead tear it down. The choices the United States makes now will shape both America's place in the world and the rights of millions of people within and beyond our borders. But the answer equally depends on the determination of other states, institutions, and advocates to resist America's attempted dismantling and imagine better alternatives.

As a human rights practitioner, I remain an optimist. Not because I believe that the arc of history bends naturally toward justice, but because I've seen it bend when people push. Time and again, I have watched survivors insist that the law recognize their humanity and their dignity. I have supported them as they turned to courts, treaty bodies, truth commissions, and other mechanisms seeking remedies and accountability. While far from ideal, these forums offer tools to contest power, language to reframe narratives, and spaces to secure some measure of justice. With or without American leadership, we must protect this system while also seizing the opportunity to make it even more just and effective.

44

THE UNITED STATES AND INTERNATIONAL CRIMINAL JUSTICE: THE END OF A LONG RELATIONSHIP

ALEX WHITING

After World War II, the United States was central to creating new institutions and law to hold political and military leaders accountable for international crimes. As this initiative grew, first from the Nuremberg and Tokyo tribunals, to the ad hoc tribunals including those for the former Yugoslavia and Rwanda, and then to the International Criminal Court (ICC), the United States found itself playing a dual role. It was both at the forefront of the project, playing a critical role in the creation and success of new tribunals to prosecute international crimes, and on the outside, refusing to join the ICC and submit to its jurisdiction. This delicate balance was challenging, but manageable, as the U.S. could claim that its dual stance was justified by its unique leadership role in the world and its ultimate commitment to justice in its own national courts.

However, in the last year, the U.S. has undermined both its role as a champion of international justice and the project of international criminal law itself by its sharp turn away from accountability for war crimes. This is a crippling loss both for the United States' moral stature and for the international community.

Initially, the commitment of the Allies after World War II to legal accountability for international crimes was uncertain—at one moment there was discussion of simply executing suspected war criminals—but ultimately the United States' embrace of a legal approach proved decisive, and the accused were tried before the Nuremberg Military Tribunal and Far East Tribunal. As Justice Robert Jackson famously declared in his opening statement, "That four great nations, flushed with victory and stung with injury stay the hand of vengeance and voluntarily submit their captive enemies to the judgment of the law is one of the most significant tributes that Power has ever paid to Reason."

International criminal justice then went quiet for nearly fifty years, a casualty of the Cold War, but when it was reborn in the early 1990s, the United States again played a critical role in its creation and development. When stories emerged from the wars in the Balkans of ethnic cleansing, detention camps, and sexual violence, evoking powerful and vivid memories of the crimes of the Holocaust, the U.S. led the push to establish an international tribunal to hold the alleged war criminals accountable. At the UN Security Council meeting in 1993 to create the International Criminal Tribunal for the former Yugoslavia, U.S. Ambassador Madeleine Albright, a prime mover in that effort, declared, "There is an echo in this Chamber today. The Nuremberg Principles have been reaffirmed." Then through funding, staffing, and political and diplomatic support, the United States proved essential to the success of that court, as well as to the accomplishments of later tribunals established to address atrocity crimes in Rwanda, Cambodia, Sierra Leone, and Kosovo.

The United States' support for international criminal accountability became more complicated with the establishment in 1998 of the International Criminal Court (ICC), a permanent international court to prosecute war crimes, crimes against humanity, genocide, and the crime of aggression. On the one hand, the United States provided important support to certain ICC investigations. For example, it backed UN Security Council votes to grant the ICC jurisdiction to investigate crimes in Sudan in 2005 and Libya in 2011, and it materially supported the ICC's investigations in Uganda and Ukraine with evidence and diplomatic support. And from its creation, American prosecutors have held senior positions within the ICC Office of the Prosecutor, making important contributions to the work of the court.

But on the other hand, the United States has consistently resisted taking the ultimate step, that of joining the ICC and submitting to its jurisdiction. Even beyond that, the U.S. has further asserted that it will not permit the court to prosecute U.S. nationals, even if they were to fall within the court's jurisdiction. When the court became operational in 2002, for example, Congress enacted the American Servicemembers' Protection Act, authorizing the president "to use all means necessary and appropriate to bring about the release" of any U.S. nationals detained by the court. Because "all means necessary" includes military force, this statute became known derisively in the Netherlands as The Hague Invasion Act.

The United States has not always necessarily seen itself as immune from international criminal accountability. Although the post-World War II tribunals were later criticized for being one-sided, Justice Jackson believed that the law outlawing aggressive war would apply equally to the Allied countries going forward, including the United States. In his opening at the Nuremberg trial, he said, "And let me make clear that while this law is first applied against German aggressors, the law includes, and if it is to serve a useful purpose it must condemn, aggression by any other nations, including those which sit here now in judgment. We are able to do away with domestic tyranny and violence and aggression by those in power against the rights of their own people only when we make all men answerable to the law."

So why hasn't the United States, a champion of international accountability for atrocity crimes, joined the ICC? For presidents before the current one, the refusal to join has not been to escape accountability for operating outside of the law, as some critics might allege. Rather, the reasons for staying out of the ICC have been both cultural and pragmatic. Culturally, Americans have long harbored a suspicion of international institutions and commitments, no doubt reinforced by its geographic distance from much of the world. It is why, even as an undisputed superpower, the U.S. has at times imagined that it could disengage from the rest of the world. Accordingly, it would likely be difficult to persuade a majority of Americans to sign up to an international court that could, in theory, criminally prosecute U.S. soldiers.

Pragmatically, there is a recognition that, despite its moments of isolationism, the United States frequently finds itself militarily engaged across the globe. The crimes prosecuted by the ICC have both legal and political meaning, and a feature of modern conflict is that accusations of war crimes, crimes against humanity, and even genocide fly in all directions. A commitment of the modern tribunals, partly in reaction to criticisms of the post-World War II tribunals, has been to investigate all sides to a conflict, and at times these courts have stretched to prosecute both sides, sometimes with disastrous results. If the United States were engaged in an unpopular war with significant civilian casualties, would the ICC prosecutor be able to resist calls from aggrieved nations and human rights groups to prosecute U.S. nationals, even when the evidence of crimes was lacking? Uncertainty on this question has made it feel risky to join the court.

For these reasons, no U.S. administration has even considered joining the court. Remarkably, with regard to the rest of the world, the U.S. has largely been able to defend its dual role: supporting international criminal prosecutions on the one hand while refusing to submit itself to the jurisdiction of the ICC. In part this balancing act has worked because the ICC's jurisdiction is complementary to national jurisdiction, and so the U.S. could plausibly claim that there is no need for it to join the ICC because it will address any criminal allegations against U.S. nationals "in house." It may also be that the 125 countries that have signed up to the ICC, including some of the United States' closest allies, hope that over time, especially if the ICC develops a strong track record of responsible prosecutions, the U.S. will see its way to joining the court.

Today, however, this delicate balance is fraying and may have already broken. The U.S. has broadly turned away from international commitments and institutions. In the last year, the United States has violated the UN Charter on the use of force, retreated from commitments to domestic accountability for war crimes, and ratcheted up its attacks on the ICC. The President has committed acts of aggression against sovereign states and threatened them against others. He has pardoned soldiers prosecuted by the military for conduct amounting to war crimes. His Secretary of Defense has made statements suggesting that the military will not be constrained by rules of engagement and has reduced the Pentagon staff dedicated to civilian protection in war. And the administration has imposed devastating sanctions—ordinarily reserved for terrorists, war criminals, and the leaders of drug cartels—on prosecutors and judges at the ICC because of its ongoing cases regarding Palestine and Israel.

These steps undermine the United States' role in the international criminal justice project, and may put at risk the entire project altogether. The United States is surrendering the moral and legal leadership it showed since Nuremberg, and it will be difficult for other countries to continue to look away. Although in the past, states have found ways to accept the

United States absenting itself from the ICC's jurisdiction, largely because of the U.S.'s fundamental commitment to the rule of law, the current government's actions are something else altogether: they betray a wholesale abandonment of accountability for international crimes. Increasingly, other states will likely reconsider their own commitments to justice for international crimes in light of the United States' retreat. Ironically, and tragically, the international criminal justice project could be fatally undermined by the country that made it possible.

45

The United States, International Engagement, and the Need to Look Both Back and Outward

Bill Alford

There is a temptation to see the recent withdrawal by the United States from scores of international organizations and agreements, and the broader repudiation of the so-called rules-based international order as a singular product of the current administration. Even as we acknowledge that this administration, as it proudly proclaims, is seeking to redefine America's position in the world, we would be remiss if we failed to situate these actions in the broader scope of American history.

Over the course of our history, the United States has had a profound ambivalence about international engagement, fluctuating between seeing it as essential (at times to the point of initiating it) and treating it as something to be avoided (even if doing so at times undermined our efforts at initiating it). We see this pattern from the earliest days of the Republic, with George Washington in his Farewell Address of 1796, writing that "The great rule of conduct for us in regard to foreign nations is in extending our commercial relations to have with them as little political connection as possible"—this notwithstanding the crucial role of French military, diplomatic, and financial support in our War of Independence.

That pattern has repeated itself throughout American history. Consider, for example, the Wilson administration, in the aftermath of World War I, proposing the creation of a League of Nations only to sound its death knell by refusing to join it. Or the United States, in the immediate aftermath of World War II, advancing the idea of a robust International Trade Organization which, owing to Senate opposition, never got off the ground, leaving in its stead a flawed General Agreement on Tariffs and Trade. Or the initiation, under President Nixon, of a convention to govern the law of the sea, which we have refused to ratify, even as our own

Navy has voluntarily adhered to the principle of freedom of navigation that undergirds the convention. Or the establishment in the 1990s of a World Trade Organization, imbued with the vision of American lawyers, that both Democratic and Republican administrations have subsequently undercut because of unhappiness with how that vision has played out.

Parallels abound in a host of other areas. These include the United Nations Convention on the Rights of Persons with Disabilities (said to be inspired by the Americans with Disabilities Act developed by the George H. W. Bush administration); the Convention on the Rights of the Child (in the formation of which the United States played an important role but which we remain the only UN member not to have ratified); and the Rome Statute of the International Criminal Court (which bears the imprint of the US-led Nuremberg and Tokyo war crimes tribunals but which President Clinton, after signing, did not submit to the Senate for ratification).

As important as it is to understand the current administration's posture toward the international legal order in historical context, it is no less vital to identify what is different now. To be sure, that order has fallen well short of its own stated ideals and been freighted with hypocrisy as many a critic from the right, left, and center have argued over many years. But no previous American administration (or allied government) has attacked it in as frontal, thorough-going and unabashed a manner, with profound and enduring human and reputational costs.

What also is different is the possibility that China may fill the void. To be sure, from the earliest days of our Republic, American views of China have fluctuated much as have our views on global order, consistent only in typically painting China in monochromatic tones, be they positive or negative. For Franklin, Paine, and Jefferson (among other key revolutionary era figures) China was a source of inspiration for its culture and institutions, in part as a foil to Europe. Indeed, Jefferson went so far as to extoll China's guarded approach toward international engagement. A century later, fear of what came to be known as the Yellow Peril led to our nation's first major racially-based immigration law, the so-called Chinese Exclusion Act of 1882. In the late twentieth century, giddy ahistorical "end of history" accounts assumed a China eager to converge toward legal, economic, and perhaps even political institutions akin to ours. That account, in turn, has given way in this century to near-uniform depictions of an unremittingly sinister mortal enemy bearing outsized responsibility for what ails our nation.

The precise shape of the challenge the People's Republic of China poses regarding global order remains to be seen. China speaks increasingly of crafting an alternative, based on enduring Chinese values, to what it calls the "hegemonic western world order." But for decades it has forcefully advanced an extremely traditional Westphalian view of sovereignty emanating from that very "hegemonic . . . order." Witness, for example, the ways in which it invokes sovereignty to denounce concerns from abroad about its Uyghur population in Xinjiang and other human rights issues.

Some analysts suggest that the People's Republic may seek global leadership by endeavoring to fill part of the gap resulting from the massive cutback in humanitarian aid left by the United States (which has been exacerbated by smaller, but still significant, cutbacks by Canada, France, Germany, Sweden, and the United Kingdom). Others note opportunities for China created by our disavowal of the Paris Climate Agreement, the World Health Organization and other international undertakings. But it is an open question whether Beijing is willing to make the hard domestic and external political choices (for even as it is increasingly authoritarian, it is not a monolith) and expend the necessary funds to make any of this a reality. To take but one illustration, even as innovation in the PRC regarding EVs, batteries, solar panels, and wind turbines offers promise in the fight against climate change, it remains the world's largest emitter of greenhouse gases, continues to build coal-fired plants at home and abroad, and through its model of state subsidization has undercut panel and turbine production in the United States, Germany, and elsewhere.

As the United States, at the 250th anniversary of the Declaration of Independence, looks ahead, we need also both to look back and to look outward. We need to be mindful of the dueling strands of our own history and their contemporary implications. And we need simultaneously to take into account that other nations are complex in their own ways and that, often, what they accomplish and how they fail are interwoven. China in our lifetime has had historic successes, with more than one billion citizens lifting themselves out of poverty (approximate annual per capita income rising over the past half century from US $165 to US

$14,700). But it also has had epic calamities, as evidenced most starkly by its draconian one-child policy (which so overrode citizen autonomy that, even with its official ending in 2015, the nation faces a demographic crisis of unprecedented proportions).

Confronting complexity and contradiction will not resolve enduring tensions in our own body politic. Nor will it provide ready answers to profound external challenges. But, surely, fuller understanding is an indispensable step as we hope to secure a better future for our children, grandchildren, and beyond.

PART XII

WAR

The Declaration of Independence was, among other things, a declaration of war, complete with a list of reasons and justifications for initiating armed conflict against Britain. In its detailed solemnity, the Declaration makes clear that the Founders appreciated the heavy costs of the decision to go to war. Today, the legal authority for such decisions is highly contested even as the full costs of war are both obscured and unequally distributed. Jill Lepore explains that the Constitution expressly confers on Congress, not the president, the power to "declare war" because the Founders considered it undemocratic to permit the executive branch to declare war on its own. Abraham Lincoln similarly described the power to declare war as "the most oppressive of all Kingly oppressions." And yet, notwithstanding this history, ever since the 1960s American presidents have frequently engaged in military action without congressional approval, from Vietnam to Iran. Lepore concludes that Congress effectively undermined its own war power by having repeatedly failed to assert it. Daniel Nagin reminds us that it is military servicemembers who pay the heaviest costs of these controversial, contested political decisions. And yet, as he catalogues, the federal government has failed our military veterans in myriad ways, imposing lifelong disabilities, denying them benefits, and abandoning too many of them to lives of poverty, homelessness, and incarceration. Nagin argues that these injustices are directly contrary to the spirit of the Declaration itself, noting that "the plight of soldiers and veterans was plainly front of mind for the drafters and the others assembled in Philadelphia." Reminding us that going to war is a definitional national decision, these scholars teach us how that decision has been made, managed, and contested over the centuries.

46

Do U.S. Presidents Have the Power to Declare War?

Jill Lepore

Whether a U.S. president has the power to declare war is a matter of American constitutional law. That question can be answered doctrinally, politically, or historically. Whichever way, everything hinges on the year 1964. And the story told by the events of that year, and of the decades since, is the story of the slow erosion of congressional power.

On August 2, 1964, North Vietnamese torpedo boats attacked the U.S.S. Maddox in the Gulf of Tonkin. Following a much-disputed report of a second attack, President Lyndon B. Johnson ordered a bombing raid and asked Congress to pass a joint resolution of support. Johnson had been angling for such a resolution since the last weeks of 1963 and had begun discussing it in earnest the following February. "Being sprung from the loins of the Congress," Johnson's adviser Jack Valenti later said, "he was very, very disgruntled and discontented with the fact that we were messing around in Southeast Asia without congressional approval." As a senator, Johnson had particularly objected to Harry Truman having sent troops to Korea without seeking support from Congress. If any president tried to get away with that while Johnson was Senate Majority Leader, Valenti said, "Lyndon Johnson would have torn his balls off."

Pressed by Johnson to prop up the Administration's actions in Vietnam, Senator J. William Fulbright of Arkansas, the chair of the Senate Foreign Relations Committee, set to work wrangling his colleagues immediately following the attack on the Maddox. On the Senate floor, he offered reassurance that the measure was exceedingly narrow, but it was also clear that at least some members of the Senate understood the breadth of the resolution.

MR. BREWSTER: My question is whether there is anything in the resolution which would authorize or recommend or approve the landing of large American armies in Vietnam or in China.

MR. FULBRIGHT: There is nothing in the resolution, as I read it, that contemplates it. I agree with the senator that that is the last thing we would want to do. However, the language of the resolution would not prevent it. It would authorize whatever the Commander-in-Chief feels is necessary.

On August 7th, Congress issued a joint resolution declaring its support for "the determination of the President, as Commander in Chief, to take all necessary measures to repel any armed attack against the forces of the United States and to prevent any further aggression." Johnson was delighted, remarking that the Tonkin Gulf Resolution, "like grandma's nightshirt . . . covered everything."

Fulbright came to regret both the vote and the war whose conduct it authorized. In 1967, he presided over hearings investigating American military operations in Vietnam. Johnson, furious at what he considered a betrayal, said, "You know when you're milking a cow and you have all that foamy white milk in the bucket and you're just about through, when all of a sudden the cow switches her tail through a pile of manure and slaps it into that foamy white milk? That's Bill Fulbright." In 1971, weary of the war in Vietnam, Congress repealed the Tonkin Gulf Resolution. Two years later, determined to prevent "another Vietnam," Congress jointly passed the War Powers Resolution; that measure aimed to claw back for the legislature its exclusive constitutional power to declare war, limiting the circumstances under which a president could do so to "a national emergency created by attack upon the United States, its territories or possessions, or its armed forces."

In 1964, the House voted unanimously in favor of the Tonkin Gulf Resolution, and only two senators voted against: Ernest Gruening, a Democrat and former governor of Alaska, and Wayne L. Morse, a Democrat from Oregon and a former dean of the Oregon Law School. Gruening, who trained as a doctor, spent his early career as a foreign-policy journalist, and was an editor at *The Nation*. His position regarding U.S. involvement in Vietnam dates to his opposition to the U.S. occupation of Haiti.

A so-called peace progressive of the Wilsonian era, the anti-imperialist, pro-democracy Gruening had objected to American involvement in foreign wars since the 1920s. Elected to the Senate in 1958, he had consistently warned against U.S. entry into the war in Vietnam, questioning American intelligence and calling it, in March of 1964, an "impossible war." During the debate over the Tonkin Gulf Resolution, Gruening said the "allegation that we are supporting freedom in South Vietnam has a hollow sound."

Morse's dissent is the more interesting case. Morse, a progressive Republican from Wisconsin and an avid Cold Warrior, had been elected to the Senate from Oregon but left the Republican Party in part because of its failure to denounce Joseph McCarthy and, in 1955, became a Democrat. In 1957, he objected, unsuccessfully, to a resolution that Dwight Eisenhower presented to Congress, seeking pre-authorization for military action in the Middle East, calling it "constitutionally dangerous." After the Bay of Pigs fiasco, in 1962, Morse predicted that "we are in a situation in which we shall probably never again see Congress pass a declaration of war prior to the beginning of a war." History proved him right.

Morse so frequently opposed unauthorized military action, and so often spoke at the end of the day, before an empty chamber, that he earned the nickname the Five O'Clock Shadow. In 1963, the week before John F. Kennedy was assassinated, Kennedy admitted to Morse, privately, "Wayne, I want you to know you're absolutely right in your criticism of my Vietnam policy." In the spring, when Johnson sought a military appropriation, Morse accused him of "trying by indirection to obtain congressional approval of our illegal, unilateral military action in South Vietnam without coming forward with a request for a declaration of war."

In August, Morse objected to the Tonkin Gulf Resolution on constitutional grounds, calling the resolution a "predated declaration of war," an "evasion of congressional responsibility," and a de facto amendment of the U.S. Constitution. He warned his colleagues that "the American people will quickly lose their liberty if you do not stop feeding the trend toward Government by executive supremacy." In 1965, when Johnson ordered the bombing of North Vietnam and sent fifty thousand troops to South Vietnam—"This is really war," the president said that summer—Morse became a leading speaker at rallies in the growing antiwar movement.

In 1787, the U.S. Constitution explicitly gave Congress the power to "declare war." When, at the Constitutional Convention, Pierce Butler of South Carolina raised the possibility that the president should wield this power, Elbridge Gerry of Massachusetts responded that he "never expected to hear in a republic, a motion to empower the Executive alone to declare war."

Abraham Lincoln, serving in Congress sixty years later, agreed. He said the delegates had understood the power to declare war to be "the most oppressive of all Kingly oppressions," and had therefore resolved "that no one man should hold the power of bringing this oppression upon us." If a president were to be granted this kingly power, to wage war "whenever he shall deem it necessary," Lincoln warned, "you allow him to make war at pleasure."

That later presidents did indeed engage in military action without consulting Congress, creeping in on a power reserved for the legislature, is a fact of the past century and a half of American history, including during the Trump years. Does the fact of that frequent practice alter the Constitution? This question has been a subject of heated legal dispute since the late 1960s.

Reviewing the state of the debate in 1971, the Yale legal scholar Alexander M. Bickel addressed the contention that the provision of the Constitution that grants only Congress the power to declare war had been informally amended by the executive's regular exercise of this authority. After all, as Louis Brandeis had written, the Constitution "is capable of growth." Bickel was unpersuaded. Growth there might be, he argued, but you can't extend the length of a presidential term, or abolish the Electoral College, by "growth," and neither can you grant the executive the power to declare war by force of habit. To be clear, Bickel opposed the U.S. war in Vietnam. But his argument, here, was merely the constitutional one: "No one should ever reasonably have assumed that the United States could go to war by presidential say-so."

Much ink and blood have been spilled on this question since Vietnam, especially with regard to U.S. military action in the Middle East, in Iraq, in Afghanistan, and in Iran. The debate still tends to fall into two camps. One camp sticks strictly to the claim that Congress alone has the power to declare war. The other camp argues that the President has the power, as Commander-in-Chief, to engage in military action to defend Americans in case of emergency. Both of those statements can be true and yet this can scarcely be said to be a stalemate, or even a proper separation of powers. Congress, having repeatedly failed to exercise its war power, no longer effectively can. And, as to what constitutes an emergency, the president gets to decide, allowing him, as Lincoln put it, to make war at pleasure.

This essay is an adaption of an earlier version that appeared in *The New Yorker*.

47

A Declaration for Those in Uniform

Daniel L. Nagin

War, war fighting, and war fighters are central to the Declaration of Independence. By July 4, 1776, the armed conflict between the soldiers of the Continental Army and royal troops had already been ongoing for more than a year. The Declaration of Independence set forth justifications for both the armed rebellion already well underway and, implicitly, armed rebellion in other places and times. Meanwhile, as a bill of particulars, the document contained no fewer than six references to abuses of power related to the King's armies, soldiers, and mercenaries. And, as a formal declaration, the very first power of "Free and Independent States" cited by the document was the "full Power to Levy War." For these and other reasons, the Declaration of Independence can be understood as a document particularly concerned with the martial.

Against this backdrop, the Declaration of Independence has a distinctive salience for our modern era of endless war. (As I write this, the country is not yet forty-eight hours into what is being labeled as "major combat operations" against Iran.) Yet the salience I want to draw out here most pertains to a modern battle of a different sort.

That modern battle is the battle that too many military veterans must fight with their own government. I am thinking most especially about the growing number of veterans who leave service with an unjustly imposed less than honorable discharge—whether because of the effects of combat trauma or military sexual trauma, or other stressors, traumatic brain injuries, *de jure* or *de facto* discrimination on the basis of race and ethnicity, sex, religion, and LGBTQ+ identities, or capricious decision making at the command level.

Tragically, these discharges can relegate veterans to lives on the margins, marked by higher rates of poverty, homelessness, incarceration, mental illness, and suicide. Shamed, cast aside, and deprived of supports, veterans are denied a meaningful chance to live lives of stability and dignity. In theory, an avenue exists to obtain redress. But, in a cruel twist, the tribunals responsible for providing relief from the stigma and harm of unjust discharges suffer from some of the same defects of arbitrary government action that were cataloged in the Declaration of Independence's bill of particulars.

At the end of World War II, Congress directed the Department of Defense to establish military review boards that would be duty bound to correct errors, improprieties, injustices, and inequities in discharges and records. Today, in some quantum of cases, these boards fulfill their charge as intended. However, as advocates, journalists, scholars, and federal oversight mechanisms have well demonstrated in recent years, the boards are also plagued by widespread distortions of power and responsibility—the character of which bring us back, dismayingly, to the words of the Declaration of Independence.

Among other things, the Declaration of Independence railed against a sovereign that would erect barriers to the citizenry's access to government records. "He has called together Legislative Bodies at Places unusual, uncomfortable, and distant from the Depository of their public Records, for the sole Purpose of fatiguing them into Compliance with his Measures." The military review boards do not maintain their written decisions in any kind of consistent, comprehensive, and accessible way—preventing veterans from finding support for their claims for relief.

The Declaration of Independence condemned how the sovereign's delay and inaction in the face of urgent needs left the people vulnerable to manifold harms. "He has refused for a long Time, after such Dissolutions, to cause others to be elected; whereby the Legislative Powers, incapable of Annihilation, have returned to the People at large for their exercise; the State remaining in the mean time exposed to all the Dangers of Invasion from without, and Convulsions within." The military review boards are beset by pernicious delays, often taking years to issue decisions and leaving already vulnerable veterans exposed to ongoing harms.

The Declaration of Independence inveighed against a sovereign that would install "an Arbitrary Government." At alarming rates, the military review boards deny relief, often using boilerplate language and with little, if any, evidence that the facts of the case and the arguments of the veteran informed the outcome.

The Declaration of Independence enumerated the "repeated" efforts to bring about change in the sovereign's conduct, all with unsatisfactory results and "repeated injury." Through policy directives, legislation, litigation, and other means, the military review boards have been told what they must do to reform their ways; but these instructions have produced only uneven and limited change.

The miliary review boards are not, of course, somehow modern-day King Georges. Nevertheless, we should be troubled by the extent to which the founding charter of American Independence—a document preoccupied with the martial—shines a spotlight on the way our present government fails military veterans. Even though the Declaration of Independence made no explicit mention of the new nation's duty to care for those who were taking up arms in support of the principles announced therein, the plight of soldiers and veterans was plainly front of mind for the Drafters and the others assembled in Philadelphia that spring and summer. The nation was then struggling to muster the troops necessary to carry forward the nascent rebellion and to determine in what ways it would—or even could—care for those who borne the battle.

Indeed, just two weeks before the Declaration of Independence was adopted, the Second Continental Congress established a committee "to consider what provision ought to be made for such as are wounded or disabled in the land or sea service, and report a plan for that purpose." And a little over two months later, the Second Continental Congress created the first "American" compensation system for injured and disabled veterans. But lacking funding and an effective plan for implementation, this first framework for veterans benefits never took shape and collapsed.

In these ways, the nation's founding charter speaks to the injustices being visited upon some of our most at-risk veterans today. What is more, in our current era, when the institutions and mechanisms of democracy are themselves under attack, when war has become a kind of permanent state of affairs, when the lawfulness of military orders must be scrutinized with fervor, and when a diminishing percentage of the population enters service and actually bears the burden of armed conflict—in an era such as this, the unique voice of the veterans community is as indispensable as ever. For history teaches that veterans have often been essential voices for democracy at home. Perhaps the most powerful example can be found in the pivotal role black veterans—returning home following World War II and the Korean War and at extraordinary personal peril—played as warriors for democracy in the U.S. South.

While every community member has a role to play in promoting and safeguarding democracy, our current moment requires us to recognize anew the link between how we treat *all* veterans and the preservation of democratic ideals. Yes, we have a legal and moral obligation to ensure that those who take the oath do not find themselves wrongly jettisoned by the military, that the government does not turn its back on those same veterans when they seek to restore their dignity, and that those veterans receive full membership in the circle of veterans and our wider polity. Also hanging in the balance is the democratic imperative itself, first proclaimed in the Declaration of Independence 250 years ago.

PART XIII

LEGAL REASONING IN A DEMOCRACY

In order to have a "government of laws" and not merely the raw exercise of power, law must be different from politics, which means that legal reasoning needs to be different from political reasoning. Ben Eidelson describes the "magic trick" of legal thinking as the ability to separate out issues that seems inextricable. We can value free speech, for example, even if the content of that speech does not seem good or valuable to us. Eidelson identifies this legal ability to extricate questions as indispensable to the rule of law, and he mourns the many ways that it is being openly abandoned across the political spectrum. Stephen Sachs takes on the debate over whether laws written centuries ago should still govern our modern polity. He points out that by its nature, "law is an imposition of past rules. At least until we devise time machines . . . a new law can have its effects only in the future." The Founders' law is therefore not the dreaded "Dead Hand of the Past," he argues, but part of an ongoing living practice—relying on old laws even as we pass new ones. And he muses that with all their flaws, the Founders "built better than they knew: the words of slave owners like Jefferson would be invoked for the abolition of slavery; the political freedoms defined by men would be deployed to campaign for women's suffrage."

Form and process are also constitutive aspects of legal reasoning. John Goldberg notes that the Declaration was a kind of legal complaint, and he celebrates the powerful role that the formal complaint can play in a democracy, giving voice to individual grievances and rights' violations. He maintains that this empowering role is even more vital in the rationalized, mass anonymity of modern society. Charles Nesson celebrates the legal interpretive power of the jury to acquit against the evidence, even when the letter of the law has technically been satisfied. Nesson describes the jury's legal authority as a vital check on governmental power, and he argues that it has been stolen by modern doctrines that assert, incorrectly, that the jury has no discretion to ignore laws it deems unjust. Intisar Rabb traces another tradition of legal reasoning—Islamic law—and its presence throughout American legal history: from petitions filed in Arabic by enslaved people seeking their freedom, to the powerful role played by Black Muslims in the civil rights movement. She urges us to keep engaging with these religious and legal precepts of liberty and justice as we grapple with the modern persistence of racial inequality. And finally, Scott Brewer offers a unique philosophical rumination on the impossibility of apolitical law. Juxtaposing quotes from Frederick Douglass to Nietzsche, he invites us to rethink how we read legal texts. He ends by sharing the famous line from Joseph Heller's novel *Catch-22* that captures the tense relationship between law and power: "Catch-22 says they have a right to do anything we can't stop them from doing."

48

THE "LEGAL MIND" AS CULTURAL ACHIEVEMENT

BENJAMIN EIDELSON

"If you can think about a thing that is inextricably attached to something else, without thinking of the thing which it is attached to, then you have a legal mind." So said Thomas Reed Powell, a well-known constitutional scholar (and Harvard professor) a century ago. Powell was calling attention to the fundamental strangeness, even obtuseness, of much legal reasoning. And yet he put his finger on something indispensable to legal education, to effective lawyering, and, I think, to the vague ideal of "the rule of law."

When we use our legal minds, in Powell's sense, we don blinders—training our vision on certain things by blocking out others. It is not so different from when a professor blind-grades exams or when an orchestra auditions musicians from behind a screen. In those cases, though, the "things" in question (say, how a violinist sounds and how they look) are easy to prise apart. What makes Powell's formulation arresting is the thought that, with practice, we might learn to do something similar even when the things in question are "inextricably attached."

Now, if that sounds like a magic trick—extricating the inextricable—that was probably Powell's point. Even so, we can demystify and redeem the idea by tweaking it to say that "a legal mind" is one for which much that might have seemed inextricable proves, upon reflection, not to be. When we "think like a lawyer," that is, we can perform feats like separating the value of speech from its truth—making it so that insights and errors are, for First Amendment purposes, indistinguishable. We can say that nobody should be disfavored for their religion, even as we insist that nobody's treatment of others should be insulated from scrutiny just for being grounded in their faith. We can maintain that the rules for elections should be fair, because this is good for society, and yet that the fairness of an election procedure does not depend on whether the candidates whom it tends to help are good for society. And we can hold that prosecutors' decisions should be insulated from politics even as we know that sometimes those same decisions have political implications of immense significance.

This capacity for nuance and restraint is a key part of what we are now seeing dismantled—not incrementally or under cover of darkness, but with abandon. When a giant banner of Donald Trump hangs on the side of federal agency headquarters throughout Washington, DC, that is less an assault on any particular norm than on the very idea of norms—of role-specific expectations and obligations that define institutions, and give them integrity, by circumscribing the considerations that matter for them in particular. In this vision, there is no separation between the person of the President and the government of the United States, just as there is no distinction between a licit consideration and an illicit one or between a policy's legality and its merits. Rather than donning blinders, everyone is supposed to see their work through the prism of its repercussions for the President and his conception of the greater good (which may come to the same thing).

And while there is no equivalence between this attack on American institutions and the resistance it has engendered, a great danger of this period, in my view, is that the new contempt for boundaries and role morality will take root and spread. That contempt may not look like Trump's all-caps charges of disloyalty against the Justices who struck down his tariffs, but it will build on the crude absolutism and scorecard mentality that he has made inescapable. Something like this is already discernible in the resurgence of "moral clarity"—invariably understood as willingness to take categorical stands on all sorts of questions—as a measure of leadership, as if being clear-eyed could not lead one to see contextual distinctions or cause for restraint.

One reason this shift represents a loss is that a person's ability to speak their legal mind, as it were, depends on their faith that other people will hear them as doing so. You might think it important to explain why vitriolic anti-Israel protests are lawful, for instance, but not want to opine on whether those same protests are admirable or pernicious. As feats of mental extrication go, that one is not very difficult. But your ability to say one thing without saying another depends less on how *you* think than on how other people do. Indeed, if you know that your audience will hear both A and B when you say "A," then to go ahead and say "A" pretty much *is* to say "B," too. Sometimes you can adapt by saying "A" and taking pains to disclaim "B" (that is what I did at the start of the last paragraph). But that tends to gum up the communicative works. And you won't really have avoided signaling a stance toward "B" anyway; you'll be seen, rightly, as deliberately distancing yourself from it.

If others' attitudes toward nuance and boundaries shape our opportunities for expression, something similar is true about our very capacities to think and act with integrity. Judge Richard Posner once observed that judges tend to decide cases on their legal merits for "the same reason that many people do not cheat at games even when they are sure they can get away with cheating." "The pleasure of judging is bound up with compliance with certain self-limiting rules that define the 'game' of judging," he explained, "and judges for the most part are people who want to be—judges." But that was thirty years ago. What happens when enough of the players and onlookers assume that most of the players cheat? When someone volunteers to serve as a "judge" against that backdrop, what game should we think they are signing up to play? Even for a traditionalist who would prefer to play the old game, the pure satisfaction of that role is surely much diminished—and so less likely to counterbalance the pressure toward delivering a preferred result—when one is left to play that game alone and without the prospect of recognition for playing it well.

All of this is to say that the capacity for granularity that characterizes a "legal mind" is not really an internal feature of individual minds; it is a cultural achievement.

By the same token, the erosion of this culture affects us in ways that go beyond weakening institutional norms and role morality. It is the same facility with extrication, after all, that makes it possible for us to admire a friend's courage in advancing a moral outlook that we find strange and wrong, or to recognize a concern as sincere and understandable but misplaced. Not coincidentally, a legal mind is more likely to be an open one too—better able to isolate and extricate the kernel of truth in an aversive idea, and better able to envision taking that element on board without worrying overmuch that it will taint or destabilize everything else.

As with any culture, people have sustained this one by conducting themselves publicly in a manner that manifests the value that they place on it. But as with any culture, that demonstration works best when it is a happy side effect of something automatic, not a self-conscious display. Someone who is seen to be making a bid for recognition as above the political fray will also be seen, fairly, as doing something awfully like politics. Like other cultures, in other words, the "legal mind" thrives when it does not need to make the case for itself and may be in trouble as soon as it does.

49

The Living Hand

Stephen E. Sachs

Celebrating the Founders' achievements, 250 years on, is broadly welcomed today. But letting their choices govern us—as our legal system claims they do—is rather less so. The American Revolutionaries rebelled against an established order; the Constitution they adopted a decade later was a break from tradition too. So why should we, today, be bound by their decisions? If they thought "the earth belongs in usufruct to the living," why should today's majorities hold our powers of self-government in entail? And why should the choices of an eighteenth-century elite, a group of rich white men who paired a theory of natural rights with a practice of human slavery, still dominate the diverse, egalitarian country we've become? Thus the dreaded "Dead Hand of the Past": the claim that eighteenth-century Americans, and the laws they wrote, have no authority to govern us today.

Yet the Dead Hand of the Past can't govern us, not really. *We do this to ourselves*, and for good reason too. We use the Founders' law because it's the only one we have; because it's tolerably democratic and just; and because we, today, have enough in common with each other that we can look past our differences with the past.

The core mistake of the Dead Hand is that law *is* an imposition of past rules. "At least until we devise time machines," the D.C. Circuit has explained, a new law "can have its effects only in the future." Imagine legislators voting on a bill this afternoon: their decision, *today*, makes no difference unless it still binds people *tomorrow*, in whose eyes it will already be *yesterday*'s rule. That's what James Madison meant by "parchment barriers": The parchment can't reach out and shake you until you comply. Only living people can do that—and as Judge Easterbrook once put it, "We the living" enforce old laws so that *our* legislatures can make new ones.

So the law's hand is always a living one, because only living people can apply it. And our living law happens to answer a great many questions (who elects the president? how many houses of Congress are there? who gets to appoint judges or remove them?) the way they were answered back then. People today can always pick new answers, but since we don't all agree on those answers—which we don't!—we have a rule to keep using the ones we have. Besides, the People can't speak for themselves, and everyone who might claim to speak for them (presidents, Congress, judges, state governors) was chosen for jobs with existing powers under existing law, not as Tribunes of the People empowered to remake the law. And if we *were* electing unconstrained Tribunes of the People, who could accept the risk that the other side might win? Limited powers are the price we pay for democratic stability, with the promise that if you lose one election, you'll still be around to contest the next one.

But why should these democratic majorities accept rules that majorities can't change? This isn't a question of law so much as democratic theory—and nothing in democratic theory tells you when a national majority should get to outvote a majority in Montana or in Massachusetts (on inheritance law? on the governor?), any more than a U.S. majority can be outvoted by a majority across the Western Hemisphere or across all nations beginning with "U." Like the European Union, the United States—whether under the Continental Congress, the Confederation, or the Constitution—has always been a complex polity, "neither wholly federal, nor wholly national," with neither feature more democratic than the other. The usual bugbears of the Dead Hand (the Senate, the Electoral College, enumerated powers, Article V) are really just reflections of federalism, and of our complex rather than consolidated government.

In fact, our legal system is more democratic than it seems. A bare majority in each state and congressional district might be enough for a constitutional amendment to sail through; Article V isn't a *supermajority* requirement so much as a geographic *distribution* requirement. And the states would never have joined together if an *un*distributed majority could have changed the deal as soon as they did—and that's a democratic decision too.

Nor do the democratic failures of the Founding make our system meaningfully less democratic today. Japan is a democracy, though

America imposed on it a constitution after World War II; what matters is whether that constitution allows for self-government now, not whether it reflected true democracy then. And while the democratic failures of the Founding were deep, no one knows which way they cut. To assign a broader meaning to the Commerce Clause, say, because only propertied white males ratified it is to reverse the counterfactual; if anything, the excluded women and less-propertied white men who couldn't vote would likely have favored *less* federal power than the merchants, professionals, and elite landowners who could. The same flawed ratification process we used for the parts of the Constitution you don't like was also used for the parts you do (say, Article III); throwing some out informally and piecemeal would make our system less democratic, not more so.

But why, in the end, should we obey—or even feel any kinship with—a generation of Founders we *know* were morally flawed? Part of the answer is that we don't follow their rules for their personal virtue: The legal status of the Telecommunications Act of 1996 doesn't turn on the virtues of Bill Clinton or Newt Gingrich. Part of the answer, too, is that they built better than they knew: The words of slave owners like Jefferson would be invoked for the abolition of slavery; the political freedoms defined by men would be deployed to campaign for women's suffrage; and the system built by a narrow propertied elite would come to offer unknown and unexpected millions a hope for a better life.

And part of the answer, too, is to consider *our* hope for such kinship regardless of our own virtues. You don't have to think our generation's own flaws, whatever they may be (whether inequality or fossil-fuel use or abortion or irreligion or meat-eating or what have you), nearly as awful as American slavery to imagine future generations, with different priorities, rejecting kinship with us because of them. But we may still feel a sense of kinship with *them*, our own descendants and posterity, for whom we seek to build a better world. We should see in the Founding generation not some alien people distant from ourselves, but our political ancestors, sharing with us a commitment—however halting—that all men are created equal, endowed with inalienable rights, which governments are instituted to secure. And if we still rely on that government today, two and a half centuries later, a little celebration is hardly out of place.

50

TOM, MEET MAX

JOHN C.P. GOLDBERG

It is not hard to detect Thomas Jefferson's legal training in the Declaration of Independence. As Gary Wills once noted, Jefferson would later refer to it as an "appeal"—what lawyers today would call a complaint. Hence, its somewhat hyperbolic allegations of unlawful conduct and injury, as well as its demand for a form of legal relief—namely, the bestowal by other countries of the recognition that, under international law, would confer nationhood on the colonists.

Commonplace in everyday life, complaints warrant ambivalence. My mother was fond of mailing hand-written grievances to companies whose products fell short of her expectations. (This usually earned her a prefabricated apology and sometimes a coupon.) "Admirable," I thought at the time. It's good to stand up for oneself. But a little cringey, too. It's possible some mountains were being made of molehills.

Within the genus of complaints, legal complaints are a distinctive species. They are part of a system that enables individuals and entities to vindicate important rights and interests. As such, they promise to hold us accountable to each other, and government officials accountable to the persons they purport to serve. Like non-legal complaints, however, they are sometimes unfounded or better left unpursued. Also, to a much greater extent than grumpy missives, they can make life difficult for their recipients (not to mention the complainants themselves). This is why we have rules that specify appropriate grounds for complaints and that govern how they are made and resolved.

Jefferson's "complaint" itself garnered an ambivalent reception. It was celebrated—and still is—as a bold assertion of the rights of the individual against government. It was also dismissed by some as frivolous litigation (so to speak). And it was called out for its morally mistaken assumptions about who among us are endowed with unalienable rights.

250 years later, legal complaints carry a potential significance they could not have in the Revolutionary era. For we are now well on the other side of the crucible that Max Weber sought to capture under the heading *rationalisierung*—"rationalization." My basic contention is that, in our rationalized world, complaints offer a distinctively valuable mode of asserting individual voice and value.

Here's a crude rendering of Weber's thesis. Life has been scaled up: We are a mass society. Narrow means-ends rationality pushes aggressively into all domains (including, most relevantly for this audience, education and the professions). Impersonal, bureaucratic and legalistic modes of interaction crowd out the informal and spontaneous. What started as a quest for salvation through hard work and self-discipline has taken on a life of its own, "disenchanting" the world by crowding out "non-rational" modes of interaction, eroding small communities and traditional values, and leaving many to lead diminished lives as glorified cogs in vast machines that operate apart from any broadly shared sense of overarching purpose or value. Harvard sociologist Talcott Parsons, serving as translator, memorably had Weber describing us as trapped in an "iron cage." But Parsons was himself engaging in a bit of hyperbole. Weber's vibe was more stoical than melodramatic or tragic. He offered his diagnosis in the thought that it might help individuals live as responsibly as one can live in a world of irreducible value-conflict and inevitable compromise.

One needn't endorse all the different aspects of Weber's complex diagnosis to grant that it captures legitimate concerns about the place of the individual in mass society. In doing so, it also implicitly identifies why, in such circumstances, there is value in having loci of individual empowerment. Yet, although the development of modern legal systems figured prominently in his work, so far as I am aware, Weber didn't have much to say about the place of civil litigation in a routinized world. Through the invocation of yet another historical figure, we can nonetheless imagine how he might have.

Enter Roscoe Pound. As John Fabian Witt has recounted, in the 1950s, with careful cultivation by leading plaintiffs' lawyers (including the colorful Marvin Belli, the "King of Torts") Pound flipped his own script. An early champion of the administrative state as a superior alternative to the vagaries of the common law, Pound—then in his 80s and preoccupied, like many others, with the specter of Communism—began proselytizing for the traditional common law's decentralized, complaint-driven apparatus as central to the preservation of liberty.

Pound made a case for complaints in the argot of a Cold Warrior. But it doesn't take a sharp turn of the wheel to redirect his analysis to address potential problems within an advanced liberal-capitalist state such as our own. Weber saw ours as a depersonalized, anonymized world; one in which, to paraphrase *Casablanca*, the problems of the ordinary person don't amount to a hill of beans. If there is something to this contention, a system for complaints, by enabling individuals to assert themselves and vindicate their interests, might serve as a bit of a check and balance.

Whether this promise is realized will depend on whether such a system distinguishes valid from frivolous complaints, and whether it operates with rules that provide both broad access and efficient and fair resolutions. If not, it will offer little more than occasions for random, spasmodic bits of self-assertion. Again, this is why, in a liberal-democratic government, complaints must be governed by substantive, procedural, and remedial law that both empower and restrain.

It is also important to appreciate that complaint systems themselves, no less than other modern institutions, are subject to rationalization. The bureaucratization of civil litigation—think of thousands of claims being resolved through lawyer-created settlement grids barely influenced by client input, or claims being commodified through certain kinds of litigation finance—is by now a familiar phenomenon. So too is the displacement of litigation not only by bureaucratic regulation but by its absence, which is sometimes construed (under the doctrine of preemption) as precluding litigation in domains of potential regulation. Subsumption and displacement of this kind are not inevitable, however. They are the result of, and thus can still be affected by, the design and application of the rules for adjudicating complaints.

To the extent we today live in Weber's world, we have good reason, 250 years later, to recall the power of Jefferson's complaint.

51

PALLADIUM OF LIBERTY: CONSCIENTIOUS ACQUITTAL AND THE RESTORATION OF THE AMERICAN JURY

CHARLES R. NESSON

Our Founders fought a revolution for liberty. In the Declaration of Independence they "pledged our lives, our fortunes, and our sacred honor" to secure it. When We the People later drafted and ratified our Constitution, our overwhelming concern was the protection of that liberty. We adopted a governmental structure of separated powers, checks and balances, designed to prevent the concentration of unchecked power that might threaten it.

Of all the checks on power, none was more important than trial by jury in prosecutions in which the state claimed the right to take a person's liberty away. Alexander Hamilton captured this shared understanding in *Federalist 83*:

> The friends and adversaries of the plan of the convention, if they agree in nothing else, concur at least in the value they set upon the trial by jury; or if there is any difference between them it consists in this: the former regard it as a valuable safeguard to liberty; the latter represent it as the very palladium of free government.

This was the substance of our liberty, secured through and against the procedural power of the state. The state could not take the liberty of one of us away, even by proving a statutory violation, unless a unanimous jury agreed. This was not only a protection for a defendant but a right of the people built into the architecture of our government. As Thomas Jefferson would later put it, "I consider trial by jury as the only anchor ever yet imagined by man, by which a government can be held to the principles of its constitution."

The concept of the Palladium was, for the Founding generation, more than a graceful classical allusion; it was a precise architectural claim about the survival of the republic. In the ancient world, the Palladium was the sacred statue of Pallas Athena, a celestial anchor believed to render the city of Troy impregnable so long as it remained within the citadel. To describe the jury as the "Palladium of Liberty" was to identify it as the indispensable talisman of the American constitutional order—the "sacred anchor" that tethered the abstract power of the State to the living moral conscience of the People. The fall of Troy began not with the breach of its walls, but with the secret theft of the statue from its heights.

For the American jury, the theft of our palladium of liberty was perpetrated by our Supreme Court in *Sparf v. United States* (1895). Before *Sparf*, the jury's exercise of conscientious acquittal was understood not as a subversion of the rule of law, but as its ultimate moral validation.

The *Sparf* decision created a profound imbalance. By reducing the jury to a mere fact-finding instrument, the Court granted the prosecutor and judge a monopoly over liberty, unencumbered by the community's sense of right and wrong. This departure from our constitutional design has had grave, wide-ranging consequences, transforming the trial (and the plea-bargaining by which the prosecution avoids trial) into a lopsided exercise of state power. Yet a jury's judgment of conscience is not a violation of the "Rule of Law"; it is its completion. It ensures that the law remains a reflection of the people's consent rather than a tool of executive vengeance.

Sparf substituted in its place a system sustained by deception. In the modern courtroom, a judge delivers a solemn instruction: "As your moral obligation under the oath you have taken, you must apply the law as I give it to you." Both the judge and the legal establishment know this is only part of the truth. They know the jury possesses an unreviewable power to acquit against the evidence. Yet that power is suppressed, spoken of only to be denigrated and dismissed as "jury nullification." What once stood at the center of our constitutional design is now treated as unauthorized misbehavior by a judiciary that has stolen the palladium of our liberty. As a result we have lost a critical check upon the power of the prosecutor, and destabilized our constitutionally crafted system of checks and balances.

The conflict did not originate with *Sparf*. Rather, the events that led to its unhappy result were precipitated by the partisan clash between

Federalists and Republicans over the Sedition Act of 1798. Battle was fought over whether the jury possessed the power to determine questions of law against the instructions of the court. Federalist judges of the era asserted their exclusive authority to declare the Sedition Act constitutional, while Jeffersonian defense lawyers argued that the jury could decide the law was unconstitutional regardless of what the trial judge said.

By framing the jury's power as a right to "declare the law unconstitutional," the Jeffersonian lawyers accidentally walked into a trap. They claimed for the jury a "legislative" or "supreme court" power that the jury was never designed to have. This allowed Federalist judges (and eventually the *Sparf* Court) to frame the issue as a choice between "The Rule of Law" and "Anarchy."

In retrospect, this was a false issue, misframed in a way that obscured the jury's true substantive role in judging justice. The jury is not, and never was, a body designed to legislate or to strike down statutes. Its power to acquit is limited to the single case at hand and to be voiced only through the words "not guilty." Its reach extends only to the defendant before it. An acquittal has no precedential consequence; the statute remains in full legal force.

Properly understood, the judge's role is to say what the law is and whether the proof is sufficient; the jury's role should have been understood as deciding only, and ultimately, whether depriving the defendant of his liberty in the specific instance before it would serve the ends of justice.

When the Supreme Court addressed the issue in *Sparf*, it accepted this historical misframing. In affirming the judge's role of declaring the law, the Court swept aside (and under the rug) the jury's justice function without paying any heed to the original constitutional understanding. Instead, the Court performed a rhetorical sleight: The moral responsibility that great judges of the past—like Marshall and Story—had urged upon juries to act to prevent wrongful convictions was transformed into a command to the jury that, if the letter of the law and the facts appeared to match, its sole responsibility was to *convict*. The shield was turned into a sword.

Restoration requires that the jury be explicitly informed of its duty to decide two distinct issues in reaching a verdict:

1. Has the government proved beyond a reasonable doubt that the defendant committed the acts alleged in the indictment?
2. Is taking the defendant's liberty a just application of the law in this case?

The second question provides the formal mechanism for conscientious acquittal. It allows the community to say 'No' to the State, not by ignoring the law, but by honoring a higher principle of justice. Returning the jury to this central role is the critical first step to righting the balance of power, reestablishing the jury as a respected representative of the people and a visible, accountable branch of government. This shift moves the jury's power to acquit out of the shadows of what is pejoratively labeled 'nullification' and into the light of conscientious acquittal as a recognized constitutional duty. It ensures that the power to condemn is legitimate only when it is twice-blessed: once by the Law of the Bench and once by the Conscience of the People. By returning this judgment to the jury, we strengthen the Rule of Law by grounding it, as the Founders intended, in Rule by the People.

52

ANTEBELLUM SHARĪʿA, CIVIL RIGHTS SHARĪʿA, AND AMERICAN FREEDOM

INTISAR A. RABB

In 1776, as the United States declared independence in the name of freedom, a young boy in Senegambia was preparing to pursue a twenty-five-year education in Islamic scripture and law (sharīʿa). That boy, Omar ibn Said, would be enslaved decades later—where, in 1809 he became the "talk of the town" for writing fluent Arabic on the walls of a Fayetteville, NC jail cell. His story invites a reconsideration of American legal history: What if sharīʿa—present from the nation's beginning—had been legible to the nation's founding debates about freedom? And what does it mean for the American experiment that it is now?

Although largely forgotten, there was once an "antebellum sharīʿa." Enslaved people petitioned for freedom in Arabic, invoking religious precepts of liberty and challenging the morality of slavery. Thomas Jefferson himself received at least two such petitions from fugitives who were likely transported across the Middle Passage on the same vessel as Omar, in 1807. At that time, the petitioners' legal-moral framework was suppressed and largely disregarded. But it found new life over one hundred years later in a "civil rights sharīʿa"—a reemergent and influential force in the twentieth century that demanded lawmakers make good on American promises of freedom and fairness. And it offers insight into the current assault on fundamental rights and freedoms—as we struggle to better define and enact the requirements of justice in America today.

I.   ANTEBELLUM SHARĪʿA: DISPLAY AND DISMISSAL

Omar ibn Said was no ordinary enslaved person. Before his capture at age thirty-seven, he had spent decades studying Qur'anic interpretation,

Mālikī legal jurisprudence, and related disciplines. His training was in Futa Toro under the rule of Almaami Abdul Kader Kane (r. 1776–1807), a scholar-ruler who came to power promising abolition and who used sharī'a to argue against the enslavement of Muslims. For Omar, sharī'a was not abstract theology but a lived moral and legal system oriented toward freedom and justice. Yet when Omar arrived in the United States, that moral framework, once situated in the American slaveholding South, was decidedly excluded from any meaningful debates about freedom or justice.

Omar's Arabic writings on the jail walls drew fascination from local leaders. James Owen, a plantation owner and future congressman, posted bond to take Omar home while ostensibly searching for the runaway's owner. James and his brother John used Omar as an exotic prop, both displaying and dismissing the man they proceeded to hold as property. John Owen encouraged Omar to document his life story even though, once Owen became governor, he helped pass laws criminalizing teaching enslaved people to read or write. The brothers made Omar write in Arabic before gatherings of the legal elite. Rather than exhibit him for physical prowess, as happened with other enslaved Africans, the Owens brothers ironically valued Omar for his intellect, recognizing in his literacy and genteel bearing a man they believed could advance their cause. Together, they promoted a public narrative of Omar as a "grateful slave" who had converted to Christianity and preferred to remain on the plantation. Omar's writings indicated otherwise.

In 1819, Omar wrote a letter in Arabic (his English being extremely limited) to the Owens brothers petitioning for his freedom and return home. Drawing on his scholarly training, the letter uses religious rhetoric— shared between Muslims and Christians—to suggest that only God holds true ownership over men, and to question the morality of his enslavement. Seeking a translation, Omar conveyed the letter to the state's first chief justice, John Louis Taylor, who passed it on to American anthem author Francis Scott Key—both lawyers from the Owens brothers' circles. These men had their own motivations: They hoped that Omar's high level of academic training and "good breeding" could make him a bona fide convert to Christianity and perhaps a valuable representative for their cause as members of the American Colonization Society, which opposed abolition of slavery and promoted the return of free Blacks to Liberia. Key passed the letter on to Professor Moses Stuart at Andover Theological Seminary in Massachusetts (now part of Yale University), who professed to know Arabic and co-founded the American Oriental Society for the study of the languages and civilizations of Asia and the Islamic world. Stuart, however, was unable to read the letter. He instead gave it to the library, where it languished unread for over a century.

The problem was not merely linguistic. It was legal and epistemic. Sharīʿa, as Omar articulated it, was illegible and insidious to proponents of American slavery. To engage it would have required recognizing an enslaved Black man as a legal thinker and scholar whose claims to freedom were grounded in a coherent moral or legal tradition.

To be sure, the legal elite—from Thomas Jefferson to the Owens brothers—could well have found Arabic translators if so motivated to engage. After all, in 1786, Jefferson and his representatives had successfully negotiated with Arabic-speaking envoys for Moroccan recognition of the United States (though unsuccessfully to avoid tariffs in exchange for safe passage of American ships through the Strait of Gibraltar—second only to the Strait of Hormuz for maritime trade and geopolitical power). Further, he had familiarized himself enough with Islam to argue (along with James Madison in *Federalist 10*) for an expansive notion of religious freedom that included the "Mahometans."

Yet that same legal elite chose not to engage enslaved Muslims' petitions for freedom. Instead, antebellum sharīʿa was a dead end: a sophisticated legal tradition embodied in multiple petitions for freedom present within the United States at the Founding but excluded from its legal discourse.

Omar died still enslaved in 1863, six months after the Emancipation Proclamation.

II. CIVIL RIGHTS SHARĪʿA: ENGAGEMENT AND EVOLUTION

A century later, the descendants—both literal and spiritual—of figures like Omar (estimates place the population of enslaved Muslims at 10–30 percent reintroduced Islamic views of freedom and justice into American legal and political discourse. No longer confined to Arabic texts, Black Muslims now articulated a "civil rights sharīʿa."

Two figures exemplify this shift.

Malcolm X reframed racial injustice as a civil rights and human rights challenge, grounded in a moral vision shaped by Islamic thought. Repeating the Muslim refrain drawn from the Qur'ān (2:191, 217), that "oppression is worse than slaughter," he challenged prevailing assumptions about policing and prisons, promoted equity and economic self-reliance over integration, and more. His influential work sometimes extended into the courts. In *SaMarion v. McGinnis* (1966), Malcolm successfully argued to a lower federal court in New York that Muslim prisoners at Attica retain religious rights. (Two years prior, in *Cooper v. Pate* (1964), a landmark Supreme Court decision had significantly expanded prisoners' rights, allowing challenges to violations of religious freedom and other constitutional rights, after a Muslim inmate in Illinois petitioned for his ability to freely practice his faith.) By considering the Muslims' arguments, the courts engaged Islamic claims on their own terms as they coincided with American values, and thus expanded rights for all prisoners.

Muhammad Ali famously transformed legal doctrine as well, at great cost to his boxing career at its height. His refusal to be drafted into the Vietnam War, given his Islamic sense of morality and justice, led to *Clay v. United States* (1971), in which the Supreme Court expanded the definition of conscientious objection to include nontraditional religious beliefs. Through eventually (and narrowly) engaging Muhammad Ali's claims, the Court strengthened protections for religious freedom and dissent for all Americans.

Together, these figures did what Omar could not: they made sharī'a-informed claims legible within American law and public discourse. Taken seriously, they and the courts reshaped the legal landscape by motivating engagement with and ultimately expanding understandings of both Islamic moral reasoning and American constitutional principles, for the better.

III. AMERICAN FREEDOM TOOLS: MINORITY PERSPECTIVES ON RIGHTS AND JUSTICE

Americans have long grappled with a history of racial subordination rooted in slavery and its aftermath. Throughout that history, sharī'a has served many—particularly as articulated by Black Muslims—as a moral framework for resisting oppression and advancing claims to freedom and dignity. (Of course, many others—particularly waves of immigrants from the Muslim world after the Immigration and Nationality Act of 1965 lifted racial and national origins quotas favoring Europeans, and after politicians ostensibly responded to violence at home and abroad— would recast sharī'a and "American Muslim" as connected to questions of immigration, national security, and distant homelands.) Throughout that history, too, the role of American sharī'a has been uneven: Antebellum sharī'a was dismissed from legal and moral discourse while civil rights sharī'a (although not often featured in civil rights histories) helped advance law and discourse about the requirements of justice. The lesson is that America loses when we ignore such perspectives, and gains when we engage.

Today marks a third phase. Despite important gains since the Founding, we grapple with continuing inequalities along racial justice lines. American descendants of slavery are at or near the bottom of nearly every metric of social wellbeing, according to official data from the U.S. Census, the Federal Reserve, the CDC, and the National Center for Education Statistics: the lowest median household income and wealth, highest poverty and unemployment rates, lowest home ownership rates, second-lowest college degree rates, and highest incarceration rates. If we are to address these tragic failures, the American experiment must continuously expand understandings of and engagement with sophisticated perspectives on freedom and justice, civil rights sharī'a arguments included. Those committed to meaningful scholarship, law, and policy to that end will need to equip themselves with a wide array of tools to do so. At a moment in history when such engagement is more necessary than ever, the difference between the two approaches to sharī'a is the difference between repeating the past and learning from it.

FOR FURTHER READING

Much of Omar's history and writings, interpreted here through a legal lens, come from Mbaye Lo and Carl W. Ernst, *I Cannot Write My Life: Islam, Arabic, and Slavery in Omar Ibn Said's America* (Chapel Hill: University of

North Carolina Press, 2023); his life story was popularized by Rhiannon Giddens, who co-wrote the 2023 Pulitzer Prize-winning opera *Omar* with composer Michael Abels. For further reading on histories of Muslims in early America, see Jeffrey Einboden, *Jefferson's Muslim Fugitives: The Lost Story of Enslaved Africans, Their Arabic Letters, and an American President* (Oxford: Oxford University Press, 2020); Denise A. Spellberg, *Thomas Jefferson's Qur'an: Islam and the Founders* (New York: Knopf, 2013); Ala Alryyes, *A Muslim American Slave: The Life of Omar Ibn Said* (Madison: University of Wisconsin Press, 2011); Michael A. Gomez, *Black Crescent: The Experience and Legacy of African Muslims in the Americas* (Cambridge: Cambridge University Press, 2005); John O. Hunwick, "I Wish to be Seen in Our Land Called Āfrikā: ʿUmar b. Sayyid's Appeal to be Released from Slavery (1819)," *Journal of American and Islamic Studies* 5 (2003–2004): 62–77; Sylviane Diouf, *Servants of Allah: African Muslims Enslaved in the Americas* (New York: New York University Press, 1998); Allan D. Austin, *African Muslims in Antebellum America: A Sourcebook* (New York: Garland Publishing, 1984).

53

REAL LEGAL NIHILISM

SCOTT BREWER

In the endarkening and spreading umbra of rule by unargued judicial proclamation, in hot wars, in cold ICE[1]: power demands everything, without concession.[2]

". . . all that means, let us dare to grasp it, *a will to nothingness*, an aversion to life, a rebellion against the most fundamental prerequisites of life, but it is and remains *a will*! . . . And, to conclude by saying what I said at the beginning: man still prefers to *will nothingness*, than *not* will . . ."[3]

Nowhere is now here.[4]

NOTES

1. *See, e.g., Dep't of Homeland Sec. v. D.V.D.*, No. 24A1153 (U.S. June 23, 2025) (6–3 unsigned order with no merits briefing or oral argument staying—in effect overruling—federal district court order). Sotomayor, J., dissenting, joined by Kagan & Jackson, JJ.:

> In matters of life and death, it is best to proceed with caution. In this case, the Government took the opposite approach. It wrongfully deported one plaintiff to Guatemala, even though an Immigration Judge found he was likely to face torture there. Then, in clear violation of a court order, it deported six more to South Sudan, a nation the State Department considers too unsafe for all but its most critical personnel. An attentive District Court's timely intervention only narrowly prevented a third set of unlawful removals to Libya. Rather than allowing our lower court colleagues to manage this high-stakes litigation with the care and attention it plainly requires, this Court now intervenes to grant the Government emergency relief from an order it has repeatedly defied. I cannot join so gross an abuse of the Court's equitable discretion. . . . The Due Process Clause represents "the principle that ours is a government of laws, not of men, and that we submit ourselves to rulers only if under rules." *Youngstown Sheet & Tube Co. v. Sawyer, 343 U. S. 579, 646 (1952)* (Jackson, J., concurring). By rewarding lawlessness, the Court once again undermines that foundational principle. Apparently, the

Court finds the idea that thousands will suffer violence in farflung locales more palatable than the remote possibility that a District Court exceeded its remedial powers when it ordered the Government to provide notice and process to which the plaintiffs are constitutionally and statutorily entitled. That use of discretion is as incomprehensible as it is inexcusable. Respectfully, but regretfully, I dissent.

See also McMahon v. New York, No. 24A1203 (U.S. July 14, 2025) (6–3 unsigned order with no merits briefing or oral argument, staying—in effect overruling—federal district court order). Sotomayor, J., dissenting, joined by Kagan & Jackson, JJ.:

> This case arises out of the President's unilateral efforts to eliminate a Cabinet-level agency established by Congress nearly half a century ago: the Department of Education. As Congress mandated, the Department plays a vital role in this Nation's education system, safeguarding equal access to learning and channeling billions of dollars to schools and students across the country each year. Only Congress has the power to abolish the Department. The Executive's task, by contrast, is to "take Care that the Laws be faithfully executed." U. S. Const., Art. II, §3. Yet, by executive fiat, the President ordered the Secretary of Education to "take all necessary steps to facilitate the closure of the Department." Exec. Order No. 14242, 90 Fed. Reg. 13679 (2025). Consistent with that Executive Order, Secretary Linda McMahon gutted the Department's work force, firing over 50 percent of its staff overnight. In her own words, that mass termination served as "the first step on the road to a total shutdown" of the Department. Dept. of Ed., Press Release (Mar. 11, 2025); *infra*, at 7. When the Executive publicly announces its intent to break the law, and then executes on that promise, it is the Judiciary's duty to check that lawlessness, not expedite it. Two lower courts rose to the occasion, preliminarily enjoining the mass firings while the litigation remains ongoing. Rather than maintain the status quo, however, this Court now intervenes, lifting the injunction and permitting the Government to proceed with dismantling the Department. That decision is indefensible. It hands the Executive the power to repeal statutes by firing all those necessary to carry them out. The majority is either willfully blind to the implications of its ruling or naive, but either way the threat to our Constitution's separation of powers is grave. Unable to join in this misuse of our emergency docket, I respectfully dissent.

2. *Compare* Frederick Douglass, *Address on West India Emancipation* (Aug. 3, 1857) ("Power concedes nothing without a demand. It never did and it never will."). *See also* Joseph Heller, *Catch-22*, pp. 374–75 (1994) (1955):

> "There must have been a reason," Yossarian persisted, pounding his fist into his hand. "They couldn't just barge in here and chase everyone out."
>
> "No reason," wailed the old woman. "No reason."
>
> "What right did they have?"
>
> "Catch-22."
>
> "*What?*" Yossarian froze in his tracks with fear and alarm and felt his whole body begin to tingle. "*What did you say?*"
>
> "Catch-22," the old woman repeated, rocking her head up and down. "Catch-22. Catch-22 says they have a right to do anything we can't stop them from doing."
>
> "What the hell are you talking about?" Yossarian shouted at her in bewildered, furious protest. "How did you know it was Catch-22? Who the hell told you it was Catch-22?"
>
> "The soldiers with the hard white hats and clubs. The girls were crying. 'Did we do anything wrong?' they said. The men said no and pushed them away out the door with the ends of their clubs. 'Then why are you chasing us out?' the girls said. 'Catch-22,' the men said. 'What right do you have?' the girls said. 'Catch-22,' the men said. All they kept saying was 'Catch-22, Catch-22.' What does it mean, Catch-22? What is Catch-22?"

"Didn't they show it to you?" Yossarian demanded, stamping about in anger and distress. "Didn't you even make them read it?"

"They don't have to show us Catch-22," the old woman answered. "The law says they don't have to."

"What law says they don't have to?"

"Catch-22."

3. Friedrich Nietzsche, *On the Genealogy of Morality III*, § 28, at 120 (Keith Ansell-Pearson ed., Carol Diethe trans., rev. student ed. 2006) (German: ". . . das alles bedeutet, wagen wir es, dies zu begreifen, einen *Willen zum Nichts*, einen Widerwillen gegen das Leben, eine Auflehnung gegen die grundsätzlichsten Voraussetzungen des Lebens, aber es ist und bleibt ein *Wille*! . . . Und, um es noch zum Schluss zu sagen, was ich anfangs sagte: lieber will noch der Mensch *das Nichts* wollen, als *nicht* wollen . . .").

4. *See fruitfully* Samuel Beckett, "Dante . . . Bruno. Vico.. Joyce," lead essay in *Our Exagmination Round His Factification for Incamination of Work in Progress* (1929). ("Here form is content, content is form. You complain that this stuff is not written in English. It is not written at all. It is not to be read—or rather it is not only to be read. It is to be looked at and listened to. His writing is not about something; it is that something itself.")

PART XIV

THE LEGAL PROFESSION, LEGAL EDUCATION, AND THE RULE OF LAW

Law is not self-executing, nor does law teach itself. Lawyers and law professors both play special roles in maintaining the integrity and humanity of the legal process, often against strong odds. David Wilkins emphasizes the democratic importance of an independent bar, noting that a "government of laws and not of men" requires a legal profession prepared to defy state authority to protect the rights of individuals. He also acknowledges the many modern challenges to this ideal, and exhorts the legal profession to invest collectively in its own independence and integrity. Good lawyering also requires broad and deep understanding. Eloise Lawrence opines that law students cannot truly understand the U.S. legal system without exposure, through clinical education, to our overburdened state courts where most Americans actually experience the law. Much of that system does not function fairly as it should. But, Lawrence informs us optimistically, when students see the inequalities of the legal process for themselves, often "they are inspired to make our system more just." Dehlia Umunna likewise describes the joy of teaching law students the principles of zealous representation and the constitutional ideals embodied in the right to counsel. She emphasizes the importance not only of legal skills and knowledge, but the obligation to represent and care about clients as full human beings. And finally, Elizabeth Kamali takes us back to the lawyer Thomas Jefferson's bookshelf, which contained not only legal treatises, but "translations of the Qur'an and the Mishnah, several works of canon and Roman law, Paulus Orosius's *Historiarum adversus paganos*, and Stephen White's cutting-edge treatise on bee-keeping." Kamali exhorts law students and lawyers alike to maintain their curiosity and "a thirst for human understanding grounded in history, philosophy, theology, and other disciplines."

54

REIMAGINING PROFESSIONAL INDEPENDENCE

DAVID B. WILKINS

As we celebrate the nation's 250th birthday, the need for an independent legal profession dedicated to upholding the public purposes of the law has never been more important. But the structural conditions that allowed lawyers to play this role in the past, however imperfectly, have changed dramatically since bar leaders confidently extolled the value of an independent legal profession during the bicentennial celebrations in 1976. If America hopes to "keep" our republic by the tricentennial, to invoke Ben Franklin's famous quip, we will need to articulate and reinforce an understanding of professional independence that inspires lawyers to uphold their public duties in a world in which they are no longer insulated from the state and the market.

Lawyers are proud of their role at the Founding: twenty-five of the fifty-two signers of the Declaration of Independence; thirty-one of fifty-six members of the Continental Congress. The presence of so many lawyers is meant to symbolize the nation's commitment to creating a "government of laws, not of men," with lawyers as both architects and guardians of the rule of law and independent judiciary at the core of the American democratic project. To be sure, this normative vision of lawyers as the "social curators of legalism," in the legal historian Robert Gordon's evocative phrase, has always been more aspirational than real. But the *ideal* of an independent legal profession, where lawyers act as "officers of the court" prepared to challenge state authority, creatively advocate for unpopular clients, and work to dissuade powerful interests from acting in ways that undermine the law's public purposes remains a cornerstone of America's commitment to the rule of law. And, while it is easy to point to the many ways in which lawyers have failed in these duties, there are also many instances, large and small, where lawyers have stood up coura-geously to protect the rule of law.

As we enter the middle decades of the twenty-first century, however, the structural conditions that have supported lawyers in exercising this kind of independence have been eroding for some time. Traditionally, the bar has insisted that for lawyers to be independent, the profession must be "self-regulating," structurally insulated from both the power of the state and the corrupting influence of the market. Like the normative ideal of professional independence, this vision of structural self-regulation has always been more aspirational than real. Lawyers have always been sub-ject to state laws that apply to all citizens and, as market actors, to the laws of supply and demand. But the degree of control over the profession by the market and the state has increased dramatically even in the fifty years since the bicentennial and is likely to rachet up even further in years to come.

In 1976, there were fewer than 350,000 lawyers in the United States, 70 percent of whom practiced alone or in small loosely organized firms in ways that were broadly similar to the average practitioner when the American Bar Association staked the profession's claim to autonomy and self-regulation a century before. Similarly, bicentennial lawyers still oper-ated within a broad state-granted monopoly reinforced by norms of def-erence to professional expertise that largely insulated practitioners from bureaucratic control, external competition, and the reach of state power.

For better and for worse, this world no longer exists. There are now more than 1.3 million American lawyers, the majority of whom now work in organizations of increasing size and scope where they are subject to direct supervision and bureaucratic norms that incentivize efficiency and profit over craft and independence. Far from the days in which formal rules and informal norms limited competition, practitioners now inhabit a fiercely competitive legal services ecosystem rapidly being reshaped by alterna-tive providers, artificial intelligence, and blurring boundaries between law and other professional services. These changes have undoubtedly helped to make legal services more accessible and accountable—although far too many Americans still have no realistic access. But these changes have also made it harder for practitioners to prioritize professional inde-pendence over market norms.

Moreover, it is now abundantly clear that the legal profession is squarely in the sights of government actors in the United States and around the world who seek to turn lawyers into an instrument of state power and a means of undermining the independence of the judiciary. Politicians are increasingly willing to deploy the instrumentalities of the state to dissuade government lawyers, and lawyers whose clients are dependent on government (which is virtually every client) from being too "independent" from the wishes of those who wield state power. This rise of "autocratic legalism" puts mounting pressure on the many lawyers who do not support this new Alice in Wonderland legal world to stand quietly by as those who do turn their privileged position as officers of the court into opportunities to sabotage the independent judiciary and the rule of law.

These pressures in turn make coordinated action by the profession to protect professional independence even more challenging. Fewer than a quarter of all lawyers even belong to the American Bar Association, down from the 50 percent who were members in 1976, diminishing its ability to speak as a strong collective voice for professional norms. At the same time, the failure of the community of large law firms to mount a united response to President Trump's Executive Orders—which attack the professional independence of certain firms for the clients they represent—underscores how market pressures make collective action outside of professional organizations increasingly difficult.

Given these structural conditions, it is not sufficient—if it ever was—simply to urge lawyers to be independent. Although personal courage and a commitment to the ideal of professional independence are necessary conditions, they have never been sufficient to produce independence in fact. And such exhortations will certainly fail in a world in which even the vestiges of the kind of self-regulatory deference to professional norms and expertise that helped to insulate lawyers in the past from the reach of the state and the pressures of the marketplace have largely disappeared.

Instead, we must begin to build an account of professional independence that addresses these complex realities. This account must begin in law school. For most of the last one hundred years, legal education has concentrated on teaching students to "think like a lawyer" with very little attention to the realities of legal practice in which these future professionals will be called upon to exercise this skill. If we want lawyers to act independently in practice we must arm them with a deep understanding of the ways in which institutions, norms, and practices put pressure on professional independence, while providing them with tools to help navigate these pressures in ways that preserve space for independent judgment.

This account of professional independence must not only inspire lawyers. It must also persuade citizens who are increasingly skeptical of the legal profession's value, and even more alarmingly, of the value of the rule of law and democracy itself. Lawyers are partly responsible for this skepticism. Far too often, the profession has been on the side of blocking innovations that might make legal services more accessible, while lending support to powerful interests that manipulate the rule of law for private gain and stall the operation of democratic institutions. In a world in which technical legal analysis will increasingly be done by machines whose speed and accuracy will soon far outpace that of humans, it is imperative that the legal profession articulate the value of independent human judgment in ways that resonate with citizens as well as lawyers.

Recent events underscore both the difficulty and the urgency of this task. As we celebrate this important milestone in our country's history, the legal profession would do well to spend less time commemorating the role of lawyers at the Founding and more time on the difficult process of forging a vision of professional independence fit for the complex challenges lawyers face today.

55

LAW, LEGAL EDUCATION, AND STRUCTURAL INJUSTICE

ELOISE P. LAWRENCE

Two hundred and fifty years after our nation's Founders declared that it was a self-evident truth that "all men are created equal," a proper legal education should include the simple question of whether this truth is reflected in our justice system. To answer that question accurately, a law student needs exposure to our crowded, overburdened state courts—the core of our legal system—where 70 to 80 million cases are filed every year. Clinical legal education provides that exposure. In a direct service clinic, a law student experiences the quality of justice delivered to tenants, workers, immigrants, children, parents, people accused of crimes—in short, the millions of everyday Americans involved in our legal system. When law students learn how the law works in fact, how the legal system functions in practice, and how often it fails to deliver equal justice, they are inspired to make our system more just.

A law student of mine learned these lessons on a recent morning spent in housing court. When we arrived at the courthouse in the heart of downtown Boston, a long line of people snaked out the door. Young, old, disabled, able-bodied, mostly people of color stood exposed to the New England winter waiting to be screened by courthouse security. Attorneys, primarily white and able-bodied, skipped the line, showed the court officers their bar cards, and were admitted expeditiously into the warm courthouse.

After my law student made it through security, he and I climbed the stairs to the fifth floor, passing the crowded criminal court, the probate court, and the small claims court on the way to the housing court. As we waited in the courtroom for our case to be called, we observed how the structural unfairness, first experienced at the courthouse entrance, was repeated and reinforced throughout the morning. Indigent, unrepresented people, many of whom did not speak English, were forced to navigate a landscape of unwritten rules in an attempt to keep a roof over their heads.

A representative case that morning involved a pro se middle-aged black man who was asking the court to "stay the levy" on a writ of execution. In other words, he was asking the court to prevent his eviction: the constable moving him and his possessions out of his single room in a building intended for low-income people. The gentleman explained to the judge that he was experiencing an emergency and fully intended to pay his rent. "What am I supposed to do?" he asked the judge. "I was hurt on the job a few months ago and I am seeking worker's compensation. I have always paid rent before my injury, and I will pay again as soon as I can." Instead of answering the tenant's valid question, the judge posed his own hostile question: "Why aren't you like the man who walks into the grocery store and takes a bottle of milk and doesn't pay for it?" The tenant did not answer, and the judge repeated, "Why isn't what you are doing the same thing?" The obvious implication: this man was a criminal for being poor. He was stealing from the landlord.

Realizing it was not a rhetorical question, the tenant took a step back from the counsel table as if pushed by the judge's words, and said, "I don't know." While this tenant knew instinctively that this analogy was false and unfair, he did not have the basic legal knowledge and language that a law student might have. Based on her first year Property course alone, a law student might have reminded the judge about the difference between real property and personal property, or about the fact that the housing court is a court of equity as well as law. In other words, she could have demonstrated that the judge was wrong as a matter of law and equity. But, the man did not have a lawyer to make this argument on his behalf. As a result, the judge denied the tenant's motion and allowed the landlord to evict.

In a later hearing, this same judge stated: "I am in the business of evicting people . . . [even though] I don't like it, [I am compelled] to apply the law as written." The court's view that housing court judges are in the business of evicting people may be an accurate description of the day-to-day operations of the court, but it is not actually how Massachusetts law is written. Rather, the state legislature created housing courts to ensure the health, safety, and welfare of people living in residential properties, and to determine when a dispute arises who has a superior right to possess a residence. The state's common law, law of equity, and statutory laws create a complex scheme that balances the interests of landlords who have chosen to give possessory rights of a housing accommodation to a person or persons but now want those rights back, and the interests of the tenant who resides in that housing accommodation. In short, the "law as written" does not dictate that the housing court must evict a man who is struggling to survive. Instead, it is the pressure of large caseloads, overwhelming power imbalances, and unacknowledged biases that lead the housing court to rule routinely against tenants.

The lessons from this particular morning are repeated daily in courthouses all over the country, in housing, criminal, and family courts. The law of these courts is not the doctrine taught in law school classrooms. Often, the law is the judge—her mood, attitude, and opinions. In many instances, the judge reinforces existing hierarchies along racial, ethnic, class, and language lines. In addition, millions of Americans are forced to navigate the legal system alone or with overwhelmed, under-resourced counsel even when their lives and fundamental liberties are at stake.

This lack of legal assistance is often referred to as the "access to justice problem." This gap between the demand and the supply for legal assistance is due in part to the strict ethical rules that prohibit non-lawyers from helping people unable to afford a lawyer. Recently, I observed the court prevent a woman from assisting her elderly, hearing-impaired mother in an eviction case because the woman was not a lawyer. The daughter was told by the court to step back behind the bar and her mother was provided a headset by a court officer. Elderly, hearing-impaired, and alone, the tenant was forced to defend her right to stay in her home. At a time when wealth inequality grows wider every year, we can expect that the number of unrepresented or underrepresented people will continue to grow as well. Presently, almost 40 percent of this country (130 million people) qualify for Legal Services Corporation-funded programs, which serve only households at or below 200 percent of the poverty level. Only one in four eligible litigants receive representation from legal aid due to lack of funding for such programs.

State bars and national bar associations must do more to fill the access to justice gap, including loosening the monopoly of providing legal assistance. But even where indigent people do receive counsel, representation alone does not mitigate the power imbalances, biases, and unfairness that millions of people experience in our justice system.

The larger challenge is to build a justice system in the twenty-first century that reflects our nation's stated values and self-evident truths. Clinical education is a start, because it teaches future lawyers how the law is applied to the least resourced Americans in the nation's busiest courts. It also teaches them the unique role and responsibility that lawyers have within the system. My hope is that all law students will learn these lessons in law school, and when they become lawyers, they will accept the responsibility to create a system that delivers equal justice for all.

56

HUMANIZING THE ACCUSED IN THE PURSUIT OF THE RULE OF LAW

DEHLIA UMUNNA

I met Ms. X in 2022. Her first words to me were through the metal bars of holding cell number three at Roxbury District Court. She was visibly angry and defiant, and made it clear that she did not trust me. She ignored my attempt at a handshake and responded with hostility when I inquired about her well-being. Ms. X wore sweatpants and a T-shirt. Her attire was unsuitable for a New England winter, but it was what she had been wearing when police arrived at her home and arrested her for assault with a dangerous weapon—a baseball bat. Her cell was filthy and reeked of urine. She needed her medication, and her two small children were now with a relative due to her arrest.

Over the years, her icy exterior softened. Ms. X came to appreciate that my representation extended beyond demonstrating expertise in her legal matter. Since our initial meeting, she has faced various criminal charges—the kind that Rule 3.03-certified students at Harvard Law School's Criminal Justice Institute (CJI) are trained to handle under my supervision.

As my students and I learned more about her circumstances, we uncovered the story of a woman deeply harmed long before she entered a courtroom. The legal system that would later prosecute her had never intervened when she struggled in school, nor when she endured emotional and physical abuse as a child. It did not protect her when a trusted neighbor sexually assaulted her, nor did it provide meaningful support when she became a teenage mother.

Her experiences are not unique; they reflect the lives of thousands of individuals enmeshed in the American criminal legal system every day. For twenty-seven years, I have had the honor and privilege of representing hundreds of indigent men, women, and children, like Ms. X, accused of crimes at every stage of the criminal process, from simple assaults to murders. I approach my work with great personal commitment, as no other profession offers such direct exposure to human suffering and trauma, while also revealing the resilience of the human spirit in overcoming stigma, poverty, and systemic racism.

This work embodies the constitutional ideal of equality under the rule of law, and the principle, articulated decades ago by the Supreme Court, that "any person . . . too poor to hire a lawyer cannot be assured a fair trial unless counsel is provided for [them]." This right is especially important now because the law has become more politicized. We see this trend through recent Supreme Court decisions and as the criminal legal system is increasingly weaponized for political retribution. The right to counsel ensures that everyone is entitled to due process and zealous advocacy, no matter who they are or what they believe. Put simply, public defenders protect us all.

Now more than ever, it is critical to teach students the importance of careful, comprehensive advocacy. Instilling the values of holistic, empathy-based advocacy prepares students to meet these responsibilities with clarity and integrity.

As a clinical law professor, I pair my advocacy work with the joy of teaching hundreds of HLS students to represent clients zealously. My main goal at CJI is to prepare students to embrace the responsibility of providing effective, persuasive criminal defense in a system designed to strip the accused of the most basic constitutional rights. I strive to instill in my students the enduring values of ethical advocacy. Competent counsel demonstrates the legal knowledge, thoroughness, and preparation necessary for effective client representation. This standard requires a clear understanding of the client's objectives, adherence to ethical principles, and the application of relevant legal expertise to each case.

I find profound fulfillment in teaching Harvard Law School students to become capable and zealous advocates as they represent clients through their roles as student attorneys at CJI. My students find tremendous growth in applying their legal knowledge and skills to pursue equal justice under the law and to serve individual human beings.

As public defenders, our job is to bring the context of our clients' lives into the courtroom. Effective counsel doesn't end with persuading the court of our client's lack of culpability—it requires telling the complete story of the individual being prosecuted. For each of my students, it's crucial to develop the skill of telling their client's story in a persuasive and compelling way when the system denigrates the client's basic humanity. Through clinical education, I teach my students to care. I teach them to care enough to leave our clients in a better place than we found them.

Many of my students from the past decade now lead public defender offices or teach in their own criminal law clinics. Their work reflects the values I strive to instill: competence, integrity, and an unwavering commitment to human dignity. They are living proof that clinical education shapes not only skilled lawyers, but principled advocates.

Ms. X still has pending cases; one is scheduled for trial in eight weeks. We have earned her trust and respect because we represent her with the ferocity of zealous advocates who see beyond the sum of her legal matters and recognize her humanity. As she puts it, "I have had many lawyers, but I have never had lawyers like you. You saw me, you heard me, and you treated me like I was a person, and that means more to me than y'all will ever know."

I hope that future generations of students will continue to uphold the rule of law, stand beside the marginalized, and recognize that representing the accused is both a privilege and a profound responsibility. And that is why I teach HLS students.

57

On Cats, Codices, and the Common Law Curriculum

Elizabeth Papp Kamali

Two hundred and fifty years ago, the lawyer Thomas Jefferson had on his bookshelf translations of the Qur'an and the Mishnah, several works of canon and Roman law, Paulus Orosius's *Historiarum adversus paganos*, and Stephen White's cutting-edge treatise on bee-keeping, to name just a few of his carefully curated volumes. Josiah Quincy, Jr., co-counsel to John Adams in the controversial defense of British soldiers implicated in the Boston Massacre, had in his commonplace book, compiled during his legal training, a collection of the most practical of lawyerly tidbits, such as the idea that a writ might be executed on its day of return, alongside Latin maxims conveying fundamental rule-of-law principles, such as *nihil aliud potest rex quam quod jure potest*, or a king can do nothing but what he can do by law.

Legal education then was apprenticeship-based. Today, in Harvard Law School's unparalleled clinical program we might find echoes of that tradition and of the practical education of aspiring common lawyers in England's Inns of Court. If we look closely enough, we can also find in pockets of our vast curriculum the modern equivalent of Jefferson's bookshelf and of Quincy's collection of textual treasures that could at once guide him through the fine points of pleading and yet also provide moral and ethical counsel for grappling with an exceedingly unpopular defense or, for that matter, an approaching revolution. (Tragically, Quincy died in 1775 at age thirty-one, never seeing the revolution that his words and actions helped actuate.) An HLS student today might take Justice Abella on law and literature, Rabb or Stilt on Islamic law, Stephenson on Shakespeare, Lanni on ancient Athenian law, Tallarita on Cicero. Would that more would do so, and that more would venture into Harvard Yard for an elective further afield. A lawyer will continue to learn the technicalities of law throughout her career; she will arguably never have a comparable time in her life when she can quench, in such a thoroughgoing fashion, a thirst for human understanding grounded in history, philosophy, theology, and other disciplines, a thirst universities like Harvard were historically designed to satisfy.

Legal scholarship has also moved away from that thirst. Not long after the American Revolution, newspapers published cutting-edge constitutional law scholarship in the form of *The Federalist Papers*, reaching a broad readership. I suppose there is some equivalent, in concept if not depth, in the occasional op-ed penned by law professors today. However, legal scholarship of the tenure-securing variety has grown increasingly insular and byzantine (not in the eastern Roman sense). With some notable exceptions, flagship law reviews publish the fashionable and familiar—often the constitutional and administrative law debates of the day. Authors learn how to write with an eye toward catching student editors' eyes, employing the ritualized format of repetitive argument mapping and an excessive and obsessive footnoting style less attuned to avoiding plagiarism than to boosting citation statistics.

This insularity imposes numerous pressures on historically minded legal scholarship. To publish a work of legal history in a law review, an author must frame it as "forgotten" or "lost" or "uncovered," as if historians were sifting through legal rubble to find a holy grail while archivists and librarians slumbered nearby, unaware of the treasures awaiting the breathless arrival of the next Indiana Jones of future law journal fame. Similarly, when history appears in the jurisprudence of our highest court, it is typically in an instrumentalized form that treats the past as oracle to the present, as something to be divined by dipping into crisply composed and now word-searchable treatises, typically the usual suspects—Bracton, Coke, Hale, and Blackstone.

We like our history in neat packages. But the work of historians is rarely tidy, requiring the intellectual equivalent of donning one's patched overalls to labor in an unruly garden. It also requires sustained reading, sometimes of dull, serial records, and sometimes of the treatises so beloved by our courts. What if instead of word-searching Bracton for a passage on the legal issue of the day, law clerks were to read the treatise, or a portion of it, straight through, along with Samuel Thorne's footnotes identifying Bracton's eclectic sources? Were they to do so, they would engage a plethora of unruly questions. Why does Bracton refer to wailing and gnashing of teeth when describing the professional responsibilities of judges? What is the context of Bracton's passage on insanity, often cited as the source of the wild beast test? Why does Bracton quote from Azo of Bologna (cutting-edge Roman-law scholarship) and Raymond of Peñafort (cutting-edge canon law) in describing early thirteenth-century English common law?

My hope for the next generation of Harvard lawyers is that perhaps in response to the latest technological advances, law students will opt, where they can, for the low-tech. Faced with novel challenges to the rule of law, they might foment a new revolution of sorts, one bent upon dein-strumentalizing legal history, otherwise known as engaging in history for history's sake. As is already true for many of my students, they might, for example, take a class on English legal history not because it might make them a better originalist or a more effective anti-originalist, but because it might provide space for pondering questions like: Was the ordeal, the *iudicium dei*, literally understood to be the judgment of God? Why did King Edward III need a secret password to correspond with Pope John XXII in the 1330s? Why did the medieval English coroner, in compiling a Latin record, slip into the vernacular to name the types of weapons used in a homicide, and what kind of knife was a *thwytel* anyway? Why were medieval registers of writs and statute collections (like those found in the Harvard Law Library) bespoke codices, and who was using them for what?

Looking beyond England, modern lawyers might learn a great deal about negotiation from the story of Skarphéðin in Njáls Saga and about the interplay between law and society from the treatment of cats in medi-eval Welsh law. They might begin to wonder: Why are most major reli-gious systems undergirded by law? Why was St. Paul so conflicted about law's value? What "laws" govern other aspects of our lives? (My own household lives by what we call the *lex cati*, according to which a person upon whom a cat has fallen asleep may demand of the nearest cat-free person a cup of tea or retrieval of a book or the like to avoid getting up and disturbing a feline's forty winks.) Law is, or ought to be, a profession of profound curiosity. Lawyers need, above all else, a moral and ethical compass, and committing to memory the rules that will get one past the bar and professional responsibility exam are no substitute for a lifelong commitment to humanistic learning and formation of conscience. To what extent is law fundamental to human flourishing? I suspect Jefferson had a book on his shelf and Quincy a marginal note in his commonplace book that beckons toward an answer.

What's on your shelf?

PART XV
COMMUNITY AND CIVIC VIRTUE

At the end of the day, law is both a product and prerequisite of community. It both reflects and constitutes the values and virtues of the polity. As birthdays often do, the 250th anniversary invites us to reflect deeply on what those values and virtues should look like. Justice Stephen Breyer exhorts us to go back to first principles, those contained in the Declaration and in the Gettysburg Address, to reinvest in the civic virtues needed for a successful republic. Ronald Sullivan likewise emphasizes the Founders' ethical commitments to civic virtue or *arete*: the idea that our individual interests must sometimes give way to the common good. To get a more accurate sense of what the Founders actually valued, Jim Greiner encourages us to sit down and reread the words of the Declaration. Doing so reveals the sorts of policies that the Founders originally thought would make American great: openness to immigration and trade, for example, and a commitment to reasoned, fact-based decision-making. In this same spirit of accuracy, Bruce Mann warns against the temptations of revisionism. "History," he writes, "is not a record of inevitable progress along a high moral path. History is struggle." Remembering and understanding America's ethical struggles with war, slavery, religion, and equality are part of building a democracy that honors and includes us all. And finally, Molly Brady quite literally brings us home with a rumination on the devolution of modern American community in the age of suburban sprawl and digitized connection. She points out that law is partially responsible for both phenomena: "our property law choices have invited disinvestment and physical decay, [even as] the law has done all it can to enable technological growth with neither regulation nor liability." In concert, all these authors exhort us to use the legal tools at our disposal to further community, to promote democratic values such as civility and respect, and to build a stronger republic for the next generation.

58

A Nation of Documents

Stephen Breyer

Joanna, my wife, once promised our grandchildren that she would give twenty dollars to each of them who learned Lincoln's Gettysburg Address by heart. Most did. Almost all of them learned at least the first two sentences. Those two sentences are important, for they help explain, then and now, why we think of our country as a Nation of Documents and not a Nation of a Single Tribe.

Consider the first sentence: "Four score and seven years ago our fathers brought forth on this continent a new nation, conceived in liberty and dedicated to the proposition that all men are created equal." What had happened eighty-seven years before? Lincoln's reference is to the Declaration of Independence, not the Constitution. Why? In part because the Declaration, not the Constitution (at that time), referred to equality, a major goal of the Civil War. In part because the Declaration, to a greater extent than did the Constitution, set forth yet more words that encapsulate this Nation's basic aspirations.

Those words made their author, Thomas Jefferson immortal. Jefferson wrote: "We hold these truths to be self-evident, that all men are created equal, that they are endowed by their Creator with certain inalienable rights, that among these are life, liberty, and the pursuit of happiness—That to secure these rights governments are instituted among men, deriving their just powers from the consent of the governed."

By the time I grew up, just after World War II, we had elaborated further upon these basic "inalienable rights." We are a democracy, we search for equality, but we do more. We protect basic liberties, such as free speech, free press, and others listed in the Constitution. We insist upon a separation of powers, vertically (states, federal government) and horizontally (three branches of the federal government) so that no group of individuals becomes too powerful. We follow a "rule of law," self-governance through laws that we make collectively and not through the exercise of brute power. And some historians tell us that the words "pursuit of happiness" reflect an effort to devise a nation of laws based upon reason and not simply upon emotion or what Madison called "faction."

That first sentence thus encapsulated the basic values that have offered us guidance since the Founding and to which Lincoln in the midst of the Civil War referred. They are values that Joanna wanted our grandchildren to understand.

But she wanted our grandchildren also to become familiar with Lincoln's second sentence. It says, "Now we are engaged in a great civil war, *testing whether that nation, or any nation so conceived and so dedicated, can long endure.*" The word often used to describe that to which Lincoln refers here is "experiment." The "Great Experiment," as George Washington wrote on January 9, 1790, represented "the last great experiment for promoting human happiness." It is an "experiment" in a republican form of government, written into our Constitution, which will continue to exist only (as Benjamin Franklin told the women outside Independence Hall) "if you can keep it." It is an experiment in government, "of," "by," and "for . . . the people," as Lincoln later pointed out at Gettysburg.

Can we keep it? There are some today who fear not. But I am not so pessimistic. I would invite the pessimists to come with me when I describe the constitutional job of the Supreme Court to law school, or university, or high school students. I tell them that this document, the Constitution, is now theirs; they are the ones who must make certain the great experiment succeeds. And they look interested; it is what they want; they will help.

I tell them something I first learned working on the Senate staff. When you foresee opposition to your proposal or point of view, find someone, whom you believe intelligent, who genuinely believes the opposite to you, and talk to them. Talk civilly. Wait. Don't talk too much. Listen. Eventually they are likely to say something you genuinely agree with. Then say, "Stop. *You* have made a good point. Let's see if we can work with that." And you often, not always but often, will be able to work out a compromise. If you get 30 percent of what you want, great! Take it. Don't hold out for 100 percent of nothing. And the students look interested. It is what they want. They will help. This is what makes me an optimist.

Interest alone, of course, is not enough. The next generations, my grandchildren and their children must learn how our governments work—federal, state, and local. They must learn about the wisdom and values in our foundational documents. They must learn how to participate. And they must start early. As my colleague Sandra O'Connor pointed out, "The practice of democracy is not passed down through the gene pool. It must be taught and learned anew by each generation." She was a fan of what used to be called, "Twelfth Grade Civics" and so am I. There are groups of teachers and citizens who are trying to see that civic knowledge is taught once again throughout the nation: iCivics, the Annenberg Center, the Miller Center, the Federal Judicial Center, and many others. They are trying to help. Perhaps even more importantly, we must continue to learn and to practice what may be an American specialty: working together. This also starts early. We learned to work together at grammar school where my fifth-grade teacher would divide us into groups of four, assign a project to each of the groups, and give one grade to each. Such lessons paid off when we saw the country work together during the COVID-19 pandemic where, in city after city, people would form groups to check up on old and vulnerable people to see that they were all right, that would help those who needed help.

If we want practical instruction, we can still read the words of Alexis de Tocqueville, that great French scholar of the United States. He wrote in the 1830's that when he approached the United States, he heard "noise," and endless arguing. But he knew that was a virtue not a vice. He feared a silent "aristocracy" producing inequality and suppressing liberty. That "noise," he believed, was the noise of associations, many different associations, ranging from book groups to civil liberties unions, to town halls. When faced with problems, their members would debate, discuss, argue, and suggest experiments. And those problems included all sorts of civic problems, from livestock grazing to elections. Perhaps today they would include how we should deal with the internet or artificial intelligence. de Tocqueville would probably stress the need for broad and inclusive association that does not turn our nation of documents into groups of individually exclusive, indeed tribal, cultures. But he would not fear experiment. After all, he said that the "greatness of America lies not in being more enlightened than any other nation, but rather in her ability to repair her faults."

Let me end with a remark about one of our special documentary virtues, a virtue that helps to support the others. I speak, perhaps because I am a judge, of the rule of law, and its capacity to protect us against our worst impulses. In this spirit, I always suggest to my students that they read Camus's book, *The Plague*. It is ostensibly about a lethal plague that hit the city of Oran in Algeria. But, more likely, it is about France when occupied by the Nazis. When the plague left the city, there was great joy. But Camus wrote that "such joy is always imperiled. . . . [T]he plague bacillus never dies or disappears for good." It goes into remission. It can lurk for years in "furniture and linen-chests . . . in bedrooms, cellars, trunks and bookshelves." He warned that perhaps the day would come to the misfortune or education of mankind, when it would re-awaken its rats and "sen[d] them forth to die in a [once-]happy city."

The rule of law, I believe, is a weapon that not only helps to support our constitutional values but militates against the re-awakening of that "plague germ" of unchecked power. Along with those values, it uniquely helps to assure the success of our American Experiment. My grandchildren, indeed the children of the twenty-first century must learn the history of those values, discuss them with others (including those who disagree), and use them to lead the world by example. I hope they do so.

59

On Civic Virtue

RONALD S. SULLIVAN, JR.

"We the People of the United States, in Order to form a more perfect Union . . ."

These opening lines of the Preamble to the Constitution of the United States reach across time and space to remind generations that our democratic project is always already in progress, incomplete, developing—not a static, fully-formed Union, but an experiment that requires our constant tinkering. Even the Founders, although demonstrably imperfect actors, recognized that the document that they were about to sign was not perfect, nor was the new government that would be born out of that document.

Our Constitution is not self-actualizing. Instead, concrete human beings, citizens of all stripes, must animate its principles. "We the People" are the enzymes that catalyze the norms deeply embedded in our democratic traditions. And "We the People" must vigilantly defend the constitutional norms foundational to the success of this democratic experiment.

The Federalist Papers are instructive on this point. Both Madison and Hamilton remind us that in order for a democratic republic to work, we must embrace a civic virtue—the notion that both citizens and their representatives must be willing to subordinate their individual interests in favor of the public good. Here, the Founding generation draws from the then-well established Aristotelian notion of *arete*, the view that virtue exists on both individual and public registers simultaneously. But importantly, their view of civic virtue was moderated by the Enlightenment's intervention that married civic virtue with institutional design as co-requisites of a robust republican form of government. Indeed, as Madison recognized, "If men were angels, no government would be necessary." We need both *arete* and a functioning government for the republic to prosper.

Regrettably, over time, *arete*, as partner to institution building, has lost its import in popular thinking. The concept of virtue is seen as old-fashioned, ephemeral, and too imprecise a currency to have purchase in the real world. Talk of virtue is relegated to the marginally relevant musing of the philosopher and given minimal real-world significance. That is unfortunate. *Arete* is the Republic's failsafe. Language, the *urstoff* of statues, rules, and regulation, can only do so much. Our democracy relies on, and is animated by, a civic virtue that recognizes that the character of the citizenry matters in sustaining our traditions. Madison, in *Federalist 48*, gives voice to this view with his admonition that "parchment barriers" alone are insufficient to protect our traditions. Character matters; civic virtue is a necessary aspect to a good-working republic. While a rule is insufficient to constrain behavior of a scoundrel, a virtuous citizen will privilege the public good even when not obligated by law.

Our democratic traditions are currently being stress-tested like never before in modern history. The President has haphazardly eschewed the norms that have served as ordering pillars of our democracy for generations, recklessly promoted a political vocabulary that has coarsened public dialogue to something akin to a junior high school locker room, aggressively returned to a form of gunboat diplomacy that bespeaks a form of imperialism long ago rejected, and blatantly turned government operations into a business transaction divorced from any normative commitments that have informed the development of our democracy. Dealmaking and personal profit rule the roost; ideals are deeply subordinate. Even more, the way the President disregards positive law and long-standing norms combines to produce a brute show of power designed to bend the government to his narrow desires.

The foregoing list is by no means exhaustive; rather, its intent is to highlight the breadth of injury to our democracy as we face its 250th anniversary.

The country faces a President who either does not know or does not care to know the elemental principles that bind the republic. Whether ignorance or mendacity explains the casual disrespect to our constitutional norms, the behavior of the sitting president should challenge the citizenry to garner the resolve and demonstrate the public virtue necessary to protect our traditions.

The problem I describe, however, is not one of the President alone; rather, too many citizens imagine the United States as a white republic instead of a beacon of freedom, as Princeton scholar Eddie S. Glaude Jr. so aptly puts it. Too many citizens are unwilling to acknowledge the warts on our body politic; but rather, they promote a revisionist history that situates America as a beautiful, finished product—a perfect union, ordained by the Creator to do whatever it will. It is this exceptionalist understanding of America that allowed chattel slavery, Jim Crow segregation, and relocation camps, to name a few—all under a Constitution that calls for equality under law. This idea of America is both wrong-headed and dangerous and will inevitably morph our democratic project into an imperial Leviathan that is destined to go the way of every empire in history.

This does not have to be America's fate.

Dr. Martin Luther King, Jr. once famously wrote that the "arc of the moral universe is long, but it bends toward justice." Although written in the passive voice, King's public life and ministry show us that people must bend this arc; it will not bend by itself. Instead, citizens of good character—virtue—must bend the moral arc of the universe toward justice. This will take courage, sacrifice, and selflessness. And humility. We must be humble enough to recognize that America is an unfinished project that requires our constant attention, care, and vigilance. We cannot let America become a museum, a historical artifact stuck in a bygone era. America must always live and grow and evolve into better versions of itself.

History teaches us that this is doable, but we must look to our better angels, roll up our collective sleeves, and do the work necessary to achieve our democracy.

60

EMPIRICAL TRUTH AND THE DECLARATION OF INDEPENDENCE

D. JAMES GREINER

When I received the invitation to participate in this volume, I considered how a hardcore empiricist could contribute to a memorialization of the Declaration of Independence. Start by rereading it, I thought. That exercise proved astonishing for someone living in 2026. In short, the Founders were empiricists, at least of a sort. And the Declaration of Independence supports policies at odds with much of today's popular politics.

The name of the dominant political movement of our era, Make America Great Again, suggests that in an unspecified past, what is now the United States became and was great because it pursued certain favored policies. The further implication is that when what is now the United States stopped pursuing those favored policies, it became mediocre. Chief among these favored policies of the past that deserve revival, we are told, are a sharp curtailing of illegal and legal immigration, a sharp curtailing of international trade, and a sharp curtailing of reliance on facts discernible from scientific sources. To make what is now the United States great again, we must refocus on these and other policies that served us well in the past.

Rereading the Declaration of Independence demonstrates that the truth is more complicated.

First, regarding the assertion that a sharp curtailing of illegal and legal immigration once made America great: the seventh grievance that the Declaration of Independence asserted against King George III was that the Monarchy was "obstructing the Laws for Naturalization of Foreigners; refusing to pass others to encourage their migrations hither."

Second, regarding the assertion that a sharp curtailing of international trade once made America great: the fifteenth grievance that the

Declaration of Independence asserted against King George III was that the Monarchy was "cutting off our Trade with all parts of the world."

Third, regarding the assertion that a sharp curtailing of reliance on facts discernible from politically neutral sources once made America great: matters are more complex. The wholesale adoption of a scientific method that depended on objective observation, a statement of a falsifiable hypothesis, an empirical test, and a resulting refinement of understanding was in its infancy in 1776. But the members of the Second Continental Congress that adopted the Declaration of Independence were empiricists of a sort. They believed in a form of natural law that partially encompassed what we would now characterize as empirical facts. Natural law, in their view, stemmed at least in part from principles of the world discoverable from the exercise of pure reason coupled with observation and measurement. Those principles included political and ethical ones. So, for example, Continental Congress members believed that a statement like "all men are created equal," which modern thinkers would classify as a moral statement, was similar to what in modern eyes would be a more empirical statement, like "The [European] rein deer could walk under the belly of our moose." (Thomas Jefferson reportedly so told French nobleman Count Buffon to refute the latter's theory that American animals, and therefore American humans, were "degenerate" copies of their European counterparts.)

The key point is that our great thinkers of that era believed in, and believed that government policy should rely on, a nascent version of scientific truth. The Declaration's preamble cites "the Laws of Nature" (distinct from the laws "of Nature's God") as a source of the "truths" that were "self-evident." Thus, it is not hard to picture the reaction of the members of the Continental Congress to attempts to rest government policy on empirically falsifiable untruths, for example, that the COVID-19 inoculation was the deadliest vaccine ever made; that childhood vaccines cause autism; that the measles vaccine causes all the illnesses that measles itself causes; that fluoride in drinking water is associated with bone cancer; that HIV may not be the cause of AIDS; or that 5G data networks are used to control human behavior. One can imagine the reaction of our great thinkers from the Declaration era to government policy based on the empirically falsifiable, and false beliefs that global warming is a con job;

that prenatal acetaminophen use causes autism; that researchers should study whether irradiating human bodies with ultraviolet rays is an advisable treatment against a virus; or that raking is an effective way to prevent forest fires.

Reading the Declaration accurately does not determine modern policy. There may be good reasons to pursue a policy of sharply reducing legal and illegal immigration or of sharply reducing international trade. There may be good reasons to pursue policies that balance other considerations, such as economic security or personal autonomy over one's body, against the lessons of science. There is no good reason, however, to distort the past. And there is no good reason to deploy the past to undermine belief in scientific sources, however inconvenient.

The great thinkers who adopted the Declaration of Independence believed that the principles they articulated there were important enough to start what would become an eight-year war, the second-deadliest in our history as measured by the fraction of our population that perished. They articulated their beliefs in a document that they signed knowing that it would be their death warrant if they lost that war. On the 250th anniversary of their achievement, an empiricist invites you to start by rereading what they wrote.

61

HISTORY AS POWER

BRUCE H. MANN

Historians are the indispensable public intellectuals. They engage the past to help us understand who we once were, how we became who we are now, and how we can strive toward better versions of our collective selves in the future. For historians, it is both a professional and a moral imperative to confront the past clearly and unflinchingly and to teach that past to the present so that others may teach it in the future.

Some people prefer not to be taught. Instead, they believe that the only past worth claiming is a celebratory one that affirms their own beliefs, their own sense of who they are and what their place in the world should rightfully be. They are the originalists who pretend a special insight into the minds and words of the Framers to justify conclusions that, curiously, tend almost invariably in one political direction—a direction that turns away from the unfulfilled promise of the Declaration of Independence. They are the parents and school board members who believe that a proper civic education requires a history stripped of the dark chapters—slavery, native displacement and extermination, oppressive labor conditions, racism, and bigotry—chapters that are as much a part of who we are as a people and a nation as the brighter chapters they would reduce history to. They are the authoritarians whose need to present themselves as the guardians of a pure and noble history drives them to try to erase all public memory of the parts of our collective history that are not pure and noble—removing all references to slavery from a memorial to the men and women George Washington held in bondage while president, deleting exhibits on the oppressive labor conditions of young women and immigrants in nineteenth-century textile mills that profited from the oppression of those same young women and immigrants. These are the people who would reduce history to a single thread that excludes anyone and anything that contradicts the stories they tell themselves about themselves or questions their monopoly of the "truth."

But history, even American history, is not a record of inevitable progress along a high moral path. History is struggle. History is a tapestry of struggles for survival, for wealth, for power, for enlightenment, for knowledge, for peace. History is also a struggle for who gets to tell it. The tapestry is the history of humanity, warts and all. The contest over who will control that history is why historians are a threat to anyone who twists history to legitimize their own dominance.

A case in point: Statues and monuments have always been contested. After all, the decision about whom to honor in marble or bronze rests with people in power—people who have declared themselves history's "winners" and who therefore have the power to ennoble their version of history to the exclusion of others. But, on occasion and over time, the once-powerless become empowered and assert their claim to history. We live in such a moment.

In recent years, Americans of all races have demanded the removal of the hundreds of monuments to the Confederacy that occupy places of honor in our public spaces. Supporters and opponents of removal both took their stand on history. Opponents claimed that the statues and monuments—like the Confederate battle flag—represent their "heritage" and honor men who fought honorably to defend a cause they believed in: states' rights. Supporters of removal argued that cause—the "Lost Cause"—was fought by traitors who took up arms against their country to defend the immoral institution of slavery and that symbols of that cause do not deserve places of honor in our public spaces. These are not mere differences of opinion. They are competing versions of history—one a self-serving invention, the other drawn from the words and deeds of the actors themselves. Which version we listen to matters because each version has consequences. Each one has the power to shape not just the present, but also the future.

History is complicated. It consists not so much of facts, although facts there surely are—Robert E. Lee really did surrender to Ulysses S. Grant— as it does of the interpretive narratives we weave from those facts—was Lee a traitor or a hero? These narratives attempt to explain the past, but they also reveal much—often more—about the narrators. For most of the first half of the twentieth century, white professional historians accepted the narrative of defeated Southerners that slavery was a largely benign institution, that the Civil War was fought over states' rights rather than slavery, that Reconstruction was a vindictive regime of white carpetbaggers and scalawags and Black freedmen propped up by federal troops, and that true peace and natural order were restored only after Reconstruction ended in 1877 and the former enslavers of the defeated South were returned to their rightful positions of authority. Historians' acceptance of that narrative made them complicit in the resubjugation of African-Americans by the long-lived legal mechanisms of Jim Crow.

No professional historian today thinks any of that is true. Instead, historians know that the statues of Confederate military and political leaders are monuments to men who took up arms against the United States to defend and preserve slavery. They know that the statues honor those men *because* they were traitors and enslavers of human beings, not despite that. They know that the statues were not erected in the mournful wake of the Civil War to honor the dead but rather decades and even a century later as defiant declarations of white supremacy to remind the Black citizens of every town in which they stood that the rights and freedoms guaranteed to them by the Thirteenth, Fourteenth, and Fifteenth Amendments to the United States Constitution meant nothing as far as their white neighbors were concerned. But even as history renders judgment, the recent return of some of the statues and restoring the surnames of Confederate traitors to military bases remind us that the struggle over who gets to tell history continues.

Statues may be symbols, but the stakes in the struggle for who gets to tell history are not symbolic. Thousands of people die each year because a bare majority of the United States Supreme Court adopted a version of history of the Second Amendment that most historians reject. The myth that the United States was founded as an explicitly Christian nation has been deployed to empower a white Christian nationalist minority that believes that the only religious rights deserving of protection are their own and that anyone who does not share their beliefs must yield. The reproductive rights of tens of millions of women were stripped away in an opinion that channeled the misogyny of a seventeenth-century English jurist and seemingly willfully distorted subsequent history, creating a world in which pregnant women risk death for want of the care they could have received until just a day earlier.

Each of these examples demonstrates how ill-minded advocates mine history selectively or fabricate it outright to advance self-justifying ends, wielding their versions of history as cudgels to claim primacy as the sole inheritors of American "values." Each is an expression of power—the power to declare what history is, the power to determine who matters and who does not, the power to control the future, or at least to try.

History done well requires humility. Humility to recognize where we have failed as well as where we have succeeded. Humility to understand that the past is inescapably pluralistic, filled with many often-quiet voices that deserve to be heard and that have shaped the present every bit as much as the louder self-proclaimed "winners."

The imperative for law and governance going forward is to reclaim history from those in power who would falsify it for the purpose of legitimizing the future they are determined to impose on the nation. What is at stake is a chance to build on our shared history a future that honors all of us, not just the privileged few. Historians can help point the way by revealing the tapestry of struggles that brought us to the present, a tapestry that teaches us that the future is a choice.

62

PROPERTY LAW IN PURSUIT OF COMMUNITY

MAUREEN E. BRADY

The 250th anniversary that this collection marks is an occasion to reckon with two historical forces that have shaped the last century of American life in ways that would have been impossible to envision at the Founding. The first is the slow unraveling of physical community, caused by auto-fueled sprawl, suburbanization, and economic disinvestment. The second is the explosive rise of forms of digital connection that promised to fill the void. Law has been the architect of both.

The areas to which I am devoting my life—property, land use, and local government law—are to blame for much of the first problem. Zoning regulations have forced us farther and farther apart; school district boundaries entrench lines of inequality; and the cost of housing is so astronomical that homeownership rates in my generation are lower than in any before. Millennials are a permanent renting class, at the whim of landlords and subjected to repeated economic shocks, which has structurally prevented people in my generation from investing in our physical communities. And yet, from my viewpoint, things could be different. To compete with an ever-expanding set of digital distractions, land use and property law could work to create alternatives: places for physical connection, new ways of living that challenge the solitary model that has dominated for so long.

For me, the problem is personal. I can sum up my teenage years with two vignettes that probably capture the early lives of many millennials. First, I was deeply lonely. My city in upstate New York saw its population peak around the time of the Erie Canal, suffering thereafter from distance and disinvestment. I grew up on a cul-de-sac in a nominal suburb of that dying city, and I remember worrying as a child about the news breaking that big companies—General Electric, Lockheed Martin—were moving away. I remember a bumper sticker that said, "If you're the last one out of Utica, turn out the lights." It was a mile walk to my elementary school on streets without sidewalks, and you'd have to cross a 45-mile-per-hour roadway. When I was seven, a girl five years older than me—Sara Anne Wood—was on her bike when she was abducted by a serial killer about five miles from my house. The physical world outside was not stable or safe; the omnipresent "Missing" posters proved it.

On the other hand, another world that promised safety and connection was literally at my fingertips. My parents bought our first Gateway desktop computer in 1998. I took "Computer" classes in elementary and high school, learning to type and use applications. I was an early adopter of instant messaging apps like ICQ and AOL, wrote a melodramatic Live-Journal blog, and sought connections on message boards focused on classically Y2K things like HTML coding and weight loss. I remember feeling awe as I learned about bands while chatting with girls my age in California, thrill as I pretended in weird chat rooms to be an entirely different person than I was. When I sent in my college enrollment deposit and received a harvard.edu email address, I immediately signed up for The-Facebook.com, which was then open only to affiliates of Harvard College (and maybe a few other schools). I became one of the first high school students on the site, though it did not seem like the world was undergoing such a colossal shift.

These two features of my life seemed independent, but I now recognize them as inextricably intertwined. All the way back in 2000, in his book *Bowling Alone*, sociologist Robert Putnam characterized the twentieth century as representing an enormous and troubling decline in individual participation in institutions associated with civic and social community. Putnam attributed it to dynamics as wide-ranging as television, the ethics of individualism, population mobility, and suburbanization.

At my basement computer, I was the next frontier for Putnam's statistics. My generation came of age with the Internet, and TheFacebook, and the iPhone (as I reach middle age, it's now AI). My grandparents, by contrast, were the heads of the Utica Catholic Women's Club, the Utica Rotary, the local United Way, the Utica Chamber of Commerce. I was an all-star in my share of high-school domains, but my entire community was online, even the parts that could have been off. One of my best high school friends—with whom I remain friends to this day—is someone I talked to near-daily on instant messenger. I think I've been to his house once.

Even as our property law choices have invited disinvestment and physical decay, the law has done all it can to enable technological growth with neither regulation nor liability. More is always better: more technology, more speech, more falsehood, a dysfunctional marketplace of ideas. Who would choose to grapple with the complexity of real human beings when you can find a community of your choosing at the click of a button—whether birders, Real Housewives fans, or Holocaust deniers. American law elevates platforms and their profit margins over other kinds of infrastructural and physical investment, fearing how we might fall behind globally if it were otherwise. It is a great irony of our moment that a social media app, Nextdoor, arose to "connect" physical neighborhoods. Any quick internet search will show that it is as poisoned as any other social media site. If you spend enough time on technology these days, when you come across a video snippet of strangers in real life being helpful or acting silly, you'll often find a wistful comment that says: "The people yearn for community."

I know more about property than technology, and while I am unsure how to fix the latter, I do believe that the former can do better. My scholarship is partially devoted to exploring how the common law and regulation can further community. Property law, at its common law core, was never just about individualism. It was a system of mutual obligation: the law of nuisance required neighbors to tolerate one another's reasonable uses; easements and covenants structured ongoing relationships across property lines; doctrines from adverse possession to transfer of title rewarded those who developed a reputation or asked around in the neighborhood. These doctrines assumed that people would live near one another, interact repeatedly, and bear responsibility for the effects of their choices. The common law, in short, was built to promote community.

Although it was in some ways tailor-made for the opposite purpose, land use regulation can be redirected toward the same end. Single-family zoning was born at the turn of the twentieth century from a mix of motives: genuine anxiety about safety in an era of industrialization, panic about race and class integration, and fears about disease. Policymakers watching the Russian Revolution in 1917 hoped that by making it possible for everyone to own a literal piece of America, they would have a stake in both capitalism and the country. Ironically, zoning has kept young people hopeless, disaffected, unable to envision an American dream. It has had help from other policies, like property tax caps, that simultaneously redound to the benefit of older homeowners and throttle the capacity of local governments to raise funds.

We owe it to future generations to make different choices. Some places are already doing just that, using regulatory change to smooth the pathway for accessory dwelling units, duplexes, and triplexes, new forms of co-housing that create genuine common spaces and real community governance. Right now, when local governments invite neighborhood participation, in-person public hearings draw out those with the most time and the most fervent opposition. Yet during the COVID-19 pandemic, we learned simple technological tweaks—remote meetings—would marshal a greater range of voices. Numerous places are experimenting with governance that gives neighborhoods or streets formal involvement in solving hard local problems. Neighborhoods need not be mere bulwarks against change. The same social ties that generate resistance can also produce welcome: not just potlucks, but political will to fuel corner stores, affordable housing, and small business.

Community is important for its own sake, but it also requires and fosters other values: civility, some degree of give-and-take. Ideologies on opposite sides of our current moment might consider civility to be either a tool of the privileged or a weakness for the foolish, but I strongly reject both. I believe that mutual respect is essential to both democracy and society.

I hope that in the United States, and at Harvard Law School—an institution that gets a reputation for training adversaries rather than neighbors, and where the open letter can become a substitute for conversation—we will be able to lean into community as against efforts to stoke or celebrate conflict. And there is much community here, if you know where to look. When I walk the hallways—at least when I am not looking at my phone—I see students deep in conversation with beloved baristas or security guards, 1L classrooms bursting with energy, cookies left on a colleague's desk after a particularly challenging day. What some have called our "epidemic of loneliness" was not inevitable, but produced, by choices about roads and zoning and digital platforms—and what we owe each other as neighbors. Law made those destructive choices, and law can make different ones. While we celebrate the Declaration, I also nod to the Pennsylvania Constitution of 1776: "[A]ll government ought to be instituted and supported for the security and protection of the community as such." As that too turns 250, the sentiment is worth fighting for.

Contributor List

Bill Alford is the Jerome A. and Joan L. Cohen Professor of East Asia Legal Studies and Director of the Harvard Law School's East Asian Legal Studies program.

Sabrineh Ardalan is a Clinical Professor of Law and director of the Harvard Immigration and Refugee Clinical Program.

Yochai Benkler is the Berkman Professor of Entrepreneurial Legal Studies, faculty director of the Program on Law and Political Economy, and co-director of the Berkman Klein Center for Internet and Society. He uses history, empirics, and social theory to explain the dynamics of innovation, social struggle, and crisis in capitalism.

Sharon Block is a Professor of Practice and Executive Director of the Center for Labor and a Just Economy at Harvard Law School. Her work focuses on labor, employment and administrative law.

Nikolas Bowie is the Louis D. Brandeis Professor of Law. He is a historian who teaches courses in federal constitutional law, state constitutional law, and local government law. His research focuses on critical legal histories of democracy in the United States.

Maureen E. Brady is the Louis D. Brandeis Professor of Law. She teaches property law and related subjects. Her scholarship uses historical analyses of property institutions and land use doctrines to explore broader theoretical questions. She is also an Associate Reporter for the American Law Institute's Fourth Restatement of Property.

Scott Brewer is a Professor of Law at Harvard Law School. He teaches and writes in jurisprudence and the philosophy of law. He is co-founder of the Summer School on Law and Logic, and founder of the Logocratic Academy.

Stephen Breyer is the Byrne Professor of Administrative Law and Process at Harvard Law School. From 1980–1994 he served as Judge and later Chief Judge on the United States Court of Appeals for the First Circuit and, from 1994–2022, as Associate Justice of the United States Supreme Court.

Emily M. Broad Leib is a Clinical Professor of Law and Director of Harvard Law School's Center for Health Law and Policy Innovation. She is also Founder and Faculty Director of the Harvard Law School Food Law and Policy Clinic, the nation's first law school clinic devoted to the challenges facing our food system.

Tomiko Brown-Nagin is the Daniel P.S. Paul Professor of Constitutional Law at Harvard Law School and Professor of History in the Harvard Faculty of Arts and Sciences. She also is dean of the Harvard Radcliffe Institute for Advanced Study.

Guy-Uriel E. Charles is the Charles J. Ogletree Jr. Professor of Law. He also directs the Charles Hamilton Houston Institute for Race and Justice. He writes about how law mediates political power and how law addresses racial subordination.

John Coates is the John F. Cogan, Jr. Professor of Law and Economics, and Research Director of the Center on the Legal Profession. Professor Coates previously served as General Counsel and as Acting Director for the Division of Corporation Finance for the SEC.

I. Glenn Cohen is the James A. Attwood and Leslie Williams Professor of Law, and Faculty Director of the Petrie-Flom Center for Health Law Policy, Biotechnology & Bioethics. He is one of the world's leading experts on the intersection of bioethics and the law, as well as health law.

Andrew Manuel Crespo is the Morris Wasserstein Public Interest Professor of Law, the Founding Executive Faculty Director of the Institute to End Mass Incarceration, and a founding editor and Co-Editor-in-Chief of the award-winning decarceral magazine, *Inquest*.

Christine Desan is the Leo Gottlieb Professor of Law. She teaches and writes about the political economy of capitalism, the constitutional law of money, the international monetary system, constitutional history, and legal theory. She co-founded Harvard's Program on the Study of Capitalism and runs the website JustMoney.org.

Kristen E. Eichensehr is a Professor of Law at Harvard Law School. Her work focuses on foreign relations and national security law.

Benjamin Eidelson is a Professor of Law and Affiliate Professor of Philosophy at Harvard University. He writes and teaches about the interplay of moral and legal principles in public law, with a focus on constitutional law, antidiscrimination law, and statutory interpretation.

Jared Ellias is the Scott C. Collins Professor of Law. He writes and teaches about corporate bankruptcy law and the governance of large firms.

Susan H. Farbstein is a Clinical Professor of Law and the Director of the International Human Rights Clinic. Her legal, advocacy, and investigative work addresses war crimes and crimes against humanity, unlawful killings and disappearances, corporate accountability, and socioeconomic rights.

Noah Feldman is the Arthur Kingsley Porter University Professor, Chair of the Society of Fellows, and founding director of the Julis-Rabinowitz Program on Jewish and Israeli Law, all at Harvard University. Author of ten books, he specializes in constitutional studies.

Jody Freeman is the Archibald Cox Professor of Law, and a leading scholar of administrative law and environmental law. She is a member of the American Academy of Arts and Sciences, a Fellow of the American College of Environmental Lawyers and a member of the Council on Foreign Relations.

D. James Greiner is the Honorable S. William Green Professor of Public Law. An empirical scholar, he serves as the Faculty Director of the Access to Justice Lab, the only entity in the United States that focuses on randomized control trials in the legal profession.

John C.P. Goldberg is the Morgan and Helen Chu Dean and Professor of Law. He is an expert in tort law, tort theory, and political philosophy.

Annette Gordon-Reed is the Carl M. Loeb University Professor at Harvard. A legal historian, she has won sixteen book prizes including the Pulitzer Prize, the National Book Award, a MacArthur Fellowship, a Guggenheim Fellowship, the National Humanities Medal, the Frederick

Douglass Book Prize, the George Washington Book Prize, and the Anisfield-Wolf Book Award.

Sheila Heen is the Thaddeus R. Beal Professor of Practice, a Deputy Director of the Harvard Negotiation Project and a Founder of Triad Consulting. She is co-author of two *New York Times* bestsellers, *Difficult Conversations: How to Discuss What Matters Most* and *Thanks for the Feedback: The Science and Art of Receiving Feedback Well.*

Howell E. Jackson is the James S. Reid, Jr., Professor of Law. His research interests include financial regulation and federal budget policy. He is co-author of *Fiscal Challenges: An Interdisciplinary Approach to Budget Policy* (2008, Cambridge University Press) as well as numerous other publications on financial regulation and budget policy.

Elizabeth Papp Kamali is the Austin Wakeman Scott Professor of Law and an Affiliate of the Department of History. Her research focuses on the medieval English common law and the history of criminal law, with a particular interest in the early criminal trial jury.

Randall Kennedy is the Michael R. Klein Professor of Law. Author of numerous books, he is a member of the American Law Institute, the American Academy of Arts and Sciences, and the American Philosophical Association.

Michael Klarman is the Charles Warren Professor of Legal History. He has won numerous awards for his teaching and scholarship, which are primarily in the areas of Constitutional Law and Constitutional History.

Adriaan Lanni is the Touroff-Glueck Professor of Law. Her research focuses on ancient law and society and modern criminal justice reform, with a focus on restorative justice. She has been awarded fellowships from the Guggenheim Foundation, the Radcliffe Institute for Advanced Study, and the Loeb Classical Library Foundation.

Eloise P. Lawrence is a Clinical Professor of Law and the Faculty Director of the Harvard Legal Aid Bureau, the country's oldest student-run civil legal aid clinic.

Richard J. Lazarus is the Charles Stebbins Fairchild Professor of Law. His primary areas of scholarship are environmental law and Supreme Court decisionmaking. Professor Lazarus has represented the United

States, state and local governments, and environmental groups in the United States Supreme Court in forty cases.

Jill Lepore is the David Woods Kemper '41 Professor of American History and Professor of Law at Harvard University. She is a staff writer at *The New Yorker*, and the author of many prize-winning books.

Lawrence Lessig is the Roy L. Furman Professor of Law and Leadership. He is the founder of Equal Citizens and a founding board member of Creative Commons. He has received numerous awards including a Webby, the Free Software Foundation's Freedom Award, Scientific American 50 Award, and Fastcase 50 Award.

Kenneth W. Mack is the inaugural Lawrence D. Biele Professor of Law and Affiliate Professor of History at Harvard University. He is a legal historian who focuses on politics, civil rights, and economic life, and is completing a major biography of President Barack Obama.

Bruce H. Mann is the Carl F. Schipper, Jr. Professor of Law. He is past president of the American Society for Legal History.

Martha Minow holds the 300th Anniversary University Professorship at Harvard University. She is an expert in constitutional law and human rights.

Daniel L. Nagin is a Clinical Professor of Law and Faculty Director of the WilmerHale Legal Services Center, a community-based public interest law firm home to six Harvard Law School civil practice clinics. He is also Faculty Director of the Legal Service Center's Veterans Legal Clinic.

Alexandra Natapoff is an award-winning criminal justice scholar and the Lee S. Kreindler Professor of Law. She writes about criminal courts, public defense, plea bargaining, wrongful convictions, and race and inequality in the criminal system. She previously served as a federal public defender in Baltimore, Maryland.

Charles R. Nesson founded what has become the Berkman Klein Center for Internet & Society at Harvard University. He teaches about the American Jury, once the ultimate voice of the People in American criminal justice, now reduced to relative inconsequence as a subsidiary judicial fact-finder told not to be concerned with justice.

Gerald L. Neuman is the J. Sinclair Armstrong Professor of International, Foreign, and Comparative Law, and the Director of the Human Rights

Program at Harvard Law School. He teaches human rights, constitutional law, and immigration and nationality law.

Ruth L. Okediji is the Jeremiah Smith, Jr., Professor of Law and Co-Director of the Berkman Klein Center for Internet & Society at Harvard University. She is an award-winning researcher, teacher, and scholar with expertise in intellectual property, international economic law, biblical law, and legal ethics.

Mariana Pargendler is the Beneficial Professor of Law. Her prize-winning scholarship focuses on corporate law, corporate governance, and contract law from economic and comparative perspectives.

Intisar A. Rabb is a Professor of Law, a Professor of History, and the faculty director of the Program in Islamic Law at Harvard Law School—which houses the SHARIAsource Lab for Islamic law and AI. She teaches criminal law, legislation/statutory interpretation, and courses on comparative law and Islamic legal history.

Richard M. Re is a Professor of Law at Harvard Law School. His primary research and teaching interests are in constitutional law, federal courts, and criminal procedure.

Daphna Renan is the Peter B. Munroe and Mary J. Munroe Professor of Law. Her work focuses on the U.S. presidency and the design of American democracy from the perspective of administrative and structural constitutional law.

Mark J. Roe is the David Berg Professor of Law. He teaches corporate law and corporate bankruptcy and is the author of *Strong Managers, Weak Owners: The Political Roots of American Corporate Governance* and of *Political Determinants of Corporate Governance*.

Benjamin Sachs is the Kestnbaum Professor of Labor and Industry and a leading expert in the field of labor law and labor relations. He is also faculty director of the Center for Labor and a Just Economy.

Stephen E. Sachs is the Antonin Scalia Professor of Law. His research focuses on the law and theory of constitutional interpretation, the jurisdiction of state and federal courts, the history of procedure and private law, and the role of the general common law in the U.S. legal system.

Larry Schwartztol is Professor of Practice at Harvard Law School, where he teaches, writes, and advocates on democracy and voting rights, civil rights, anti-discrimination law, and federal civil procedure. He is also the faculty director of the Democracy and Rule of Law Clinic.

Joseph William Singer is the Bussey Professor of Law. He teaches and writes about property law, conflict of laws, federal Indian law, and legal theory with an emphasis on moral and political philosophy.

Carol S. Steiker is the Henry J. Friendly Professor of Law. She specializes in the broad field of criminal justice, ranging from substantive criminal law to criminal procedure to institutional design, with a special focus on capital punishment.

Nicholas O. Stephanopoulos is the Kirkland & Ellis Professor of Law. His work is focused on the intersection of democratic theory, empirical political science, and the American electoral system.

Kristen A. Stilt is Professor of Law and Faculty Director of the Brooks McCormick Jr. Animal Law & Policy Program. She is also Faculty Director of the Program on Law & Society in the Muslim World.

Ronald S. Sullivan, Jr. is the Jesse Climenko Clinical Professor of Law. He teaches in the areas of criminal law, criminal procedure, and trial practice.

Cass R. Sunstein is the Robert Walmsley University Professor at Harvard, and the founder and director of the Program on Behavioral Economics and Public Policy at Harvard Law School. A recipient of the Holberg Prize from the government of Norway, he is author of hundreds of articles and dozens of books.

Philip L. Torrey is an Assistant Clinical Professor of Law and the Director of the Crimmigration Clinic at Harvard Law School.

Rebecca Tushnet is the Frank Stanton Professor of the First Amendment, and Faculty Co-Director of the Berkman Klein Center for Internet & Society. Her work currently focuses on copyright, trademark, and false advertising law.

Dehlia Umunna is a Clinical Professor of Law and the Faculty Director of the Harvard Law School Criminal Justice Institute. She began her career as a trial attorney at the Public Defender Service for the District of Columbia and has represented indigent clients in criminal court for over twenty years. Her teaching interests and research focus on criminal law, criminal defense and theory, policing, mass incarceration, and racial justice.

Rachel A. Viscomi is a Clinical Professor and the Director of the Harvard Negotiation & Mediation Clinical Program. She has supervised dispute resolution projects across the world, from the United States and Canada to Israel and the Democratic Republic of the Congo.

Laura Weinrib is the Fred N. Fishman Professor of Constitutional Law and an Affiliate Professor in the Harvard History Department. A legal historian, she studies how social movements have transformed constitutional categories to pursue political and economic change.

Alex Whiting is a Professor of Practice at Harvard Law School where he teaches, writes and consults on domestic and international criminal prosecution issues. He has worked extensively both as an international and U.S. federal prosecutor.

David B. Wilkins is the Lester Kissel Professor of Law, and Faculty Director of the Center on the Legal Profession at Harvard Law School. He is also a Senior Research Fellow of the American Bar Foundation and a Fellow of the Harvard University Edmond J. Safra Foundation Center for Ethics.

Jonathan Zittrain is the George Bemis Professor of International Law. He is also Professor of Public Policy at the John F. Kennedy School of Government, Professor of Computer Science at the Harvard School of Engineering and Applied Sciences, and co-founder and director of Harvard's Berkman Klein Center for Internet & Society.

Publisher contact:
The MIT Press
Massachusetts Institute of Technology
77 Massachusetts Avenue, Cambridge, MA 02139
mitpress.mit.edu

EU Authorised Representative:
Easy Access System Europe, Mustamäe tee 50,
10621 Tallinn, Estonia
gpsr.requests@easproject.com

Printed by Integrated Books International,
United States of America